Learning FreeNAS

Configure and manage a network attached storage solution

Gary Sims

BIRMINGHAM - MUMBAI

Learning FreeNAS

Copyright © 2008 Packt Publishing

All rights reserved. No part of this book may be reproduced, stored in a retrieval system, or transmitted in any form or by any means, without the prior written permission of the publisher, except in the case of brief quotations embedded in critical articles or reviews.

Every effort has been made in the preparation of this book to ensure the accuracy of the information presented. However, the information contained in this book is sold without warranty, either express or implied. Neither the author, Packt Publishing, nor its dealers or distributors will be held liable for any damages caused or alleged to be caused directly or indirectly by this book.

Packt Publishing has endeavored to provide trademark information about all the companies and products mentioned in this book by the appropriate use of capitals. However, Packt Publishing cannot guarantee the accuracy of this information.

First published: August 2008

Production Reference: 1130808

Published by Packt Publishing Ltd.
32 Lincoln Road
Olton
Birmingham, B27 6PA, UK.

ISBN 978-1-847194-68-8

www.packtpub.com

Cover Image by Michelle O'Kane (michelle@kofe.ie)

Credits

Author
Gary Sims

Reviewers
Dan Merschi
Nathan Yocom
Robert La Gesse

Senior Acquisition Editor
David Barnes

Development Editor
Nikhil Bangera

Technical Editor
Ajay Shanker

Editorial Team Leader
Mithil Kulkarni

Project Manager
Abhijeet Deobhakta

Project Coordinator
Neelkanth Mehta

Indexer
Rekha Nair

Proofreader
Camille Guy

Production Coordinator
Aparna Bhagat

Cover Work
Aparna Bhagat

About the Author

Gary Sims is a freelance Linux/FreeBSD consultant and writer from the UK and has been working with open-source software since the mid 1990s. He first saw Linux while completing his degree in Business Information Systems at Portsmouth University. Then while working for Digital Equipment Corp he came in to contact with DEC's Ultrix and later Digital UNIX (formerly OSF/1). While developing enterprise software for DEC on its UNIX platforms he became more and convinced of the benefits of open source and open-source Unix-like operating systems like Linux and FreeBSD. After leaving DEC he became a software contractor and after moving to Romania in 2003 he became a freelance Linux/FreeBSD consultant and writer and started publishing articles for the Open Source Technology Group (owners of Linux.com and SourceForge.net). This then led to him writing his first book with Packt

> I would like to thank my Mum and Dad for their support and enthusiasm while I was writing this book. I would also like to thank my wife for her patience and encouragement and my children for their frequent, but yet, welcome interruptions. I would also like to thank the FreeNAS community, specifically, Olivier Cochard-Labbé, Volker Theile, and Dan Merschi, without them FreeNAS wouldn't exist. I also owe a debt of gratitude to David Barnes (and all the people at Packt) for making this book possible.

About the Reviewer

Nathan Yocom is an accomplished software engineer with a focus on network security, identity, access control, and data integrity applications. With years of experience working at the system level, his involvement in the industry has ranged from creation of software like the open source Windows authentication project pGina (http://www.pgina.org), to Bynari Inc's Linux/Outlook integration suite (http://www.bynari.net), to working on Centrify Corporation's ground breaking Active Directory integration and auditing products (http://www.centrify.com).

Nathan's own publications have included several articles in trade journals such as SysAdmin Magazine, and co-authoring the Apress book "The Definitive Guide to Linux Network Programming" (ISBN: 1590593227).

When not hacking at code, Nathan enjoys spending time at home in the Seattle, WA area with his wife Katie, daughter Sydney, and son Ethan. Nathan can be contacted via email at: nate@yocom.org.

Table of Contents

Preface	**1**
Chapter 1: All About NAS and FreeNAS	**5**
Network Attached Storage	**5**
What is FreeNAS?	**9**
Features	**10**
What Does FreeNAS Do for Me and My Business?	**12**
How FreeNAS Meet These Needs	14
Practical Uses for the FreeNAS Server	15
Consolidation	16
Summary	**16**
Chapter 2: Preparing to Add FreeNAS to Your Network	**17**
Planning Your NAS	**17**
Capacity Planning	18
Choosing Your Hardware	20
CPU	20
Disks	21
Planning for Backup	**27**
What is RAID? And, Do I Need It?	**28**
Hardware or Software RAID	30
Network Considerations	**31**
Switch or Hub?	31
What About Wireless?	32
Summary	**33**
Chapter 3: Exploring FreeNAS	**35**
Downloading FreeNAS	**35**
What Hardware Do I Need?	**35**
Warning	36

Table of Contents

Quick Start Guide For the Impatient	**36**
Burning and Booting	37
Configuring	39
Sharing with Windows Machines	42
Testing the Share	43
Detailed Overview of Installation	**44**
Making the FreeNAS CD	45
Booting from CD	45
Phoenix BIOS	46
Phoenix-Award BIOS	47
AMI BIOS	47
First Look at FreeNAS	47
Configuring the Network	47
What is a LAN IP Address?	49
Basic Configuration	**51**
FreeNAS Web Interface	52
System	53
Interfaces	53
Disks	53
Services	53
Access	53
Status	54
Diagnostics	54
Advanced	54
Adding a Disk	54
Accessing the Disk via CIFS	58
Testing the Share	60
Accessing via FTP	61
Testing FTP Access	62
Installing to Hard Disk	**63**
Embedded versus Full	66
Upgrading FreeNAS from a Previous Version	**66**
Summary	**67**
Chapter 4: Connecting to the FreeNAS	**69**
Introduction	**69**
Connecting via CIFS	**70**
Configure CIFS on the FreeNAS Server	71
CIFS Settings Explained	73
CIFS Advanced Settings	74
Options when Adding Shares	75
What does It Mean to Map a Network Drive?	75
Connecting with CIFS via Windows Millennium	76
Using CIFS with Windows XP	77
FreeNAS, CIFS, and Windows Vista	78

Accessing the FreeNAS via CIFS from Linux	79
A CIFS Connection from OS X	80
FTP	**80**
Using the Command Line FTP Client	82
Using a Web Browser for FTP	84
NFS	**85**
Using NFS from OS X	86
Mount FreeNAS via NFS on Linux	87
RSYNCD, Unison, AFP, and UPnP	**87**
Using RSYNC for Backups	88
Using Unison for Backups and Synchronization	89
Connecting to FreeNAS via AFP	89
Streaming Media with UPnP	90
iSCSI Target	**92**
Testing the iSCSI Target with Another FreeNAS Server	94
Testing the iSCSI Target with Windows Vista	96
Accessing Your Files Using HTTP and the Built-In Web Server	**98**
Summary	**99**
Chapter 5: User and System Administration	**101**
Introduction	**101**
Local User Management	**101**
Using CIFS with Local Users	103
FTP and User Login	104
Authenticating AFP Users	105
Connect to the FreeNAS Server via SSH	106
Services that Don't Use Local User Accounts	108
Using FreeNAS with the Microsoft Active Directory	**108**
System Admin	**110**
How to Change the Web GUI User Name and Password	110
Rebooting and Shutting Down	111
How to Set the Hostname of the Server	112
Configuring the Web Interface to use HTTPS	112
Changing the Web Interface Port	113
How to Set a DNS Server	113
How to Set the Language for the Web Interface	115
Date and Time Configuration	115
How to Disable Console Menu	117
How to Stop the Startup and Shutdown Beeps	117
Adding Predefined Network Hosts	117
Reset the Server to the Factory Defaults	118

Table of Contents

Simple Network Administration	118
Disabling Bonjour/ZeroConf	119
Getting Status Information About the Server	119
Sending Status Report by Email	121
Summary	**122**
Chapter 6: Configuring Storage	**123**
Introduction	**123**
How FreeNAS Handles Data Disks	**123**
UNIX Device Names	124
Adding the Disk	125
Formatting a Newly Added Disk	126
Mounting Your Newly Formatted Disks	128
Making the New Disk Available on the Network	129
Configuring Software RAID on FreeNAS	**130**
RAID All Starts with Adding the Disks	130
Configuring RAID 1	132
Configuring RAID 5	134
Configuring JBOD or RAID 0	135
Nested RAID Configurations	136
Configuring RAID 1+0	137
Configuring RAID 0+1	138
Configuring RAID 5+0	139
Configuring RAID 5+1	140
RAID 10+0 and Beyond	142
iSCSI Initiator	**142**
Summary	**143**
Chapter 7: Backup Strategies	**145**
Backup Your FreeNAS Using Windows XP's Built-In Backup Utility	**145**
Setting Scheduled Backups with XP's Built-In Backup Utility	148
Restoring a FreeNAS Backup Made with XP's Built-In Backup Utility	**151**
Backing Up the FreeNAS Configuration Files	**152**
Backup Configuration	152
What is XML?	152
Restore Configuration	153
Using Another FreeNAS Server as a Backup Server	**153**
Debugging Your RSYNC Setup	157
RSYNC Internal Backup	**158**
Debugging Your Internal RSYNC Setup	159

Mirroring vs Conventional Backups	160
Summary	160
Chapter 8: Advanced System Configuration	**161**
Disk Encryption	161
Encrypting a Disk in FreeNAS	162
Entering the Password When You Reboot	163
Encryption Tools	164
How to Unlock an Encrypted Disk—Attach and Detach	165
How to Change the Password on an Encrypted Disk—setkey	165
Checking the Status of an Encrypted Disk—list and status	165
Advanced Hard Drive Parameters (S.M.A.R.T)	166
Enabling and using S.M.A.R.T of the FreeNAS	167
File System Consistency Check—FSCK	169
Advanced OS Tweaking	170
Tweaking the Network Settings	172
MTU, Device Polling, Speed, and Duplex	172
Adding a Static Route	173
Using Wireless	174
Adding a Swap File	175
Enabling Secure Shell Connections (SSH)	176
Allow Root Login	176
Types of SSH Authentication	177
Summary	179
Chapter 9: General Troubleshooting	**181**
Where to Look for Log Information	181
Diagnostics: Logs	182
Understanding Diagnostics—Logs: System	183
Converting between Device Names and the Real World	185
Networking Problems	186
General Connection Problems	186
Using Ping	188
Using Ping from within the Web Interfaces	189
Using ARP Tables to Solve Network Problems	190
Gigabit Transfers are Slow	191
Problems Connecting to Shares (via CIFS)	191
Windows Vista Asks for My Username and Password for Anonymous Shares	192
There are Two FreeNAS Servers on the Network, but Windows Can only See One	192
Turning On Logging to Help Solve Windows Networking Problems	192
Diagnostics: Information	193

Replacing a Failed Hard Drive in a RAID Set	**194**
Rebuilding a RAID 1 Array After Disk Failure	195
Rebuilding a RAID 5 Array After Disk Failure	196
Where to Go for More Help	**197**
Summary	**197**
Chapter 10: FreeBSD and Command Line Tools	**199**
Introduction to FreeBSD	**199**
Your First FreeBSD Commands	200
Print the Working Directory with pwd	200
Directory Listings (ls)	200
Change Directory with cd	201
Copy a File and Change Its Permissions (cp and chmod)	202
Connecting to FreeBSD Using Putty	204
Monitoring your FreeNAS Server from the Command Line	206
See Which Disks are Mounted with mount	206
Check Disk Space Usage with df	206
Discover the Size of Directories Using du	206
Process Monitoring Using ps and top	207
Advanced FreeBSD Commands for FreeNAS	**209**
Starting and Stopping Services	209
Getting Drastic with kill and killall	210
RAID Command Line Tools	211
Warning	211
List and Status Commands	212
JBOD and gconcat	214
RAID 0 and gstripe	214
RAID 1 and gmirror	214
RAID 5 and graid5	215
Where the FreeNAS Stores Things	**216**
Miscellaneous & Sundries	**217**
Using ping and arp from the Command Line	217
Creating Directories and Deleting Things	218
Editing Files Using nano	218
Shutting Down Using the Command Line	219
Summary	**219**
Index	**221**

Preface

FreeNAS is a free piece of software that turns a PC into Network Attached Storage (NAS). It supports connections from Microsoft Windows, Apple OS X, Linux, and FreeBSD. It supports RAID, has a simple web GUI, and modest system requirements. Since FreeNAS is an embedded operating system, it is compact, efficient, and dedicated to just one task.

This book shows system administrators, as well as home network users, how to quickly install and configure FreeNAS.

FreeNAS has a full range of advanced features including support for Redundant Array of Independent Disks (RAID), Microsoft Active Directory, and iSCSI. The goal of this book is to show administrators how to use these advanced features and exploit the full potential of the FreeNAS software.

The FreeNAS software is suitable for home use as well as enterprise deployment and as such this book also covers the planning and administration tasks for both types of environment. This book also has a chapter dedicated to problem solving, and much more...

What This Book Covers

Chapter 1 is a high level look at Network Attached Storage (NAS), and more specifically, the FreeNAS software. We will cover the basic idea behind NAS and the philosophy of the FreeNAS server. This chapter is less hands-on than the others in this book, but it is important to understand the concepts of Network Attached Storage and where the FreeNAS server fits into your business.

Chapter 2 will look at the basic planning points including: Capacity planning, Hardware requirements, Planning for backup, Redundancy needs, and Network infrastructure.

Chapter 3 will install the FreeNAS server, and we'll start looking at the basic configuration.

Chapter 4 shall look at the different services and protocols supported by FreeNAS, and we'll also see examples of how various platforms like Windows, OS X, and Linux can use the FreeNAS server for file sharing, backup, and streaming multimedia.

Chapter 5 will look at the different system administration tasks for the FreeNAS server as well as user administration.

Chapter 6 will look at how to manage hard disks in the FreeNAS server and how to configure them to form RAID sets that improve fault tolerance and increase drive performance.

Chapter 7 shall explore the different options that exist to back up the data on the FreeNAS server including using RSYNC to a second local disk as well as to a remote machine.

Chapter 8 looks at Advanced System Configuration like disk encryption, adding a swap space, and tweaking FreeBSD.

Chapter 9 is a guide on how to solve problems with your FreeNAS server. It covers where to look for information about the problem as well as how to hunt down problems by being methodical. It also looks at the common problems people have with their FreeNAS servers including networking problems and problems with RAID.

Chapter 10 will look at some simple FreeBSD commands and also some fundamental FreeBSD administration tasks, including stop and starting different services as well as controlling RAID from the command line.

What You Need for This Book

To get the most from this book you will need a copy of the FreeNAS server software and one or more PCs on which to install it. You will need the ability to burn a CDROM and you will possibly need a USB flash disk. You will need a network and a separate client PC with a web browser. The client PC can use Windows, OS X, Linux or any other OS that support web browsing. FreeNAS can be administered using almost any web browser including Firefox, Safari or Internet Explorer.

Since the FreeNAS server is configured via a web interface, it is assumed that the reader has a basic knowledge of using browser software.

Conventions

In this book, you will find a number of styles of text that distinguish between different kinds of information. Here are some examples of these styles, and an explanation of their meaning.

Code words in text are shown as follows: "We can include other contexts through the use of the `include` directive."

A block of code will be set as follows:

```
<interfaces>
    <lan>
        <ipaddr>192.168.1.251</ipaddr>
        <subnet>24</subnet>
        <gateway>192.168.1.254</gateway>
```

Any command-line input and output is written as follows:

```
Apr 1 11:06:00        kernel: real memory = 268435456 (256 MB)
Apr 1 11:06:00        kernel: avail memory = 252907520 (241 MB)
```

New terms and **important words** are introduced in a bold-type font. Words that you see on the screen, in menus or dialog boxes for example, appear in our text like this: "clicking the **Next** button moves you to the next screen".

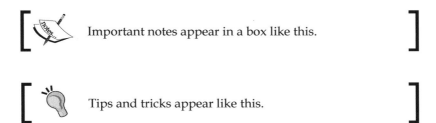

[Important notes appear in a box like this.]

[Tips and tricks appear like this.]

Reader Feedback

Feedback from our readers is always welcome. Let us know what you think about this book, what you liked or may have disliked. Reader feedback is important for us to develop titles that you really get the most out of.

To send us general feedback, simply drop an email to `feedback@packtpub.com`, making sure to mention the book title in the subject of your message.

If there is a book that you need and would like to see us publish, please send us a note in the **SUGGEST A TITLE** form on www.packtpub.com or email suggest@packtpub.com.

If there is a topic that you have expertise in and you are interested in either writing or contributing to a book, see our author guide on www.packtpub.com/authors.

Customer Support

Now that you are the proud owner of a Packt book, we have a number of things to help you to get the most from your purchase.

Errata

Although we have taken every care to ensure the accuracy of our contents, mistakes do happen. If you find a mistake in one of our books—maybe a mistake in text or code—we would be grateful if you would report this to us. By doing this you can save other readers from frustration, and help to improve subsequent versions of this book. If you find any errata, report them by visiting http://www.packtpub.com/support, selecting your book, clicking on the **let us know** link, and entering the details of your errata. Once your errata are verified, your submission will be accepted and the errata added to the list of existing errata. The existing errata can be viewed by selecting your title from http://www.packtpub.com/support.

Piracy

Piracy of copyright material on the Internet is an ongoing problem across all media. At Packt, we take the protection of our copyright and licenses very seriously. If you come across any illegal copies of our works in any form on the Internet, please provide the location address or website name immediately so we can pursue a remedy.

Please contact us at copyright@packtpub.com with a link to the suspected pirated material.

We appreciate your help in protecting our authors, and our ability to bring you valuable content.

Questions

You can contact us at questions@packtpub.com if you are having a problem with some aspect of the book, and we will do our best to address it.

All About NAS and FreeNAS

The first chapter is a high level look at Network Attached Storage (NAS), and more specifically, the FreeNAS software. We will cover the basic idea behind NAS and the philosophy of the FreeNAS server. This chapter is less hands-on than the others in this book, but it is important to understand the concepts of Network Attached Storage and where the FreeNAS server fits into your business. The main topics for this chapter include:

- What is Network Attached Storage?
- What is FreeNAS?
- What are the features of FreeNAS?
- What does FreeNAS do for me and my business?

Network Attached Storage

In the mid 80s, two popular computer companies independently started to work on ways to access files, over the network, on another computer as if the hard drive of that remote computer was attached to the local machine. These two companies were Sun Microsystems and Microsoft. The Sun Microsystems method, which was for their UNIX operating system, is known as the Network File System (NFS) and was subsequently implemented in almost all versions of the UNIX operating system including Linux. The Microsoft solution (which they actually joint developed with IBM in the initial stages) became known as SMB (Server Message Block) but in later years was renamed as the Common Internet File System (CIFS).

The general functionality of NFS and CIFS are very similar, and with either installed on a networked computer, it can read and write to the file system on another networked computer. Windows users are most used to this concept via the "Network Neighborhood" (Windows 95/98) or "My Network Places" (Windows ME, 2000 and XP) or more recently "Network and Sharing Center" (Vista). Here, you can browse the local network for other PCs and read and write files on that machine as long as the owner shared it with you.

This ability to use a remote computer (a fileserver) to store files led to many companies deploying large centralized NFS Servers or Windows Servers that were accessed by hundreds and maybe thousands of UNIX workstations or PC clients. Users would then be encouraged to store all important files on these servers as the IT staff would back up the servers regularly and so back up the important user files.

Storage space has always been an important aspect of computer systems. Today, more than ever, hard disk space is in demand. Back in the 1960s, storage was measured in bytes (8 binary digits, taking a value of either 0 or 1) and kilobytes. Then, as computers advanced, storage (including hard disks) grew to the size of megabytes (1024 kilobytes) and then gigabytes (1024 megabytes) and today with the 21st century well underway, computer storage is into the realm of terabytes (1024 gigabytes).

With modern needs for video and audio, combined with high speed local networks and the access protocols of CIFS and NFS, a new kind of storage solution has appeared: Network Attached Storage or NAS for short. A NAS server is similar to a traditional file server in many ways, especially in respects to the hardware side of the server. But a NAS server is much more specialized than a traditional office or departmental server in that it only provides access to storage via the network. It is not designed to run other applications such as databases or email servers, which other types of server might. Normally, NAS servers don't require a keyboard, mouse or monitor permanently connected to them and for day-to-day administration, a web interface is used instead.

Here is an example of the FreeNAS web interface:

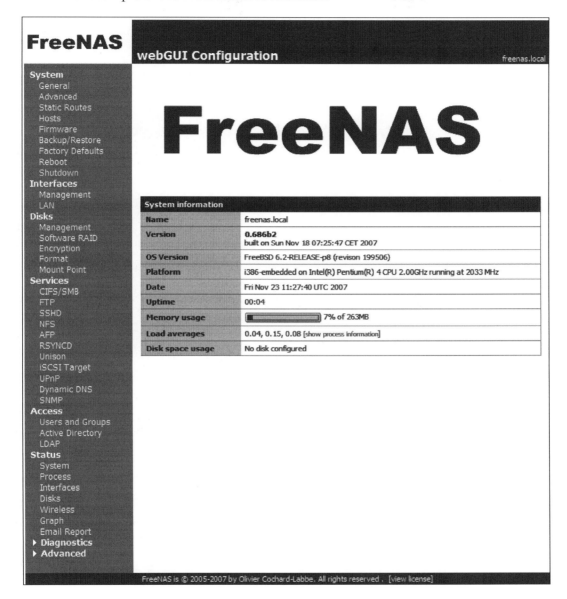

To access the data on the server, a typical NAS will support multiples access protocols and so allow Microsoft Windows clients, Apple OS X clients, and UNIX (including Linux) clients to connect and use the data on the server.

NAS servers normally contain one or more hard disks, and these hard disks can be combined to create large contiguous areas of storage or used in a way to create redundancy. In a redundancy set-up, if a hard disk fails then the system keeps working and your data isn't lost.

NAS servers come in all shapes and sizes. There are several companies that offer compact NAS servers with an embedded operating system and space for maybe two hard drives. These units are relatively cheap but offer limited room for expansion. At the other end of the scale, are dedicated NAS servers that look more like traditional file servers with good processing power and space for several hard disks (which can make the NAS capable of hosting several terabytes of data).

Here is how a NAS might fit into your network environment:

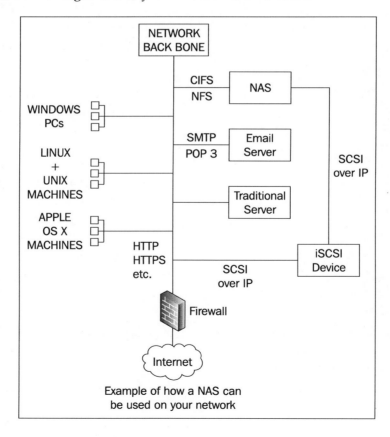

Example of how a NAS can be used on your network

Network Attached Storage has several advantages over a traditional file server in that:

- NAS offers better security. As the server is only running a dedicated operating system for providing the access to your data, there aren't other services running (like email servers and general purpose web servers) that can have potential security risks.
- A NAS server is designed to offer higher availability (less downtime). A NAS server is designed to offer redundancy models for the hard disks and so allowing for hardware failure without losing valuable data.
- A NAS server is easier to use and administer as most of the configuration is done via a web interface and that interface is designed to perform the specific tasks need to run the NAS.
- The system requirements for a NAS are modest and bleeding edge processing power isn't need.
- A NAS server works in a heterogeneous network environment and so allows diverse types of computers to connect and use its storage.

Therefore, NAS has an overall lower cost than a traditional server while allowing for expansion and increasing availability and security.

This book focuses on one implementation of NAS called FreeNAS (Free Network Attached Storage), which will turn a normal PC or server into a NAS.

What is FreeNAS?

FreeNAS is free piece of software that turns a PC into a NAS server. It supports connections from Microsoft Windows, Apple OS X, Linux, and FreeBSD. It supports hard disk redundancy, has a simple web administration interface, and modest system requirements.

FreeNAS is what is known as an embedded operating system. This means it is compact, efficient, and dedicated to just one task, in this case, NAS. Once FreeNAS is installed on a PC, the PC becomes a dedicated NAS, it can't do other general tasks at the same time.

To use FreeNAS, you need to download a copy of the software from http://www.freenas.org and boot it on the computer you want to make a NAS. We shall look at this in more detail in the next chapter.

All About NAS and FreeNAS

FreeNAS comes in two variations; the live CD and an installable kit. The live CD boots the machine as a NAS and uses a floppy disk or USB flash drive to store the configuration information. The installable version installs itself on to the server (much like a traditional operating system would) and uses the system hard drive to store the configuration data.

So why is FreeNAS free? FreeNAS is what is known as Open Source Software. It was originally written by Olivier Cochard-Labbé and is now maintained by a small international team with Oliver as the project leader. Being open source means that the FreeNAS team have licensed the software in such a way that they give unrestricted access to the software and to its source code. You are free to use and deploy FreeNAS without any restrictions. You can also obtain the source code and build or modify the software for yourself. The only restriction is that when redistributing FreeNAS, with or without modifications, the original copyright notices must remain intact. Olivier Cochard-Labbé is the copyright holder. He also holds the trademark for the name FreeNAS.

FreeNAS is made up of several different components. At the lowest level, there is the operating system (FreeBSD, see below). Then, there are various server components that provide the network services and finally, a web administration interface.

> Several times throughout this book, we will refer to the operating system FreeBSD. FreeBSD is a UNIX like operating system with lineage back to the original AT&T version of UNIX through the Berkeley Software Distribution (BSD) branch. FreeNAS is built on top of and relies on FreeBSD. Because of the high level of synergy between FreeNAS and FreeBSD, chapters 9 and 10 have been written to help you in troubleshooting problems on your FreeNAS and will deal with low level commands for the FreeBSD operating system.

Features

The capabilities of the FreeNAS software are quite impressive and the feature list is growing with every release while maintaining the goal of providing a simple NAS server. So what can the FreeNAS do?

FreeNAS installs on either a hard drive or USB flash drive and takes less than 32MB of disk space once installed.

There is support for Microsoft Windows machines using the Common Internet File System (CIFS) protocol. This is Microsoft's protocol for accessing files over the network. CIFS is also supported in the Linux operating system as well as in Apple's OS X. This means that Linux and Macintosh computers will also be able to access the NAS. With CIFS, areas of the NAS can be permanently mounted on the client machine as if they were local hard drives.

FreeNAS includes support for the Network File System (NFS). NFS is a mature network file access protocol that is most often used in UNIX-type environments. With NFS, storage areas on the NAS server can be used as if they were local disks on the client.

The File Transfer Protocol (FTP) is supported. FTP is a mature protocol for transferring files over a network. FTP is a client/server protocol and is most often used to transfer files from one machine to another in a "one off" sense. A connection is made, the files are transferred, and the connection is closed. This is a protocol that is often used to allow people to download files from the Internet. In the NAS context, it is very useful for offering a repository of software on your network (like software, company templates, and anti-virus software updates).

The FreeNAS server can be used as a backup server via different utilities like Unison and RSYNC (Remote Synchronization). With RSYNC, an entire disk or folder (and its sub-folders) can be synchronized with the backup server in an efficient manner. The advantage of RSYNC over a straight copy of the files over the network is that RSYNC only copies the portions of the files that have been changed.

FreeNAS also supports Secure Shell (SSH) for encrypted connections and data exchange, the Apple Filing Protocol (AFP) that offers file access services for Mac OS X and Classic Mac OS, and UNISON (another file synchronization protocol).

For offering both access to storage on the NAS, and also for extending the storage capabilities of your server, FreeNAS supports the Internet Small Computer System Interface (iSCSI). iSCSI simulates the presence of a local SCSI hard drive over your IP network. FreeNAS can act as an iSCSI server (exporting RAW local storage via the SCSI over IP protocol), which is technically known as being an iSCSI target. FreeNAS can also act as a client and connect to other iSCSI targets and mount iSCSI disks. iSCSI disks that are mounted locally become part of the general storage resources for the server; and the FreeNAS server can act as a gateway or head to those disks allowing other machines (like a Windows PC) to use the iSCSI disk over CIFS or FTP etc. This type of setup is very popular in the Storage Area Network (SAN) model.

FreeNAS supports several different file systems. A file system is the way files are stored and organized on the disk. Different methods of organizing files have different characteristics like speed, maximum file size, and recovery after a system crash. FreeNAS can use the UNIX File System (UFS) that is the FreeNAS default. It can use the Linux file systems ext2 and ext3 as well as the NT File System (NTFS) that is the native file system for Microsoft Windows NT/2000/XP, Windows Server 2003/2008, and Vista.

Many types of hard drives are supported, including all the popular hard drives of today (SATA/PATA, SCSI, iSCSI, USB, and Firewire). FreeNAS also handles hard drives larger than 2 Terabytes where the file system permits.

All of the popular network cards (both wired and wireless), which are supported by FreeBSD, work with FreeNAS without needing to download and install additional drivers.

FreeNAS includes hard disk fail-over and mirroring technology. Using a system called RAID (Redundant Array of Inexpensive Disks), you can configure disks into sets which work in combination to spread the data over 2 or more disks so that if a disk fails data integrity remains and your NAS continues to work. FreeNAS can use hardware RAID (where the controller card is responsible for controlling all the disks) or software RAID where the FreeBSD operating system runs the RAID sets. FreeNAS supports many popular hardware RAID cards via the drivers supplied with FreeBSD.

What Does FreeNAS Do for Me and My Business?

Network Attached Storage is a solution to a problem. To discover what a NAS and more specifically FreeNAS can do for you, we need to first look at the nature of the problem.

The problem, put simply, is the need for highly accessible storage space. Storage space demands are increasing for three distinct but yet important reasons. First, the volume of digital information created in a business is increasing. Secondly, the size of this digital information is growing, and finally, the need for comprehensive archiving and management of older data is growing, especially in countries where there are legal requirements to store data for long periods of time.

The volume of digital information created is increasing because more and more business data is being stored on computers, and businesses have become less reliant on paper. Take email for an example. 10 to 15 years ago email probably wasn't a critical part of your business. It probably existed and was used but it was not yet critical. Today, on the other hand, email has become mission critical. Online email services like Yahoo! ,Gmail, and Hotmail started by offering mailboxes with 5 or 10 megabytes, today they are offering mailboxes in gigabytes. An organization of 100 people will generate gigabytes of email data each year. If your business grows and you employ more people, then the amount of email will increase with it. As the number of your customers increases, your email data will increase and so on.

Then, if you factor in documents, contracts, accounting, inventories, presentations, sales material, and so on, you can see that the volume of data is growing. Each new sales lead, each new customer, and each support contract increases the data generated.

Secondly, the nature of digital information is changing and the size of the data is changing with it. In the years gone by, data was more text orientated but today data has gone multimedia. Photos, video, and music are normal data types today. The big difference is of course that text type data (including simple word processor documents) is small but multimedia files are much larger. This is reflected in the type of optical disks available. The humble CD-ROM was 650 megabytes which was enough for 72 minutes of music. Then came the DVD which was six times bigger at 4.7 Gigabytes (for a single layer disk). Now, there are high density disks like Blu-ray, a dual layer Blu-ray disc can store 50 GB, almost six times the size of a dual layer DVD at 8.5 GB. In parallel with this, hard disks are growing to terabyte sizes.

Thirdly, how your business manages old data is becoming more and more important. Governments around the world have passed legislation requiring businesses to keep data for longer periods of time. The value of data constantly fluctuates. What may seem to be just an old collection of files from an ex-employee can overnight become the hottest files in your system as you discover that important information is in those files. The value of old emails also fluctuates. What you consider an old email today might become important tomorrow if the lawyers want to see it due to some legal matters. Keeping your old data safe and accessible (by copying it to a FreeNAS server in conjunction with other backup methods) is critical. But by its very nature, the volume of old data will increase as every day passes and so will your need for storage.

When FreeNAS Isn't the Right Solution

FreeNAS won't be the best solution in all circumstances. The most obvious of which is if you only have a very small number of users on your network, say less than 3. In such scenarios, direct attached storage (i.e. an external USB hard drive or adding another hard drive to an existing PC on the network) is an alternative solution.

Along with the increasing demands for storage space, there is the need to have your data accessible by all different types of computer (Windows, UNIX, OS X) on your network and also for it to be available in a consistent manner without long periods of down time.

Traditionally, Windows desktop machines worked with Windows servers and UNIX desktops worked with UNIX servers, but less often did Windows and UNIX work with each other. Although many of the network protocols are available for both Windows and UNIX, the two different systems tended to be used in isolation. The Windows servers had their system managers and the UNIX machines had theirs.

To lower costs and increase availability, Network Attached Storage needs to provide access to the data from both Windows PCs and from UNIX clients. Having a single type of server that services all the clients on your network is an important aspect of managing your data.

How FreeNAS Meet These Needs

To solve this need for more storage space, you can use a NAS. But to be of value to your business, the NAS needs to be easy to use, easy to install and deploy, easy to manage, scalable, and without prohibitive licensing costs.

Ease of use—Since FreeNAS is designed to do one thing and one thing only, namely convert a PC or server into Network Attached Storage, it is simple to use and manage. From the user's points of view, it will just appear as storage. If used on the Windows platform, it will just be an extra hard drive or for the Intranet it will be an FTP repository. Most of the system administration is done via a web interface and the machine can even be rebooted via the web interface.

Easy to install and deploy—Getting FreeNAS up and running is very simple, especially when using the live CD with a USB flash drive. Just pop the CD in the drive and boot up. In the next chapter, we will do a quick install to help you become familiar with FreeNAS and its web interface.

Easy to manage—As mentioned in the 'ease of use' paragraph above, FreeNAS is dedicated NAS software. Unlike a full installation of a tradition server operating system, there is nothing to worry about except for the storage configuration. There are no overly complicated system services to configure with 101 different options. But don't be misled, FreeNAS is feature-rich and a very clever piece of software, but the management interface is simple to use while yet remaining comprehensive.

Scalability—Scalability and robustness are built-into FreeNAS as the core of its functionality comes from the FreeBSD operating system. FreeBSD has proved to be a mature and production-ready operating system. There have been many successful deployments of FreeBSD in small, medium, and large businesses and even companies like Yahoo! have relied on FreeBSD for their servers at one time or another. FreeBSD is known for its network performance and reliability which is why it was chosen for FreeNAS. The real limit to scalability will be the physical number of hard drives that can be fitted to the server. But beyond the physical drive limit, FreeNAS can use iSCSI devices on your network and so the server can scale even further.

> If you installed FreeNAS on a USB flash drive or use the live CD version, the majority of your disk space will be used for storage, which is of course the aim of a NAS. If you used a traditional operating system, several gigabytes of hard disk space could well be used up just in the initial installation.

Licensing costs — With a traditional server operating system, there are normally licensing fees to pay to the operating system manufacturer. Sometimes, this includes a "per seat" license fee that is based on the number of users in your organization. Since FreeNAS is open source, there are **no licensing fees**. This means you are free to use and deploy FreeNAS as much as you want.

Practical Uses for the FreeNAS Server

So what practical uses are there for the FreeNAS server? Here is a brief summary of some of the uses of a FreeNAS server:

- As a common storage area for resources in your business including sales material, presentations, leaflets, brochures, templates, software kits, software updates, popular office software, and popular Internet software.
- To provide each user with a folder on the network which only he/she has access to, so they can save all their work on the server and not on their local PC. This is sometimes referred to as "the network drive" meaning a hard drive accessible via the network. This has two clear advantages:
    - Backups are much easier as all the data is stored in a central place (i.e. the FreeNAS server).
    - Users aren't reliant on the PC that they use as all their data is in a central place and also the hard drives of each user's PC doesn't need to be too large and can also be wiped (for an operating system re-install perhaps) without fear at any time.
- As a central storage for large files that would quickly fill a desktop PC hard disk. If your business involves the use of large files like multimedia files (video, audio, and photographs) then a FreeNAS server can provide a convenient central storage point for these files that would otherwise overwhelm the hard drive on a desktop PC.
- As an FTP repository for your Intranet (a private, internal network which uses the same protocols as the public Internet). Assuming you have an Intranet, there are most likely common resources like presentation templates that you make available to all your employees. If your web server doesn't have enough disk space (as many don't because they are tuned for performance rather than storage) then linking to the FreeNAS server via the FTP protocol would take the burden off your web server.

- As a backup server. You can use your FreeNAS server just as a backup server. Either with the Microsoft Windows file sharing protocol (CIFS) or with RSYNC, each PC on your network can be configured to copy user data from the local PC to the FreeNAS server. Alternatively, if you are already using a general purpose server on your network, the FreeNAS server can act as a backup store for that server.
- As an iSCSI head/gateway. If you have invested in SCSI over IP technology, then FreeNAS is a good way to offer access to your iSCSI devices over multiple protocols. iSCSI devices only use one protocol, SCSI over IP, and they don't understand other protocols like the Windows file sharing protocol (CIFS) or FTP or NFS and so on. But FreeNAS understands these protocols as well as SCSI over IP. Therefore, it can act as an intermediary (a gateway) between your iSCSI devices and the computers on your network.

Consolidation

There are two aspects to consolidation (the act of reducing many servers into one) that FreeNAS can achieve. The first is consolidation based on access protocol. As mentioned previously, Windows servers and UNIX servers use different protocols for accessing their stored data. FreeNAS supports multiple access protocols including CIFS (the Windows protocol) and NFS (the UNIX protocol). A UNIX file server and a Windows file server can be consolidated into a single FreeNAS server that supports clients from both types of system. The second type of consolidation is data consolidation. If you create a FreeNAS server with high initial storage space, you can replace existing general purpose servers into one FreeNAS server. Previously, each general purpose server needed its own management (often specialized) but with just one FreeNAS server, your management workload is reduced.

Summary

This chapter has been an introduction to the concepts of Network Attached Storage and FreeNAS server. We looked at the features of the FreeNAS server and what FreeNAS can do for your business. Finally, we looked at some of the practical uses of the FreeNAS server. In the next chapter, we will look at how to plan for FreeNAS in your environment including looking at the network implications and planning for disk redundancy.

2
Preparing to Add FreeNAS to Your Network

Like all system deployments, a NAS needs to be correctly planned to maximize success. In this chapter, we will look at the basic planning points including:

- Capacity planning
- Hardware requirements
- Planning for backup
- Redundancy needs
- Network infrastructure

This chapter may seem to be less "hands on", but there are important decisions to be made and actions to be taken to successfully plan, and deploy your NAS.

Planning Your NAS

In my experience, there are two types of people in computing, those which plan meticulously before adding any new hardware or service to their networks and those who just add what they have and hope for the best. You can get busy and proper planning seems like an extra unnecessary step. But it is also equally true that fixing problems after your have deployed the system costs a lot more than resolving them before you "go live".

For example let us imagine that you didn't plan your hard disk requirements correctly and that, in fact, the server you have can't hold any more hard disks? What do you do now? Buy another server? It would have been better to get the right server to start with.

Capacity Planning

Your plans to deploy FreeNAS are constrained by two major factors, the first is the resources you have available (meaning PC or servers you already have or money to buy new ones) and how much capacity you want in your NAS.

> **Never** underestimate your need for disk space. Video files, audio files, emails, software downloads; the list of types of data we store is forever growing. I remember when I bought my first 170MB hard drive for a 386 PC that I had. I wondered how I could ever fill 170MB. Today, a short video clip is 170MB!

The more resources you have, the more capacity you can have, it is a simple relationship. FreeNAS, of course, helps this situation in a number of ways, first it is free. There are no licensing costs to pay. If you want 2 users or 20 users, the cost is the same... $0. Also, FreeNAS is on the lighter side of system requirements, you aren't going to need 4GB of memory to run this server.

So the big first question is how many users are going to use this server? If you are a home user, then the answer is probably less then 5 people. Maybe, you want the FreeNAS to act as a simple repository for multimedia files that can be accessed from any PC in your home. If you work in a small office environment then the answer is probably less than 15, and large offices less than 25. For any kind of corporate deployment, the number could be 25 and upwards.

Having established this number, you need to consider how many of these users will be writing to the NAS or in other words, will be adding files to the NAS, and how many will be just read as what is already there. We will refer to these as *write* users and *read* users. Again, in the home environment, maybe only 1 person will be actually copying files over to the NAS while 2 or 3 others maybe using them. In the office environment, it is more difficult to say, it all depends on your planned use for the FreeNAS.

Now, there is one final question for this section. How much space will each *write* user need on the server?

Now you just need to multiply:

number of write users   X   gigabytes needed

So, if we have 2 *write* users who need 5GB, each, then you need to start with 10GB of disk space. If you have 25 *write* users who each need 10GB of disk space, then you need 250BG of disk space and so on. For the home user, maybe it is only 1 write user but you want 500GB, so 1 X 500GB is 500GB!!!

Chapter 2

> **Now double it**
>
> Whatever figure you have now, double it. Somewhere you have underestimated, you don't know it but you have. Either in the number of users or in the data they need. So the safest thing to do now is double it. That way you won't be caught out with a lack of disk space in 6 months from now.

Now the next calculation is a bit trickier. We need to workout how fast your data grows. How much it will grow depends on what you are storing on your FreeNAS. For example if you are using FreeNAS as a backup server, then as your users create documents, receive emails, download things from the Internet, the amount of disk space needed to backup their PCs will increase. There aren't really any rules of thumb here, you need to work it out. Mid-range and affordable (rather than top of the range, bleeding edge, and expensive) hard disks, on average, grow in capacity about 25% to 50% per year. Their growth isn't driven by need but rather by technology so this doesn't really give us a guide how much your data grows. Having said that, there always seems to be a tendency to use all the disk space that is available. The more disk space available, the more users find ways to fill it.

I remember once working for a mid-sized IT company and the server was running out of disk space. An email was sent around asking people to delete unnecessary files from the server. Once done, over 50% of the disk space was freed.

Once you have decided how much more disk space you need each year, you can calculate your disk requirements for the next three years. For this example, we will use a 25% increase for 25 users who initially need 2GB of disk space each.

Initial space needed: 25 X 2 = 50GB

Double it: = 100GB

25% increase year 1:   100 X 25% = 125GB

25% increase year 2:   125 X 25% = 156GB

25% increase year 3:   156 X 25% = 195GB

From this, we can see that over three years, disk usage could double. Depending on your type of business and how you are using FreeNAS, your growth rates could be even higher. If the data growth rate is 40%, then the storage space needed can double in two years.

To finally tweak the equation, you could factor in any planned growth in staffing levels as every new member will require an extra 4GB of disk space initially, which translates to nearly 8GB over three years.

Choosing Your Hardware

FreeNAS runs on the PC platform. The stated minimum requirements are an "IBM PC compatible" machine with a Pentium processor, at least 96MB of memory, and a bootable CDROM drive plus hard disks for storage. However, the practical minimum requirements are a Pentium II processor and 128MB of memory, and of course, the CDROM and hard disks.

CPU

It is impossible to list every manufacturer, motherboard, and CPU that are supported by FreeNAS (or more specifically, by FreeBSD the underlying operating system) but here are some general guidelines:

- All Intel processors beginning with the Pentium are supported, including the Pentium, Pentium Pro, Pentium II, Pentium III, Pentium 4 (and its variants such as the Xeon and Celeron processors), and the Intel Core (including Core Solo, Core Duo and Core 2 Duo) processors.

- All i386-compatible AMD processors are also supported, including the Am486, Am5x86, K5, K6 (and variants), Athlon (including Athlon MP, Athlon XP, and Athlon Thunderbird), Duron, and Opteron processors.

- All of the standard PC buses are supported including ISA, AGP, PCI, and PCI-X. There is NO support for the MicroChannel expansion bus used in the IBM PS/2 line of PCs.

- PCs with more than one CPU are supported as well as PCs with dual or quad cores. FreeBSD also takes advantage of HyperThreading (HT) on Intel CPUs that support this feature. FreeBSD will detect these additional logical processors as if they were additional physical processors. FreeBSD does not attempt to optimize scheduling decisions given the shared resources between logical processors within the same CPU.

The choice of CPU is important for your NAS. Although FreeNAS will work on a Pentium 1 with less than 128MB of memory, it won't perform well for a real live environment. Although running a NAS isn't CPU intensive in terms of exotic mathematical calculations, it can be CPU intensive because of demand. If 5 people are accessing files simultaneously, the CPU will be used heavily. One of the test machines in my lab is a Pentium III running at 466Mhz. Copying large files to the FreeNAS using a very fast network connection caused the CPU to run at 100%.

Here are some guidelines to help you choose your CPU:

- If you are just experimenting with FreeNAS and are interested in using it on a small scale, then an old 233MHz or greater Pentium II machine (or AMD equivalent) will be perfect.
- For home use for backup or storing multimedia files, a minimum of a Pentium III at 1Ghz is required (or AMD equivalent). Such a machine can handle software RAID and up to 10 clients.
- For a small office environment, the smallest CPU acceptable would be a Pentium 4 running at least 1.3 GHz (or AMD equivalent).
- For large installations, a Pentium 4 (or AMD equivalent) running at 3Ghz is really the bare minimum and ideally, fast dual core or dual processor machines would be better.

Front Side Bus (FSB)

The FSB connects the CPU to the main memory. The faster the FSB, the faster data is transferred to the CPU. In general, the speed of the FSB (which is measured in MHz) scales with the speed of the CPU. However, there are some motherboard/CPU combinations that use a lower FSB even for a higher speed CPU. This will reduce the overall performance of the system. Make sure you get a machine with a good FSB speed.

Processor speed isn't the only component of the PC or server that affects transfer speeds and concurrent user capacity. The network is a very important factor and we will look at this soon, also, the type of disks in the machine is very important.

Disks

The processor's job is to co-ordinate the requests coming in on the network with the disks in the machine. If the CPU is slow then that co-ordination role will be slow and the overall performance will be slow. Equally, if the disks are slow, then the performance of the system will suffer. The end goal of a NAS is to read and write data to a hard disk. The speed of the hard disk will determine how fast the data can be read or written.

Quality

In discussing disks and the different parameters that govern their performance, it is important not to forget the quality of the disks. By quality, I mean how likely is it that the disk will fail. In your FreeNAS server, the CPU can fail, the RAM can fail, the network can fail, and so on. But if a disk fails, you are in danger of losing your data.

When looking at disks, we need to look at two things: first the way in which the disks are connected to the PC, and secondly the disks themselves.

Buses

Every hard disk is connected to the PC via a thing called an interface. An interface is a conduit or pipeline down which the data for the hard drive travels. The faster the interface, the quicker the data travel, to and from the hard disk. Over the years, PCs have sported different types of hard disk interface and with each new iteration, the top speeds have increased.

IDE/ATA — The most common hard drive interface (until around 2004) was the Advanced Technology Attachment (ATA) interface or the Integrated Drive Electronics (IDE) interface. It was developed by Western Digital in the mid 1980's and for over twenty years was the main interface for connecting hard disks and CD ROMs to a PC. There are several synonyms or variations of ATA including Enhanced IDE (EIDE) and AT Attachment Packet Interface (ATAPI) but essentially it is the same technology refined and reused. In 2003, a new interface was introduced called Serial ATA (SATA) and so ATA was retroactively renamed to Parallel ATA (PATA) to distinguish it from the newer interface. Although fading as a means to connect hard drives to a PC, ATA is still popular for connecting CD ROMs and DVD ROMs to PCs and many motherboards come with both PATA and SATA interfaces. ATA interfaces are easy to recognize as they use 40 or 80 wire ribbon cables to connect the hard drive to the PC.

SATA — The Serial Advanced Technology Attachment (SATA) interface was released in 2003 and over 2004/2005 started to grow in popularity. SATA is faster than PATA and also adds the ability to remove or add devices while operating (this is called hot swapping). SATA uses thinner cables than PATA (gone are the flat 80 pin cables) and this allows air cooling to work more efficiently in the PC.

SCSI — There has always been an alternative to PATA and SATA and that is an interface called the Small Computer System Interface or SCSI for short. Like ATA, SCSI (which is most commonly pronounced "scuzzy") has been around a long time. It has been most popular in PC servers and has also been popular with Apple for their Macintosh computers and with Sun Microsystems. Like Parallel ATA, SCSI is being replaced by a serial version using smaller cabling and running at faster speeds, these new variations are commonly known as Serial SCSI.

Each interface type has various pros and cons. If you are using an existing PC for your FreeNAS server, then the differences are largely academic as you will have to use what is in the machine. But if you are buying a new piece of hardware for your FreeNAS server, then these differences can be important.

The first differences are in transfer speeds. The last version of PATA could transfer data at 133 MB per second (MB/s). This would mean that 700 megabytes of data (the same as a CD) would copy in just over 5 seconds. SATA comes in two speeds at the moment, SATA 150, which can transfer 187.5 MB/s and SATA 300, which peaks at 375MB/s. A CD's worth of data would copy in just under 4 seconds, and just under 2 seconds respectively. SCSI has many different variations and the latest iterations Ultra-320 and Ultra-640 have transfer speeds of 320MB/s and 640MB/s. A 700MB file would transfer in just over 1 second on a Ultra-640 system. All these speeds are theoretical peak transfer rates but they do serve as a good guide to the difference in the transfer speeds.

Cost is also a difference. PATA and SATA have similar costs with SATA being slightly cheaper at the moment as PATA drives have become less popular. SCSI drives, however, have historically been more expensive. SCSI drives are mainly seen as the "professional" storage option and so have higher quality parts, but less of them are sold and so they are more expensive.

Another difference is in the number of disks that can be attached to the PC. Traditionally, ATA is limited to four disks. Most motherboards came with two IDE interfaces know as the primary and secondary interfaces. Each interface can have two drives that were called the master and the slave. In a traditional PC, the secondary master was the CD or DVD ROM drive and the primary master was the hard disk. One could expand the PC by adding another disk as either the primary slave or as the secondary slave.

$\begin{bmatrix} \end{bmatrix}$ A problem with the ATA/IDE system is that when two devices are connected to the same cable, only one device on the cable can perform a read or write operation at a time. Therefore, a hard disk on the same cable as a DVD under heavy use will find that nearly every time it is asked to perform a transfer, it has to wait for the DVD to finish its own transfer first. If the DVD isn't being used, this isn't a issue.

SATA is different in that each physical cable connects to only 1 disk. The number of SATA drives you can have on your PC depends on how many connectors there are on your motherboard. Some motherboards come with only two connectors but there are also motherboards with as many as eight connectors. It is also possible to add extra SATA connectors by installing another SATA controller in a PCI slot.

SCSI is the champion for adding extra drives to your PC or server with a standard SCSI controller allowing you to add 16 drives to it. Many servers often come with 2 or 3 SCSI controllers built-in so as many as 48 drives can be added. SCSI is a mature technology and SCSI drives are often of a higher quality than PATA/SATA disks. They are, however, more expensive.

Drives

When buying a hard drive, the first thing we often look for is the capacity of the drive, how many Gigabytes (or even Terabytes) is it. But beside the capacity, there are also issues of quality and speed. Hard disks are physical mechanisms, which means compared to computer memory or a hard disk interface, they are quite slow. When looking to buy a drive for your FreeNAS server, there are several important factors to note besides the capacity of the drive.

Hard drive performance is determined by 3 factors: the seek time, the spindle speed, and the overall transfer speed.

Seek time—In order to read or write data in a particular place on the disk, the read/write head of the disk needs to be physically moved to that place. This process is known as seeking, and the time it takes for the head to move to the correct place is the seek time. This seek time varies as it depends on how far the head's destination is, from its origin at the time of the read or write operation. Therefore, seek time is normally expressed as an average. The typical seek time for a desktop hard disk is around 7ms to 8ms (and dropping), while for a server or high end disk it is about 3ms to 4ms. This can mean that the time to find the data on the disk or the time to find the correct spot to write data to the disk can be twice as slow on cheaper hard disks. We are, of course, talking about milliseconds here but multiply that by the number of seek movements that happen on a disk and you could see significant speed improvement on higher quality disks. For big single file transfers, this won't change the performance much as once the disk has found the file (and assuming it is contiguous on the disk), it can just be read without long seek times between reads. However, in a multi-user situation, the disk will be trying to read and write to several files at once.

Spindle speed—A hard disk is made up of one or more platters coated with a magnetic material. It is from these platters that we get the word disk or sometime people like to say disc. Each platter spins inside the disk drive unit and the read/write head bobs up and down on the platter surface reading and writing data. The speed at which this platter spins is a factor in the performance of the disk. This is for two reasons: First, when waiting to find a section on the disk, the quicker the disk spins the quicker that section will come around and be under the read/write head. Second, once reading or writing has begun, the quicker the disk spins, the quicker the data can be laid down or read. Today, disks spin at a variety of speeds starting at 4200 revolutions per minute (RPM) then 5400 RPM, 7200 RPM, 10,000 RPM, and 15,000 RPM. The 10,000 and 15,000 type disks are sometimes referred to as 10K RPM or 15K RPM disks. Traditionally, laptops have used the slow disks to space battery power. A common laptop disk speed was 4200 RPM and 5400 RPM. However, there are now some 7200 RPM laptop disks. Interestingly, several high end disks manufacturers now use the 2.5 inch laptop format for servers as they are finding they can make more reliable, faster, and quieter disks in the smaller physical package and the improvements in disk drive technology has meant that these disks aren't necessarily small on capacity. Desktop machines have been the main users of 5400 RPM and 7200 RPM disks with high end servers using the expensive 10K RPM and 15K RPM disks.

Transfer speed— Now that the disk is spinning fast and the head is flying back and forth at maximum speed, the real question is how quickly can the data be read from or written to the disk. Unfortunately, this isn't an easy question to answer. There are several different types of transfer speeds that can be measured when looking at a disk. The first is the *internal media transfer rate*, which is the actual speed that the drive can read or write bits to and from the surface of the platter. This figure isn't much use to us (although I am sure there are some people who find it interesting) as it is only an *internal* transfer speed and doesn't include any seeking time. It does not reflect what comes out of the disk to the PC. A better (but not perfect) measure of disk performance is the drive's *sustained transfer rate*. This is the rate at which the drive can transfer data sequentially from multiple parts of the disk including the overheads required for seeking. However, it is worth noting that the speed of the disks external interface (for example SATA 150) does **not** reflect the drive's external transfer rate. The best drives today have a transfer rate of under 100MB/s. Now, the speed of the SATA interface is at its slowest 150MB/s and at its fastest 300MB/s. Many hard disks include a memory cache on the disk, which means that for a small fraction of a second, if the conditions are right, the disk can pump out data at the speed of the bus. But these caches are small, when compared to the size of the disk, and are just a few megabytes. So more often than not, the drive is getting the data directly from the disk platter and as such, it can **never** meet the speed of the external bus.

Multiple Disk Drives

So if the disk cannot match the speed of the disk interface, why create these ever faster specifications. Well, the good news is that because you can fit more than one disk to the PC, you can improve overall performance by reading and writing from two disks simultaneously. There are two aspects of this, first, if you install multiple disks in your FreeNAS server and offer them as separate resources, then the load on the disks will be split according to how many people are accessing files on disk one and how many are accessing data on disk two. As the disk interface can cope with both disks simultaneously, you have doubled the performance of your system. The second approach is to use the disks as an array where the disks contain copies of the same data and so the FreeNAS server can find the same data in two places and read that data from the less busy disk. This is called a Redundant Arrays of Inexpensive Disks (RAID) and we shall look at it in more detail later in this chapter.

Memory, Network Card, PCI, and USB

There are a few final things to mention when deciding on the hardware for your FreeNAS server.

The first is memory or more specifically how much memory. The minimum requirement for FreeNAS is 96MB, but if you want to use iSCSI, you need a minimum of 256MB. Having extra memory is always a good thing as FreeNAS will use the extra memory for disk caching (meaning the spare memory will be used to speed up access to the disks by storing popular bits of data in memory and so removing the need to get the data from the disk).

The next thing to consider is your network; this will be covered in more depth later in this chapter, but it is worth mentioning here that you will need a network interface to connect your NAS to the network. Many motherboards come with network interfaces on board and they are a good start, but they may not be the best thing. In short, there are 3 types of popular Ethernet network interface: 10Mb/s, 100Mb/s, and 1000Mb/s. Note that these speeds are in megabits per second **not** megabytes per second. Clearly, the faster the network interface, the more data can be transferred to and from the FreeNAS server.

However, it is worth mentioning that the performance of the network is directly related to the speed of the CPU (and the motherboard). Putting a Gigabit Ethernet card in a Pentium II will **not** increase the speed of the network transfers by ten.

To connect the network card or maybe even a hardware RAID controller to your motherboard, you will need to have free PCI slots. 99.9% of all motherboards have a free PCI slot but it is worth mentioning that the speed of PCI is limited to 132MB/s. For the network, that shouldn't be a problem but if you add a high speed hardware RAID controller, then the transfer rate to and from the controller could be more than the PCI bus. There is a new version of PCI called PCI Express. It comes in different speed configurations (1x, 2x, 4x, 8x, 16x, and 32x), but they all have much greater bandwidth than basic PCI.

Finally, your FreeNAS server will need a USB 2.0 port if you are planning on using a USB flash disk to store the configuration data or if you want to install FreeNAS on it. The configuration data can be stored on either a floppy, a USB flash disk or on a hard disk in the PC. The advantage of storing the configuration data on the USB flash disk is that you can leave the disks in the machine 100% for storage. This is also true of installing the FreeNAS on a USB flash disk. This leaves ALL the hard disks free for use as storage, as well as improving boot up time as booting from USB is faster than booting from CDROM. Note that your BIOS needs to be capable of booting from USB if you intend to install FreeNAS on a USB memory stick.

Planning for Backup

When deciding how you are going to use and deploy your FreeNAS server, you need to consider your backup requirements. Backup is sadly something that is often left as a low priority task and then suddenly something happens and everyone wants to know where are the backups.

FreeNAS doesn't come with many options for automated backup. There is no support for burning DVDs on the FreeNAS machine nor is there any support for attaching a tape drive. This leaves us with just two options:

- The first is to include enough disks in the machine so that the data can be duplicated internally, and the second is to copy the data to another machine where it can be burnt to DVD or left there as a backup server. This can be achieved in one of two ways. Double the amount of disks can be added to the machine and as a manual task the system administrator can copy the data from the "live" disks to the "backup" disks. This task can also be automated and we will look at this in more detail in chapter 7. Another way to achieve this is with RAID, which we will study in more detail later in this chapter. Using a technique known as mirroring, the FreeNAS server can be configured to automatically copy all data written to one disk to another disk and so set up a spare copy of the data. This spare copy is also used during read operations meaning that the overall storage performance increases.

> The disadvantage of duplicating the data internally, as the **only** means of backup, is that if something was to happen to the server itself then the backup data would also be lost. Secondly, this method (especially the RAID variations) doesn't allow for the recovery of mistakenly deleted files or allow for the restoration of files from a few months ago.

- The second way to implement backup for your FreeNAS server is by copying it to another machine. This second machine would either act as a backup server where the data just remains or it could be a staging point before the data is written to DVD or some other form of backup media. FreeNAS includes several ways in which the data can be copied off the server. In fact, any of the access protocols like CIFS, NFS, and FTP can be used to copy the data to another machine. Also, FreeNAS includes support for the RSYNC protocol whose primary goal is to allow the mirroring (or exact copying) of data from one machine to another. Also, RSYNC is sophisticated in that it will only copy the data that needs to be copied (because it has changed) and hence saves on network bandwidth when possible.

If you just want a backup server then another FreeNAS server would be ideal. Using the RSYNC protocol, the two FreeNAS servers can be configured to make backups at certain times. It is good practice to make sure that this backup server isn't sitting right next to the FreeNAS server. Why? Well if the roof comes down or the air conditioning decides to pour something all over your server, having the two machines side-by-side won't help your backup strategy very much!!!

If you need to get the data onto a DVD or some other type of media, then you need to use a client machine like a Windows, OS X or Linux computer to copy off the data and then put it on to DVD etc. You should investigate the backup solutions, which are available on those platforms.

What is RAID? And, Do I Need It?

It seems to be a rule of thumb for science fiction writers that once the spaceship is attacked by a hostile force, all appears to be lost until the emergency backup systems kick in, and then everything is restored to full power except for maybe a few flickering lights and the odd spark flying out of a nearby console.

Fortunately, you don't need to worry about your FreeNAS server being zapped with a laser beam, but you **do** need to worry about hard disk failures, electrical spikes, burst water pipes (or cooling systems), fires, and maybe even earthquakes.

The RAID (Redundant Arrays of Inexpensive Disks) concept isn't a magic solution for your entire backup and redundancy problems. For one, it won't save your server from an earthquake! However, as a means to improving your storage access speeds and as a way of coping with a disk failure, RAID is an excellent system.

So what is it? RAID is a system that divides and duplicates your data across several hard disks, and so provides redundancy and removes read bottlenecks. Depending on which scheme, you use your data is copied, in full or in part, across other disks in the RAID set and if one of those disks fails the other disks (with the copy of the data) continue to work and the data as a whole remains intact. RAID provides two main advantages: the duplication of data to guard against disk failure and the increase of storage performance as multiple disks can be used to read the same data and sent quickly back to the client. The minimum number of hard disks for the simplest RAID setup is two.

There are several different RAID configurations that are called RAID levels. Originally, there were 5 RAID levels of which two were most frequently used (RAID 1 and RAID 5). There are also several extensions which improve, combine or nest the original RAID levels. If a disk fails, in an array using a RAID level that has redundancy, then when a new disk is inserted to replace the failed disk, it will be reconstructed (from the other disks in the array) and the array will become fully operational again. It is also possible to designate a disk as a "hot spare", which will automatically take the place of a failed disk without external intervention. The failed disk can then be replaced and it will become the "hot spare". For RAID, all the disks need to be the same size. For the software RAID facilities in FreeNAS, if the disks are of different sizes, the small disk size will be used.

Here is an overview of the most popular RAID levels. Not all of these RAID levels are available using the software RAID functionality of FreeNAS, but they may be available if you are using a dedicated hardware RAID card.

RAID 0 (Striped set without redundancy) — RAID 0 is a way of joining two disks together to create one big disk. The data is interleaved between the two disks and so it improves performance but there is no fault tolerance. Any disk failure destroys the array and the data will be lost. On its own, this isn't very useful but it can be combined with RAID 1 in a system known as RAID 10. See below.

RAID 1 (mirroring) — Here, two disks are used with one disk mirroring the contents of the other disk. Whatever is written to disk 1 is also written simultaneously to disk 2 in a identical fashion. If either of the disks fails, the RAID continues using the remaining disk. When the faulty disk is replaced, the new disk will be synchronized with the good disk and the mirroring will continue as before. Write performance is often slightly worse than on a single device, because identical copies of the data written must be sent to the other disk but read performance is greatly improved as the data is available in two places and the read operation can be split between the two drives. The amount of storage space available is always half of the total of the two drives as one is used to duplicate the other.

RAID 5 (striped set with distributed parity) — This is one of the most popular and arguably one of the most useful RAID levels. It allows you to combine a larger number of physical disks, and still maintain some redundancy. RAID 5 can be used on three or more disks. If one disk fails, the data remains intact. RAID 5 can survive one disk failure, but not two or more. Both read and write performance usually increase with RAID 5. The size of a RAID 5 array is equal to the size of the smallest disk multiplied by the number of disks minus 1. So, if you have three 200GB disks, the total size of the array will be 200 X (3-1) = 400GB.

RAID 6 (striped set with dual distributed parity) — This is very similar to RAID 5 except that the data is distributed to two other drives, which means the array can recover from the failure of two disks. RAID 6 can be used on four or more disks. The size of a RAID 6 array is equal to the size of the disk multiplied by the number of disks minus 2. So if you have four 250GB disks, the total size of the array will be 250 X (4-2) = 500GB.

RAID 10 (mirrored stripes) — This is sometimes called RAID 1+0 and is a RAID 1 array of two RAID 0 arrays. So disk 1 and 2 are in RAID 0 configurations making a big disk A1. Disks 3 and 4 are also in a RAID 0 set making a combined disk called A2. Then A1 and A2 are used to mirror each other in a RAID 1 setup. A RAID 10 array can sustain multiple drive failures as long as the two failed drives are part of the **same** RAID 0 set. The read performance is good and the write performance is better than RAID 1 as the writing is interleaved across the two disks in the mirror.

Hardware or Software RAID

RAID comes in two forms. Arrays that are controlled by a dedicated piece of hardware often called the RAID controller or arrays that are controlled by software, more specifically the operating system, which in this case is FreeBSD.

If you have a hardware RAID controller, then you can use it. FreeBSD supports many hardware RAID controllers and the controller is responsible for managing the RAID array. With a RAID controller, performance is guaranteed as no overhead is added to the local CPU to run the array. The controller simply presents a logical disk to the operating system, which FreeNAS will "see" as one disk regardless of how many disks comprise the array. Some RAID cards also support hot swapping; allowing failed drives to be replaced while the system is running.

Beware of "Fake" Hardware RAID Controllers

There is a type of cheap RAID controller that doesn't have dedicated hardware for managing a RAID array but rather uses a combination of a standard disk controller chip with special firmware and drivers. Although described as RAID controllers, the burden of RAID processing is put on the CPU and not the RAID controller itself. These controllers are often known as "fake" RAID controllers, not because they don't implement RAID correctly but rather because they are not "true" hardware RAID controllers. FreeNAS does not support such kind of RAID controllers.

If you don't have a RAID controller, then you can use FreeNAS (with the help of FreeBSD) to run your RAID array for you. This doesn't require any extra controllers and comes free with FreeNAS. We will look, in detail, in chapter 6 about configuring software RAID on FreeNAS.

Network Considerations

As FreeNAS is **network** attached storage, an important element in deploying your server is the network infrastructure. If your network is slow, your FreeNAS server will appear slow to your users.

All modern Local Area Networks (LANs) use Ethernet or wireless. By local area, we mean confined to one local area, normally, a building like a house or office building. Ethernet was invented in the 1980s and has become the standard for wired home and office networking. Originally, it used a coax cable that went from machine to machine but today each machine connects directly to a hub or switch using an 8-wire cable called Category 5 cable (commonly known as Cat 5 cable).

The hub or switch acts as the distribution point and sends the network traffic on to the clients. There are 3 main speeds for Ethernet networking today. The first and original Ethernet network worked at 10Mb/s (notice megabits not megabytes) and was called 10BaseT, then came 100Mb/s networking called 100BaseT and more recently 1000Mb/s, which is 1000BaseT. 100BaseT is often known as Fast Ethernet and 1000BaseT as **Gigabit** Ethernet.

In simplest terms, you want to use the fastest networking possible on your FreeNAS server, which at the moment would mean Gigabit Ethernet. This doesn't mean that you need to use Gigabit Ethernet throughout your network. If your network is already established with Fast Ethernet, then you don't need to change all the network cards and switches on your network. However, you do need to ensure that your FreeNAS server is fitted with a Gigabit network card and attached to a **good** Gigabit switch.

This means that if two PCs, each with Fast Ethernet, are copying data from the FreeNAS server then both will use their maximum available network bandwidth (100Mb/s) but the FreeNAS server, being on Gigabit Ethernet, will be able to handle both requests (assuming it has the right hardware in terms of CPU and disks etc).

Switch or Hub?

To connect your FreeNAS server to your network, it will need to be connected to a piece of network equipment called a hub or switch.

Hubs are quite rare today, but in essence, it is a broadcast device that broadcasts all packets coming into a port from all the other ports. It does not try to manage the traffic in anyway or check if it is appropriate for any particular packet to be forwarded on. As a result, network collisions will occur. This means that the PC is trying to use the network, but other PCs on the hub are using it at the same time. Ethernet has a built-in system for handling this but it slows down the flow of traffic.

Because of this collision problem, only 4 hubs are allowed on a 10Mb/s network and only 2 on a 100Mb/s network. For 100Mb/s and greater networks, it is much better to use a switch.

During the cross over between 10Mb/s networks and 100Mb/s networks, a hybrid hub was produced called a dual speed hub. This hub is, in fact, two smaller hubs (a 10MB/s hub and a 100Mb/s) combined in one unit with a link between them. PCs with 100Mb/s connections would connect to the 100Mb/s hub and those with 10Mb/s to the 10Mb/s hub. There is a two port bridge between them. Like single speed hubs, such devices are rare today due to the popularity and low cost of Fast Ethernet switches.

A switch is different from a hub in that it examines the traffic coming in on a port and calculates where it should be sent. By sending each packet only to the connected device it was intended for, a network switch conserves network bandwidth and offers generally better performance than a hub.

Beware of Cheap Gigabit Switches

One thing to be aware of is that just because a switch calls itself a Gigabit Ethernet switch, that doesn't necessarily mean it can handle 1000Mb/s of traffic. Some of the cheaper switches available understand the language of 1000MB/s networks and in such are Gigabit Ethernet switches, but they don't offer the full bandwidth.

The key feature of a Gigabit switch is the support for Jumbo (meaning large) frames. Without Jumbo frame support, the increases over 100Mb/s networking will be marginal.

What About Wireless?

Wireless has become a very popular medium today for connecting home PCs to DSL (or ADSL) Internet modems and also for connecting various devices around the home like Internet radio devices, laptops or even multimedia centers which you can connect to your TV and use wireless connections to the Internet and to your desktop for streaming music and films.

FreeNAS does support a number of wireless devices and has support in the web interface for configuring a wireless card.

However, wireless isn't the best method for connecting to the FreeNAS. First of all, wireless has a limited bandwidth (54Mb/s) and is only half that of 100Mb/s. Second, the greater the distance from the wireless access point to the server, the bandwidth drops and this is especially true if the signal needs to go through walls. The practical result is that the server needs to be close to the wireless access point and since it is close, you should be able to connect to your network with a cable.

It is worth repeating that the FreeNAS server is best suited to connection to a Gigabit Ethernet switch.

Summary

In this chapter, we have looked at the decisions you will need to make to buy or prepare a server for deployment in your organization. We have considered the hardware requirements based on the numbers of users and looked at the different types of disks you can put in your server. We have also looked at some of the implications for your network.

In the next chapter, we will get our hands on the FreeNAS server and install it.

3
Exploring FreeNAS

It is time to install the FreeNAS server and start looking at the basic configuration. This chapter is divided into 5 main sections:

- Quick start guide for the impatient
- A detailed overview of installation
- Basic configuration
- Install to a hard disk
- Upgrading FreeNAS from a previous version.

Downloading FreeNAS

Before you can install the FreeNAS server, you will need to download the latest version from the FreeNAS website (http://www.freenas.org). Go to the download section and find the latest "LiveCD" version. The LiveCD version is what is known as an ISO image file and will have the .iso file extension. An ISO image is an exact copy of the structure and data for a CD or DVD disk. Using a CD burning program, you can create a FreeNAS bootable CD. We will look at this in more detail later on.

What Hardware Do I Need?

In this chapter, we will start exploring FreeNAS, so you will need a machine on which to install the FreeNAS software. At this point in time, it doesn't have to be the final machine you are going to use as the FreeNAS server. You can use a "test" machine now and having learnt all about FreeNAS, you can build, install, and deploy a production machine (or machines) later.

So, what we need now is a PC with at least 96Mb of RAM (but 128Mb or more is recommended), a bootable CD-ROM drive, a network card, one or more hard disks, and either a floppy disk drive (and a blank formatted disk) or a USB flash disk (MS-DOS formatted and empty).

Exploring FreeNAS

The hard disk will be for the data that you want to store and the floppy disk or USB flash disk will be for storing the configuration information.

For the installation and initialization stages, you will also need a monitor and keyboard (but not mouse) attached to the PC. You can remove the monitor later, once FreeNAS is up and running.

Warning

FreeNAS boots as a LiveCD, which means that it does not use the disks on the host machine during boot up. However, when you start to configure storage on the FreeNAS server (specifically, when you format drives) all the data on the disk will be LOST. Do NOT use a machine that contains important data or an operating system that you will need afterwards.

Virtualization & VMWare

The average PC runs just one operating system and inside that operating system, you would run your applications like word processing and email. There is a technology (called virtualization), which allows PCs to run more than one operating system, or to be more precise, to allow a guest virtual PC to run inside your actual PC. This virtual PC is an independent software box that can run its own OS and applications as if it were a physical computer. A virtual PC behaves exactly like a physical PC and has its own virtual CPU, RAM, hard disk, and network interface card (NIC).

You can install FreeNAS on a virtual PC and FreeNAS can't tell the difference between the virtual PC and any other physical machine, also, it appears on the network just as a real PC would, running FreeNAS.

There are lots of virtualization products available for Windows, Linux, and Apple OS X today. You can learn more at Wikipedia `http://en.wikipedia.org/wiki/Virtualization`

A very popular virtualization solution is from VMWare (`http://www.vmware.com`). VMWare have both commercial and freeware offerings and there are pre-configured FreeNAS images available for the VMWare range of products. This makes it an ideal environment for testing the FreeNAS server.

Quick Start Guide For the Impatient

If you are comfortable with burning ISO images to CDs, setting your computer's BIOS to boot from CDROM, disk partitions, and TCP/IP networking then this little guide should help you get a simple version of the FreeNAS server up and running in just a few minutes.

If, however, some of these things sound daunting, then skip this section and go on to the next one where we shall go through the installation process one step at a time.

For this example, we will use a USB flash disk to store the configuration information. You can use a floppy but be careful that during the boot process, the PC doesn't try to boot from the floppy before it boots from the CDROM.

Burning and Booting

Once you have downloaded the ISO image file from the FreeNAS website, you need to burn it to a CD. Having done that, put the CD into the PC as well as the flash disk and switch it on. Make sure that the BIOS is set to boot from CD. If it isn't, you need to enter into the BIOS and configure it to boot from CD. On many modern PCs, it is possible to select the boot device at start-up by pressing a special key (which is often either F8 or F12) to show a boot device menu. You can then select the CD as the boot device.

The boot process is in four distinct parts:

1. First, the PC will go through its POST (Power On Self Test) sequence. Here, the PC will check the amount of memory installed (which you can often see being counted on the screen) and which devices are connected (like hard drives and CDROMs).
2. It should then start to boot from the CD. Here, FreeBSD (the underlying OS of FreeNAS) will start to boot, this is recognisable by the simple spinning wheel (made up of simple text characters like | - / and \, which are animated to give the appearance of spinning).
3. The third step is the FreeNAS boot menu. This will appear for just a few seconds and you should just let it boot normally, which is the default.
4. The final stage is when the FreeNAS logo appears and the system will boot as FreeNAS server. You can tell when the system is fully loaded because the PC speaker will make some short but melodious beeps.

Exploring FreeNAS

To enable access to the web interface, the network of the FreeNAS server must be configured. Press the SPACE bar on the keyboard and the FreeNAS logo will disappear and a simple text menu will appear.

```
        built on Sun Nov 18 07:25:47 CET 2007 for i386-livecd
        Copyright (C) 2005-2007 by Olivier Cochard-Labbe. All rights reserved.
        Visit http://www.freenas.org for updates.

        LAN IPv4 address: 192.168.1.250
        LAN IPv6 address: fe80:1::20c:29ff:

        Port configuration:

        LAN    -> lnc0

Console setup
*************
1) Assign Interfaces
2) Set LAN IP address
3) Reset webGUI password
4) Reset to factory defaults
5) Ping host
6) Shell
7) Reboot system
8) PowerOff system
9) Install/Upgrade to an hard drive/flash device, etc.

Enter a number:
```

There are two aspects to configuring the network, first, you need to choose which network card to use and second, you need to assign it an address. If you have only one network card in your machine, then the FreeNAS server should have found it and automatically assigned it to be the LAN (Local Area Network) interface.

[What If My Network Card Isn't Found?

This probably means that the network card in your machine isn't supported by FreeNAS or more specifically, by FreeBSD. You will need to replace the card with one supported by FreeBSD. Check the FreeBSD hardware compatibility page for more information: http://www.freebsd.org/releases/6.2R/hardware-i386.html]

If you see something like this:

```
LAN IPv4 address: 192.168.1.250
LAN IPv6 address: fe80:1::20c:29ff:

Port configuration:

LAN    -> lnc0
```

then the network has been recognised and assigned automatically by FreeNAS.

The default IPv4 address for FreeNAS is 192.168.1.250, if this is good for your network, then you can just leave it unchanged. However, if you need to change it then press 2 followed by *ENTER*. If you want the machine to get its address from DHCP (Dynamic Host Configuration Protocol), answer yes (y) to the IPv4 DHCP question, otherwise answer no (n). If you are not using DHCP, you can now enter the desired IP address. Next, you need to enter the subnet mask. For 255.255.255.0, enter 24, for 255.255.0.0 enter 16, and for 255.0.0.0, enter 8. At this point, you can now skip the default gateway and DNS questions (by just pressing *ENTER*). If you do want to enter a default gateway and DNS server at this point, they will usually be the IP address of your Internet router. We won't be using IPv6 so the simplest thing to do now is just answer *yes* to the "Do you want to use AutoConfiguration for IPv6?" question. This will cause a small delay while FreeNAS tries (and probably fails) to get the IPv6 address but it is simpler than trying to enter the IPv6 address manually!

You are now ready to access the web interface. The FreeNAS web interface can be accessed from any machine on the network with a web browser (including Windows, Linux, and OS X machines). On this client machine, type the address of the FreeNAS server with http:// in front of it into your web browser. For example:

`http://192.168.1.250.`

Configuring

The first time you access the FreeNAS web interface, you will be asked for the username and password. The default username is *admin* and the default password is *freenas*.

Exploring FreeNAS

You should now be in the web interface. To configure some storage space, you need to work with "Disks". The logical order of working is that disks must be added, then formatted (if need be), then mounted. Finally, access is given to the various mounted disks by configuring different system services like CIFS and FTP.

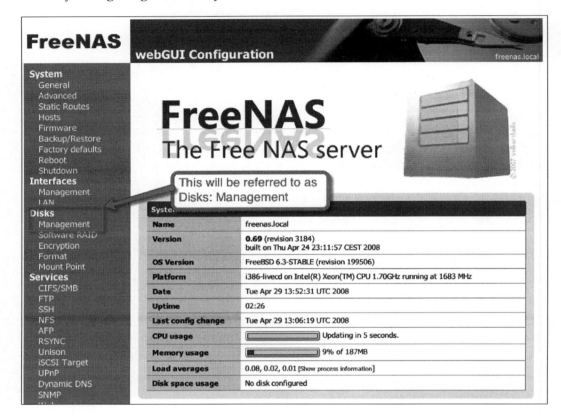

So, to add a disk, go to **Disks: Management**. There is a **+** sign in a circle on the right-hand-side of the page (it can be easy to miss first time), click on it to add a disk. On the next page, select the disk you want to add. If you click on the drop-down menu, you should see the hard disks of the machines, the CDROM, and the USB flash disk.

Chapter 3

>
> **Disk Names in FreeBSD**
> The disk naming convention in FreeBSD is:
> **/dev/ad0**: *Is the IDE/ATA Primary Master*
> **/dev/ad1** : *Is the IDE/ATA Primary Slave*
> **/dev/ad2** : *Is the IDE/ATA Secondary Master*
> **/dev/ad3**: *Is the IDE/ATA Secondary Slave*
> **/dev/acd0**: *Is the first ATA CD/DVD drive detected*
> **/dev/da0**: *Is the first SCSI hard drive, /dev/da1 the second and so on.*
> USB flash disks are controlled using the SCSI driver, so they will appear as /dev/daN drives as well.

Make sure ad0 is selected (which it should be by default). The rest of the page you can leave alone. Click **Add** to add the disk to the system. You then need to click **Apply** in order for the changes to take effect. You will now have a table showing you the disk you have added, including its size and a description.

> **Apply**
> In FreeNAS, the majority of steps need to be applied (which saves the configuration file to disk) by clicking the *Apply* button. It is normally found near the top of the page before any tables or configuration information is given. If you do not apply the changes, the interface will, on the whole, remember your changes but they will not be enacted in the system. After a reboot, unapplied changes will disappear. It is possible on some pages to make multiple operations and apply them all at the end.

Next, the disk needs to be formatted. In **Disks: Format,** select the disk ad0 (which you just added above). Leave everything else unchanged and click **Format disk**. The disk will then be formatted. The low level output of the format command will be displayed in a box. It should end with **Done!**.

Now the disk needs to be mounted. Go to **Disks: Mount Point**. Click on the **+** in the circle (which I shall refer to as the "add circle" from now on). Leave the **Type** as *Disk* and select the disk *ad0* again. You need to type in a name, *store* is as good a name as any, but feel free to use which ever descriptive name you want to.

> **Be Descriptive**
> In setting up and configuring your FreeNAS server, you will be called upon to invent various names for mount points and share names etc. Try to be as descriptive as you can without being long winded. Temp, scratch, blob, and even zob are OK for testing, but try more meaningful names like storeage1, storage60gb or backupstorage etc. Don't use spaces in the names, instead use underline and in general, the names should be no longer than 15 characters.

Although filling-in the description isn't mandatory in the web interface, it is worth using. Once you have completed the form click **Add** and then apply the changes.

Sharing with Windows Machines

Now that the disk has been added, formatted, and mounted, it is time to share it on the network and give other users the ability to read and write to it. FreeNAS supports many different types of access protocol, for this start guide, we will only look at Microsoft's CIFS protocol that primarily allows Windows machines (but also Apple OS X and Linux machines) to access the storage.

1. In Services: **CIFS/SMB**, tick the enable box (in the title of the configuration data table). At this point, you can just about leave everything else as is with the exception of the workgroup name. We will be leaving the authentication method as "Anonymous" here as this is the easiest to get working and provides unrestricted read/write access to everyone.

2. To make sure that the Windows machines are able to find the shared storage, we need to set the workgroup name, on the FreeNAS server, to be the same as the workgroup name of the Windows PC that will access the share. The default workgroup name for Windows Vista is WORKGROUP but note that the default for Window XP Home Edition was MSHOME.

3. Now click **Save and Restart**. This will save the changes you have made and restart the CIFS service.

4. Go to the **Shares** tab and click on add circle. Enter a name for the share. Repeating the name of the mount point is probably the safest policy, so in this case, store and also add a comment. Then click **...** in the **Path** section. This will bring up a simple file system browser. The files you are seeing are on the FreeNAS server and NOT on your local PC. Click **store** and **/mnt/store/** will appear in the little edit box at the click. **OK** it and you will be taken back to the shares page. Now **/mnt/store/** has been added as the path.

5. Leave everything else as it is and click **Add** and then apply the changes.

Chapter 3

So now the first hard disk of the computer is formatted, mounted, and shared to the rest of the network. Now, we will access the share from a Windows Vista machine.

Testing the Share

You can perform this test from any machine that supports the CIFS protocol including Windows 95/98/ME, Windows 2000/XP, Apple OS X, and Linux. Here, we are going to use Windows Vista.

1. Open the Network and Sharing Center by clicking **Network** on the Start menu. When the window appears, Vista will automatically scan the network for any shared network resources. When it has finished, you will see the available machines on the network including **FREENAS**.

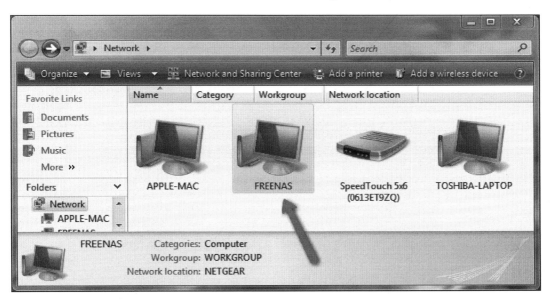

2. Open up the **FREENAS** computer and you will see store, the storage area that you configured. Double click on that and you now "inside" the FreeNAS server from within your Windows machine. Try dragging and dropping a few files in to the store area. Then try deleting them again.

Exploring FreeNAS

3. To access the FreeNAS server without using the Network and Sharing Center, click **Start**, and type **\\freenas** and then press *Enter*. This will bring up the shares available on the FreeNAS server directly:

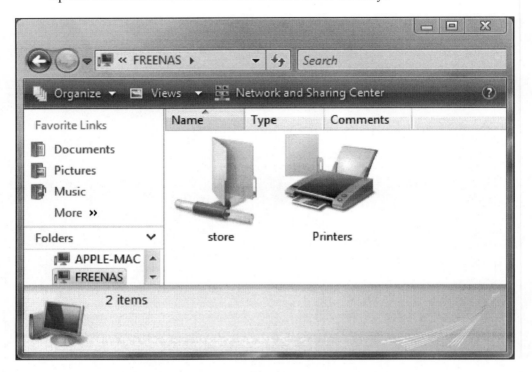

Detailed Overview of Installation

It is time to get your hands on a working FreeNAS server and to do that, we need to boot it up onto a PC. There are several steps to this. First, you must burn a CD of the ISO image file you have downloaded. Then, you need to boot the PC from the CD; this may involve changing your computers BIOS to make it boot from the optical drive. Then, you can configure the FreeNAS server to make some storage space available on the network.

When using the LiveCD to boot FreeNAS, there are two types of storage on FreeNAS: data and configuration information. The data will be held on the hard drive of the PC, but the configuration needs to be held on a floppy disk or a USB flash disk. For this example, we will use a USB flash disk to store the configuration information.

Making the FreeNAS CD

To boot the PC into FreeNAS, you need a CD. The ISO image file you have downloaded contains all the information needed for the CD, but it needs to be written onto a physical CD. This process is often known as *burning* the CD as the laser writes to the disk by heating it and marking or scorching the surface layer.

You need to use a PC with a CD-RW drive and a blank CD-R disk (I recommend using a good brand name CD-R for best results). Download the FreeNAS ISO image on to that machine. The PC with the CD writer should have some CD writing software on it (for example Roxio Easy CD or Nero). If you are familiar with the CD writing software, go ahead and burn the ISO file to the CD-R disk.

[If you aren't familiar with the CD writing software or it doesn't have any CD writing software, then I recommend ISO Recorder. You can download it from http://isorecorder.alexfeinman.com/isorecorder.htm.]

Booting from CD

Put your newly made FreeNAS CD into the CD drive of the machine on which you want to install FreeNAS, and also put the USB flash disk into a USB port. The flash disk will be used to store the configuration data. (You can also use a floppy disk. If you have both a USB flash disk and a floppy inserted, FreeNAS will save the configuration on the USB device). Now, you need to switch on the PC. When a PC starts, it goes through what is known as the Power On Self Test sequence. Here, the PC will check the amount of memory installed in the PC and find the installed hard drives. After the checks, the PC will try and boot from one of the hard drives, the CDROM, the floppy disk or even a USB flash disk. Which device the PC chooses first as its boot device can be changed by a built-in setup program. The setup program lets you modify basic system configuration settings. These settings are stored in a special battery-backed area of the computer's memory that retains the settings even when the power is switched off. During the POST sequence, there is normally a message telling you how to enter into the built-in setup program. It is normally either the *DEL* key or *F2*, on some systems it is also *F10*.

You need to enter into the setup to check and/or change the first boot device to be the CDROM so that the computer will boot into FreeNAS. Each PC has a slightly different setup program, so you will need to search around until you find what you need. The three most popular types of setup programs (also known as BIOS—Basic Input Output Program) are the Phoenix setup program, the Phoenix-Award setup program, and the AMI setup program.

[45]

Exploring FreeNAS

 There are many types of BIOS setup programs and each PC manufacturer modifies the setup program for their own use. The information below is really only a "rough guide" to help you feel your way around. Your BIOS setup program may be significantly different from the examples below. The best source of information is the manual that came with your PC or your motherboard. If you don't have one, most PC manufacturers have them available for download on their websites.

Phoenix BIOS

If your machine has a Phoenix BIOS, then normally you need to press *F2* to enter the setup program. The top of the setup program has a menu that you can navigate with the left and right arrow keys, you need to select the **Boot** menu.

On the **Boot** menu page, you can move up and down the available boot devices using the up and down arrow keys. You can expand and collapse sections with the **+** or **−** signs using the *ENTER* key. To change the boot order, you use the **+** and **−** keys. You want to make sure that the CDROM is the first device in the list. After you have changed the boot order list, you need to go to the Exit menu (by pressing the right arrow key) and select **Exit Saving Changes**. The PC will then reboot and after the POST, it will start to boot from the FreeNAS CD.

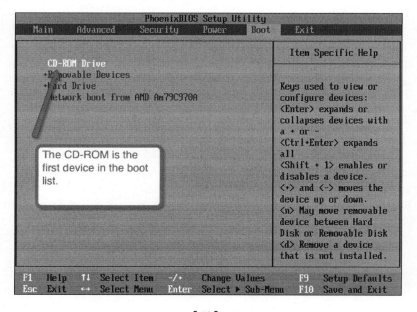

Phoenix-Award BIOS

If your PC has a Phoenix-Award BIOS, then normally, you need to press *DEL* to enter the setup program. Once inside, you can the *up*, *down*, *left*, and *right* keys to navigate around the menus. Go in to *Advanced BIOS Features* and set the *First Boot Device* to be CDROM by using the **+** and **-** keys. You now need to save your changes and exit. Pressing *ESC* will bring you back to the main menu, then select **Save & Exit Setup**. Often, pressing *F10* will have the same effect. The PC will then reboot and if you have made the changes correctly, it will boot from the FreeNAS CD.

AMI BIOS

The American Megatrends, Inc (AMI) BIOS normally displays a message telling you to **Hit <DEL> if you want to run setup**. Once inside, it is quite different to that of the setup programs for Phoenix or Award. Here, the *Tab* key is used to navigate and the arrow keys are used to change values. To go from one page to the next, press the *ALT+P* keys. This information should also be printed at the bottom of the BIOS setup page. You need to find the variable *Boot Sequence* and make sure that it is set to boot from the CDROM first.

First Look at FreeNAS

The boot process is in 4 distinct parts. First, the PC will go through its POST (Power On Self Test) sequence. Here, the PC will check the amount of memory installed (which you can often see being counted on the screen) and which devices are connected (like hard drives and CDROMs). It should then start to boot from the CD. Here, FreeBSD (the underlying OS of FreeNAS) will start to boot, this is recognisable by the simple spinning wheel (made up of simple text characters like | - / and \ which are animated to give the appearance of spinning). The third step is the FreeNAS boot menu. This will appear for just five seconds and you should just let it boot normally which is the default. The final stage is when the FreeNAS logo appears and the system will boot as a FreeNAS server. You can tell when the system is fully loaded because the PC speaker will make some short but melodious beeps.

Configuring the Network

The majority of the configuration for FreeNAS is done via a web interface, but before you can use the web interface, the FreeNAS server needs to be configured for your network. This is done via a simple text menu system using the keyboard and monitor attached to the PC with FreeNAS running on it. You probably only need to do this once, and after that this new network information will be saved on the USB flash disk (or floppy disk) and the server will boot into this configuration every time.

Exploring FreeNAS

If you press the SPACE bar on FreeNAS machine, the FreeNAS logo will disappear and a simple menu will appear.

```
       built on Sun Nov 18 07:25:47 CET 2007 for i386-livecd
       Copyright (C) 2005-2007 by Olivier Cochard-Labbe. All rights reserved.
       Visit http://www.freenas.org for updates.

       LAN IPv4 address: 192.168.1.250
       LAN IPv6 address: fe80:1::20c:29ff:

       Port configuration:

       LAN   -> lnc0

    Console setup
    **************
    1) Assign Interfaces
    2) Set LAN IP address
    3) Reset webGUI password
    4) Reset to factory defaults
    5) Ping host
    6) Shell
    7) Reboot system
    8) PowerOff system
    9) Install/Upgrade to an hard drive/flash device, etc.

    Enter a number:
```

Here, you have a number of options including options to reboot or power off the system. The first two options are about configuring the network and they reflect the two parts to configuring the network, first you need to choose which network card to use (option 1) and second you need to assign it an address (option 2).

If you have only one network card in your machine then the FreeNAS server should have found it and automatically assigned it to be the LAN (Local Area Network) interface.

[

What If My Network Card Isn't Found?

This probably means that the network card in your machine isn't supported by FreeNAS or more specifically by FreeBSD. You will need to replace the card with one supported by FreeBSD. Check the FreeBSD hardware compatibility page for more information: http://www.freebsd.org/releases/6.2R/hardware-i386.html
]

If you see something like the following screenshot:

then the network has been recognised and assigned automatically by FreeNAS.

What is a LAN IP Address?

IP stands for Internet Protocol and it is the basic low level language that computers use to talk to each other on the Internet. It is also used on private networks (in the office or at home) to connect different PCs and even printers to each other. An IPv4 address is made up of 4 sets of number (0 to 255) and is expressed in what is known as dot notation (meaning that each number has a dot between it). So 192.168.1.250 is an IP address, it also happens to be the default IP address for the FreeNAS server. Like email, the postal service and telephone, each destination (email account, mailbox or handset) needs a unique way of being identified. This is what IP addresses do; they allow each piece of equipment on the network to have a unique identifier so that messages can be addressed to the right place on the network.

>
> **Pronouncing IP Addresses**
>
> If you need to speak to someone about an IP address, the simplest way is to speak about each digit separately, so 192.168.1.250 isn't "one hundred and ninety two dot" but rather "one nine two dot one six eight dot one dot two five zero".

There are two ways in which you can obtain an IP address for the FreeNAS server. The first is to have the address assigned automatically via the DHCP service (Dynamic Host Configuration Protocol), and the second is to assign it manually.

> **What is DHCP?**
>
> The Dynamic Host Configuration Protocol (DHCP) automates the assignment of IP addresses and other IP parameters (like subnet masks and default gateway). A computer that needs an IP address will send a request to the DHCP server and the server will reply with an IP address from a pool of addresses that have been set aside for this purpose. A DHCP server can be a PC or server (running Windows, OS X or Linux) as well as small devices like modern DSL modems and firewalls.

Exploring FreeNAS

The advantage of the DHCP method is that the IP address assignment, all happens in the background and you don't need to worry about setting it yourself. The disadvantages are that first you need to have an already configured and running DHCP server on your network; and second, DHCP assigns addresses from a pool of available addresses. This means that every time the FreeNAS server boots, it is not guaranteed to have the same address as it had previously. This isn't a problem when using the CIFS protocol, however, for accessing the web interface or using protocols like FTP, it is desirable to have a stable IP address to refer to. However, for testing the FreeNAS server and learning about how it works using a DHCP assigned address could be acceptable for now.

> It is actually possible to assign fixed, permanent IP address to certain pieces of hardware, including a FreeNAS server over DHCP, but that requires extra advanced configuration changes in the DHCP server that cannot be covered in this book.

So opting for the manual IP address, you now need to obtain two pieces of information. The first is the actual IP address for the FreeNAS and the second is what is known as the subnet mask. The subnet mask will also be expressed in the dot notation and is normally something like 255.255.255.0. If you are in an office environment, you need to speak to the network administrator and he/she will be able to give you the information you need. If you are administering your own network, you need to choose an IP that isn't currently allocated to any other machine on your network (and also, isn't part of the address pool of any DHCP server on your network).

Having obtained the IP address and subnet mask, you can now configure the FreeNAS server for your network. Select option 2 on the console menu. If you have chosen to have DHCP assign the address, answer yes (y) to the first question about using DHCP for IPv4. Otherwise answer no (n).

If you are setting the address manually, you can now enter the address in dot notation, i.e. 192.168.1.240. Next, comes the subnet mask. If your subnet mask is 255.255.255.0: enter 24, for 255.255.0.0: enter 16, and for 255.0.0.0: enter 8. At this point, you can now skip the default gateway and DNS questions (by just pressing *ENTER*).

We won't be using IPv6 so the simplest thing to do now is just answer yes to the "Do you want to use AutoConfiguration for IPv6?" question. This will cause a small delay while FreeNAS tries (and probably fails) to get the IPv6 address but it is simpler than trying to enter the IPv6 address manually!

After you have successful set the IP address, there will be a small message on the screen inviting you to access the web interface by opening the listed URL in your web browser. If you have used DHCP, note down the URL listed. If you set the IP address manually, check that the URL listed is the same as the IP address you set with `http://` in front of it.

You are now ready to access the web interface.

What is IPv4 and IPv6?

The Internet Protocol has been around since the mid 1980's and when it was designed, the popularity of the Internet was not envisaged. The number of computers connected to the Internet is quickly growing beyond the addressing capabilities of the original protocol. As an answer to this, a new version of the IP protocol has been designed and has been given the name IP version 6 or IPv6 for short and the older version has taken the name IP version 4 or IPv4 for short. FreeNAS supports both versions of the Internet Protocol. In this book, we will concentrate just on IPv4 as it still remains the most popular of the two protocols.

Basic Configuration

With your FreeNAS server now being up and running, it is time to access the web interface. Open a web browser on a computer on the same network as the FreeNAS server. Enter in the URL of the FreeNAS server. This should be the same as the IP address of the server with `http://` in the front. The default URL is `http://192.168.1.250`.

The first time you access the FreeNAS web interface, you will be asked for the username and password. The default username is *admin* and the default password is *freenas*.

FreeNAS Web Interface

You should now have the web interface in your browser. The interface is split into two main sections. Down the left-hand-side are the menus, and the right-hand-side contains the pages for configuration. The menus are split into various sections: System, Interfaces, Disks, Services, Access, Status, Diagnostics, and Advanced.

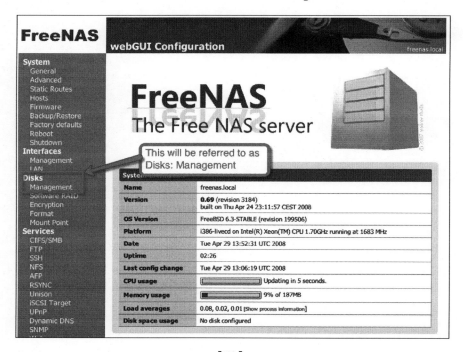

> When talking about a particular menu item, we shall use the notation Subsection: Menu Item to help you find the right menu option easily. So, the Management option, which is in the Disks subsection, will be referred to as **Disks: Management**.

System

This section is for system level configuration and operations, here for example you can change the username and password, backup and restore the configuration data, and shutdown or reboot the server.

Interfaces

Here, you can configure the network of the FreeNAS server much like you did via the console menu. You can change the network card that is used for the web interface and assign permanent or automatic IP addresses.

Be careful when you change things here as some changes won't take effect until you reboot. If you have changed any of the addressing, you will need to access the web interface with the IP address.

Disks

This section of the menu is for administering the disks on the server. Here, you can set up disk redundancy (RAID), control encryption, format disks, and mount the disks on the server.

Services

The various access protocols like CIFS, NFS, and FTP are controlled from here. Each service is administered individually and by default NONE of the services are enabled, so before you can access files stored on the FreeNAS server, you need to enable at least one of these services.

Access

Most of the services offered by FreeNAS use some form of list of users to control who has access and who does not. This section is for defining these users and the groups they belong to as well as connecting the FreeNAS server to other directory services.

Status

The status menu has several reporting tools for you to see the current state of your FreeNAS server including a general overview, memory usage, disk usage, and network usage. You can also configure emails to be sent periodically about the status of the server.

Diagnostics

The diagnostics menu contains different tools to help diagnose any problem with the FreeNAS server, including logs of all the important services and diagnostic information from the hard disks and other system modules.

Advanced

The advanced section provides some simple tools for executing commands at the operating system level and should not be used by those unfamiliar with FreeBSD.

Adding a Disk

To configure some storage space, you need to work with "Disks". The logical order of working with disks is:

1. First, FreeNAS needs to be told about the disks it can use. A disk can be a physical hard drive as well as a CD-ROM or an iSCSI target.
2. Next, the disks need to be formatted (if need be).
3. After that, the disks need to be mounted. This means that they are made available as working disk space, which can be used by the system. Before being mounted, the disks are not available to be used as storage space.
4. Finally, the storage space needs to be made available to the network via one of the access protocols, for example CIFS, NFS or FTP. To do this, the respective service needs to be enabled and configured to use the disk.

Here are the steps in detail:

1. Go to **Disks: Management**.
    - There is a + sign in a circle on the right-hand-side of the page (which shall be referred to as the "add circle" from now on), click it to add a disk.

Chapter 3

- On the next page, select the disk you want to add. If you click on the drop down menu, you should see the hard disks of the machines, the CDROM, and the USB flash disk.

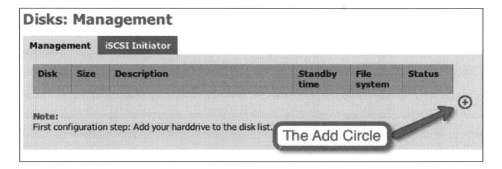

> **Disk Names in FreeBSD**
>
> The disk naming convention in FreeBSD is:
>
> **/dev/ad0**: Is the IDE/ATA Primary Master
>
> **/dev/ad1** : Is the IDE/ATA Primary Slave
>
> **/dev/ad2** : Is the IDE/ATA Secondary Master
>
> **/dev/ad3**: Is the IDE/ATA Secondary Slave
>
> **/dev/acd0**: Is the first ATA CD/DVD drive detected
>
> **/dev/da0**: Is the first SCSI hard drive, /dev/da1 the second and so on.
>
> USB flash disks are controlled using the SCSI driver so they will appear as **/dev/daN** drives as well.

- Make sure ad0 is selected (which it should be by default).
- The rest of the page you can leave alone.
- Click **Add** to add the disk to the system.

Exploring FreeNAS

- You then need to click **Apply** in order for the changes to take effect. You will now have a table showing you the disk you have added including its size and a description.

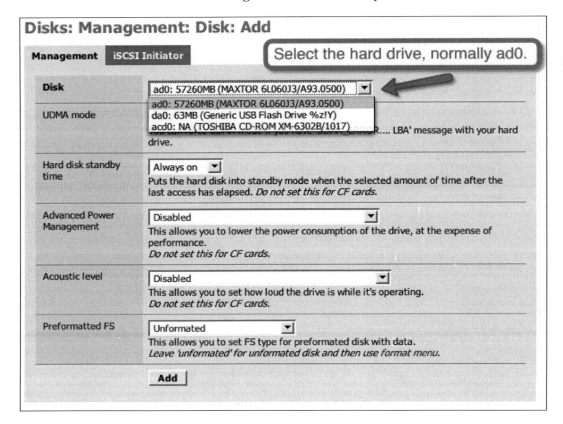

2. Next, the disk needs to be formatted. Beware all the data on this disk will be lost. In **Disks: Format**, select the disk ad0 (which you just added above). Leave everything else unchanged. By default, this means we are formatting the disk using UFS, which is the native file system for FreeBSD. You can enter a volume name if you desire. Click **Format disk**. The disk will then be formatted. The low level output of the format command will be displayed in a box. The time it takes to format the disk depends on the size of the disk. It should end with **Done!**

3. Now the disk needs to be mounted. Go to **Disks: Mount Point**. Click on the add circle. Leave the **Type** as *Disk* and select the disk *ad0* again. You need to type in a name, *store* is as good a name as any, but feel free to use which ever descriptive name you want to.

> **Be Descriptive**
>
> In setting up and configuring your FreeNAS server, you will be called upon to invent various names for mount points and share names etc. Try to be as descriptive as you can without being long winded. Temp, scratch, blob, and even zob are OK for testing but try more meaningful names like storeage1, storage60gb or backupstorage etc.

Although filling-in the description isn't mandatory in the web interface, it is worth using. Once you have completed the form click **Add** and then apply the changes.

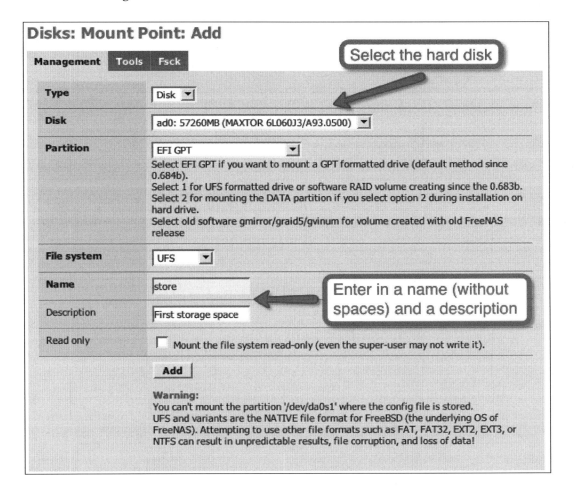

4. Now that the disk has been added, formatted, and mounted, it is time to share it on the network and give other users the ability to read and write to it. FreeNAS supports many different types of access protocols. First, we shall have a look at Microsoft's CIFS protocol that primarily allows Windows machines (but also Apple OS X and Linux machines) to access the storage. Then, our second test will be to configure the FTP protocol.

Accessing the Disk via CIFS

1. In Services: **CIFS/SMB**, tick the enable box (in the title of the configuration data table). At this point, you can just about leave everything else as is with the exception of the workgroup name.

2. To make sure that the Windows machines are able to find the shared storage, we need to set the workgroup name, on the FreeNAS server, to be the same as the workgroup name of the Windows PC that will access the share. The default workgroup name for Windows Vista is WORKGROUP, but note that the default for Window XP Home Edition was MSHOME.

> **Checking Your Workgroup**
>
> On Windows XP, you can discover your workgroup name by clicking **Start** and then right clicking on **My Computer**. Now click **Properties**. Click on the **Computer Name** tab in the **System Properties** dialog that has appeared. You can change the workgroup name by clicking the **Change...** button.
>
> On Windows Vista, you can find out your workgroup name by clicking on **Start** and then right clicking on **Computer**. Now click **Properties**. The workgroup name is in the *Computer name, domain, and workgroup settings*. You can change the workgroup by clicking on **Change settings** and then the **Change...** button.

3. Leave the authentication method as **Anonymous** here as this is the easiest to get working and provides unrestricted read/write access to everyone. Now click **Save and Restart**. This will save the changes you have made and restart the CIFS service.

Chapter 3

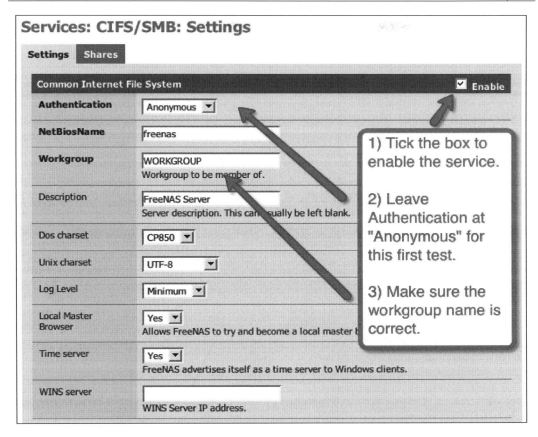

4. Now, go to the **Shares** tab and click on add circle. Enter a name for the share. Repeating the name of the mount point is probably the safest policy, so in this case *store* and also add a comment. Then click **...** in the Path section. This will bring up a simple file system browser. The files you are seeing are on the FreeNAS server and NOT on your local PC. Click **store** and **/mnt/store/** will appear in the little edit box at the click. **OK** it and you will be taken back to the shares page. Now **/mnt/store/** has been added as the path.

5. Leave everything else as it is and click **Add** and then apply the changes.

So now the first hard disk of the computer is formatted, mounted, and shared to the rest of the network. Now we will access the share from a Windows Vista machine.

Exploring FreeNAS

Testing the Share

You can perform this test from any machine that supports the CIFS protocol including Windows, OS X, and Linux. Here we are going to use Windows Vista:

1. Open the Network and Sharing Center by clicking **Network** on the Start menu. When the window appears, Vista will automatically scan the network for any shared network resources. When it has finished, you will see the available machines on the network including FREENAS.

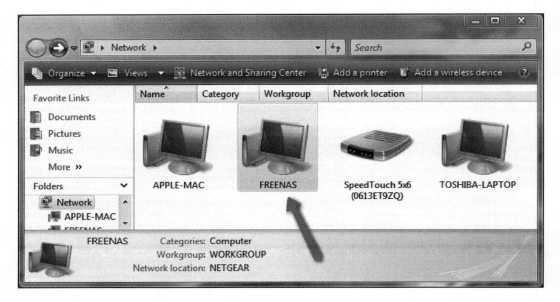

2. Open up the FREENAS computer and you will see *store*, the storage area that you configured. Double click on that and you now "inside" the FreeNAS server from within your Windows machine. Try dragging and dropping a few files into the *store* area. Then try deleting them again.

3. To access the FreeNAS server, without using the Network and Sharing Center, click **Start**, and type **\\freenas** and then press *Enter*. This will bring up the shares available on the FreeNAS server directly.

Accessing via FTP

The File Transfer Protocol is a fast and stable protocol for transferring files over a network. FTP is a client/server protocol and is most often used to transfer files from one machine to another in a "one off" sense. A connection is made, the files are transferred, and the connection is closed. This is a protocol that is often used to allow people to download files from the Internet. In the NAS context, it is very useful for offering a repository of software on your network (like software, company templates, and antivirus software updates).

1. To enable the FTP service, go to **Services: FTP** and tick enable.
2. Now click **Save and Restart**.

This will save the changes you have made and restart the FTP service. By default, anonymous FTP logins are enabled. This means that any user can log in and access the storage.

Exploring FreeNAS

Testing FTP Access

All modern operating systems including Windows, Linux, and OS X contain command line FTP clients. These are simply enough to use, but can be a bit difficult to learn if you are used to using graphic user interfaces. A good free FTP client for Windows is Core FTP and you can download it from http://www.coreftp.com.

1. To test the FTP service of FreeNAS using Core FTP, first download it and install it.
2. The first window you see when you start Core FTP is the **Site Manager**. Here, you can enter the parameters for connecting to a server.
3. In the **Site Name** field, enter **FreeNAS_Server** as a way to remember this particular server connection.
4. In **Host/IP/URL** enter the IP address of your FreeNAS server.
5. Tick **Anonymous,** which enables you to connect without a username and password (actually the username is anonymous and Core FTP will fill that in for you).
6. Now press **Connect**.

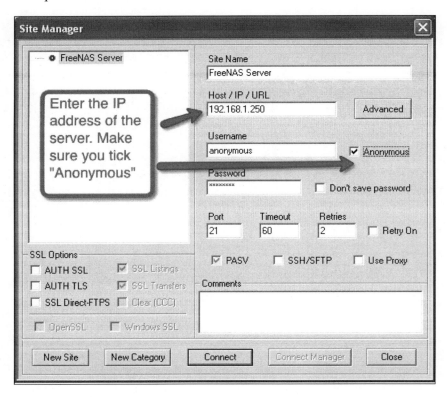

Once you press *connect*, Core FTP will connect to the FreeNAS server. On the left, you will have the file on your Windows machine and on the right, the files on the FreeNAS machine. The FTP service puts you in at the top level so you will need to double click on *store* to enter into the *store* folder that represents the disk configured earlier. You can try dragging some files over from your Windows machines and see that they will be copied over to the FreeNAS server.

As a final test, you can try to access the FreeNAS server again via CIFS (just click **start** and enter **\\freenas** and then open the *store* share) and you will see the files you just copied over using FTP.

Using Windows Built-In FTP Client

Modern versions of Windows also come with a simple FTP client built-in to Windows Explorer. You can open an FTP connection to the FreeNAS server by typing **ftp://192.168.1.250** (if this isn't the IP address of your FreeNAS server, change accordingly) in the address bar of My Computer (or Internet Explorer). From here, you can drag and drop files and use Windows Explorer very much like you would with a local hard drive.

Installing to Hard Disk

Up until now, FreeNAS has been running from the "LiveCD", which means it boots from the CD and runs from memory without needing the operating system to be copied on to the hard drive. FreeNAS has an option to install itself on a hard drive or USB flash disk and will boot from there without needing the CD. For a hard drive install, the configuration data will be saved on the hard drive rather than on a USB flash disk or floppy disk.

The preferred way to install FreeNAS is onto a USB flash disk as this frees up an IDE or SCSI channel for extra storage. FreeNAS is optimized for use with flash disks. To save wearing out the flash disk, (with too many write operations) the embedded version of FreeNAS runs from memory once the initial boot has been made from the flash disk. To use the USB flash disk version, you need to have a BIOS that can boot from a USB flash disk.

Before you proceed, you should note that installing FreeNAS on a hard drive will erase all the data on that hard drive.

When installing FreeNAS to a hard disk, you have the option to partition your hard drive into 2 parts. The first will be the boot partition which will contain the FreeNAS server. This is only a small partition and the rest of the disk will be the larger data partition.

Exploring FreeNAS

To install FreeNAS to your hard disk, you need to go back to the console (as this can't be done from the web interface).

 For more information on the difference between "embedded" and "full", see the *Embedded versus. Full* section below.

1. Select option **9** and then **2** to install the "embedded" version of FreeNAS onto a hard disk with a data partition.
2. You will be presented with a summary of what actions the installation will perform. Select **OK** to continue.
3. Next, you will be asked to confirm the device name of the CDROM (which has the FreeNAS files).
4. Then, you need to choose the hard drive on which you would like to install FreeNAS. You will be given a list of available hard drives. You need to install FreeNAS on ad0, which is the primary master IDE drive. If you have SCSI, you should choose da0. Note that if you have a USB flash disk inserted, it may be listed as da0 and this shouldn't be confused with a genuine SCSI hard drive.
5. The system will now install.

Once the FreeNAS is installed, the console will show a success message. At this point, it is important to understand a few things:

1. The disk with FreeNAS installed has now been partitioned into two parts. These are referred to as ad0 partition 1 (or ad0p1 for short) and ad0 partition 2 (ad0p2). Partition 1 contains the FreeNAS software and partition 2 is for your data.
2. You need to revisit the **Disks: Mount Point** page as the underlying structure of the disk has changed and any previous mount point may be invalid.

3. You do not need to format ad0 again. It has been formatted using UFS for you.

4. You need to remove the disk from the CD drive and reboot the machine. To do this remove the disk, press *Enter* to go back to the installation submenu, the chose *EXIT* to return to the main menu and finally, use option **7** to reboot the machine.

To mount partition 2, you need to go to the **Disks: Mount Point** page. If you have existing mount points defined for the disk when you installed FreeNAS, you need to remove them first before continuing. To mount partition 2, click the add circle, chose the disk (probably ad0 or da0), then select partition 2. This is different from when you used the whole disk. Partition 2 is the data partition while partition one contains the FreeNAS software. Fill out the name and description and click **add**.

After that, you can enable services like CIFS and FTP just like you did before.

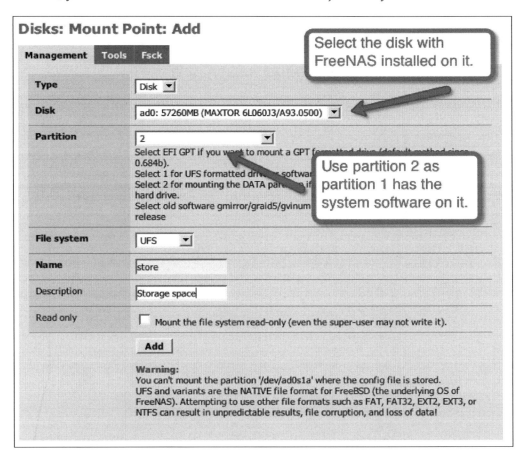

Exploring FreeNAS

Embedded versus Full

When you were in the installation submenu, you would have seen that there is also what is known as a "full" install of FreeNAS. This doesn't mean that it has any more features or is somehow more complete than the "embedded" version. But rather, it is a way to install FreeNAS like a traditional operating system. The files are installed on the hard disk and if they are edited or deleted they are done so permanently. The embedded version runs from RAM (and is initially loaded from the hard disk) and any changes made to the operating system files will only be temporary and when the system is rebooted, it will return to its original state. This means that the full version can be tweaked and changed which is good for those developing plugins for FreeNAS, but it also means that the system can be broken accidentally by those unfamiliar with FreeBSD. The embedded version, however, adds a level of protection and if anything goes wrong, a reboot will restore the system files to their installed state.

> This discussion is about the system files, not about the configuration file that is updated and controlled via the actions taken in the web interface. A reboot will NOT restore the configuration to a previous state unless the changes have not been applied.

The recommended way to install FreeNAS is to use the embedded version. You should only consider the full version if any of the following are true:

- You need to install extra FreeBSD packages to your FreeNAS server.
- You need to customize the size of the root file system.
- You are low on system RAM and need to run FreeBSD from hard disk, rather than a RAM disk.

Upgrading FreeNAS from a Previous Version

If you are running a LiveCD version of FreeNAS, then upgrading is simple. Just download the new version and burn it onto a CD and then reboot the FreeNAS server using the new CD. Always remember to check the FreeNAS website for any information about upgrading particularly with regards to internal changes like the format of the configuration file.

If you have installed FreeNAS on a hard drive (or USB flash disk), then FreeNAS can be upgraded via the web interface. On the FreeNAS website, you will find embedded versions of FreeNAS for download. These are not ISO files like the LiveCD version but rather files for upgrading an existing installation. The embedded download is a .img file. Download the correct file and save it on your hard disk. Go to the web interface and find the **System: Firmware** page, click **Enable Firmware Upload** and then locate the file you downloaded using the **Browse...** button.

Finally, click on **Upgrade firmware**. Wait patiently and FreeNAS will reboot when the upgrade is completed, your configuration data will be preserved.

DO NOT abort the firmware upgrade once it has started. You need a minimum of 128 MB RAM to perform the firmware update. You should always backup the System configuration before doing a Firmware upgrade. You can do this from the System: Backup/Restore page.

Summary

In this chapter, we have installed and configured the FreeNAS server. We booted the FreeNAS server from the LiveCD disk and configured a simple disk that was accessed by CIFS and FTP. We also looked at how to install FreeNAS to the hard drive and how to upgrade it.

In the next chapter, we shall take a detailed look at the different ways you can connect to your FreeNAS server including from Windows machines, from OS X and from Linux.

4
Connecting to the FreeNAS

The strength of the FreeNAS server is that so many different operating systems can connect to it and use its services. In this chapter, we shall look at the different services and protocols supported by FreeNAS, and see examples of how various platforms like Windows, OS X, and Linux can use the FreeNAS server for file sharing, backup, and streaming multimedia.

Introduction

The FreeNAS server is "multi lingual" in that it can talk to many different types of computers system using a variety of protocols. Before looking at each of these protocols individually, it is worth looking at them as a whole and seeing why each protocol exists and for which job is it best suited.

The table below lists each protocol along with which type of computer (Windows, Apple Mac etc) can connect to the FreeNAS server using that protocol. Some protocols are native to a particular platform, for examples CIFS is native protocol for Windows machines, but other operating systems like OS X can "talk" CIFS as well. Also listed, is the main use of that protocol.

	Windows	OS X	Linux/UNIX	Usage
CIFS	Yes. Native.	Yes. Built in.	Yes. Built in.	File sharing
NFS	Yes. Requires 3rd party software.	Yes. Native.	Yes. Native.	File sharing
FTP	Yes. Built in or you can use 3rd party software.	Yes. Built in and you can use 3rd party software.	Yes. Built in and you can use 3rd party software.	Uploading and downloading files
RSYNCD	Yes. Requires 3rd party software.	Yes. Built in and you can use 3rd party software.	Yes. Built in.	Backups and synchronization.

	Windows	OS X	Linux/UNIX	Usage
Unison	Yes. Requires 3rd party software.	Yes. Requires 3rd party software.	Yes. Requires 3rd party software.	Backups and synchronization.
AFP	No.	Native.	No.	File sharing for Apple
UPnP	Yes. Requires 3rd party software.	Yes. Requires 3rd party software.	Yes. Requires 3rd party software or a specialized distribution (see below).	Streaming media
iSCSI	Yes. Built in to some versions of Windows, e.g. Windows Vista.	Yes. Requires 3rd party software.	Yes. Built in.	Connecting to remote raw disks with the SCSI over IP protocol.

In this chapter, we are going to look in detail at the various protocols. To help you in this, it will be best if you have a test FreeNAS server up and running and you have followed the quick installation and configuration guide in Chapter 2.

Connecting via CIFS

The Common Internet File System (CIFS) is the standard way in which files are accessed on a remote Windows computer. Developed and maintained by Microsoft for use on their Windows platform, it has also been implemented on most major operating systems including OS X and Linux using 3rd party software, the most popular of which is called Samba. Samba is open source software that provides remote file access services to CIFS clients on a variety of platforms (including to Windows clients). Samba is included in the FreeNAS server.

The abilities of CIFS are actually larger than just accessing files. With it, other resources like printers can also be shared on the network, but for FreeNAS, CIFS is used to share disks on the server and make them available to other computers that understand the CIFS protocol. This means that Windows, Linux, and OS X machines are all capable of accessing files on the FreeNAS server via the CIFS protocol.

Sometimes, when reading about CIFS, you might read the term SMB or Server Message Block. SMB was the original name of the CIFS protocol and was the result of work done by IBM and then later Microsoft. In 1996, SMB was renamed CIFS.

Configure CIFS on the FreeNAS Server

Before attempting to connect another computer to the FreeNAS server via CIFS, you need to be sure that CIFS is correctly configured on the FreeNAS server.

1. Go to Services: **CIFS/SMB**. This page contains two tabs, first, the **settings** page and then the **shares** page. First of all, make sure that the service is enabled by ticking the "Enable" box in the title bar of the configuration table.

2. To get CIFS working with the default settings, you need to set as a minimum the Authentication system, the NetBios Name, and the Workgroup. Authentication should be left at Anonymous for the moment. We will look more at authentication and user management in FreeNAS in the next chapter. The NetBios Name is the name that the FreeNAS server will have on the Windows network. When you want to access the server, Windows lets you use a friendly name rather than the IP. For this example, we will use the name FreeNAS. Finally, you need to enter the workgroup. All Windows machines belong either to a workgroup or a domain.

> **Workgroups and Domains**
>
> Home networks and small office LANs use workgroups, which are essentially collections of computers that share a similar tag or designation. On a home network, there is normally only 1 workgroup called "WORKGROUP" (or MSHOME if you mainly have Windows XP machines. For the small office environment, there might be 2 or 3 workgroups, maybe "SALES", "ENGINEERING", and "ACCOUNTS". The workgroup links the machines together so that when the network is viewed, these machines will be grouped together. There are typically no more than ten to twenty computers in a workgroup and all the computers must be on the same local network.
>
> Larger business networks use domains rather than workgroups. In a domain, there is a server (called the domain controller) that controls the resources and security in that domain. Once a user has a domain account, they can log on to any computer in the domain without needing a local account on any particular machine. Domains can have thousands of computers spread across several networks.

3. Enter in the workgroup name for the FreeNAS server. It will probably be WORKGROUP or maybe XPHOME if you have many Windows XP machines on your network.

Connecting to the FreeNAS

4. The next step is to configure what disks are shared on the network. Click on **Save and Restart** at the bottom of the page and then click the **Shares** tab at the top. Here is where you add disks to be shared on the network via the CIFS protocol. You can only share previously configured disks. If you have disks that need to be added to the FreeNAS, go to the Disk: menu. For more information, see the quick start guide in Chapter 2 or for advanced information, go to Chapter 6.

5. Click the add circle. You are now in **Services: CIFS/SMB: Share: Add**. The minimum data here is the **Name** you want to give the share, a Comment or description about the share and where the share is, the Path.

6. Name and comment should be easy enough to fill in. For this example, we will use store and a storage place respectively. Now, for the path. In FreeNAS, all disks are mounted under **/mnt**. This means that the path will be something like **/mnt/diskname**. To find the right path name, click on **...** This will bring up a new window.

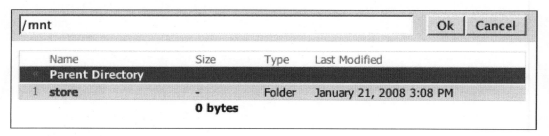

At the top, you will see **/mnt** and then further down **store**. This is the name of the disk that was configured in **Disks: Mount Point: Add**. Click on store and the path will change to **/mnt/path**.

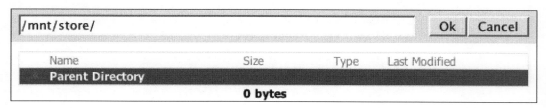

[72]

7. Click on **OK**, then on **Add,** and finally, apply the changes.

At this point, CIFS is configured and ready to go. Before looking at how the different versions of Windows, as well as OS X and Linux, can connect to FreeNAS using CIFS, let us look in details at the other parameters.

CIFS Settings Explained

Parameter	Meaning
Description	Server description. This can be left blank but you may find including a description useful.
Dos charset	This is the charset FreeNAS uses when communicating with Windows 9x/Me clients. It will talk Unicode to all newer clients. The default is CP850, which is perfect for English and other Western European Languages.
Unix charset	This is the charset used internally by FreeNAS. The default is UTF-8, which is fine for most systems and covers all characters in all languages.
Log Level	Sets the amount of log/debug messages that are sent to the log file. These can be read in Diagnostics: Logs: System. You should leave this on Minimum unless you are trying to solve a CIFS connection problem.
Local Master Browser	Allows FreeNAS to try and become a local master browser.
	Inside the My Network Places (or the equivalent in Vista), icons represent machines. The local master browser collates information to create this browse list.
	You can safely leave this at Yes, unless you are running the FreeNAS inside a domain, when it is best to set it to No.
Time server	If your FreeNAS server has an accurate clock, you can instruct it to advertise itself as an SMB time server to Windows clients.
WINS server	WINS (Windows Internetworking Name Server) allows the FreeNAS server to discover the friendly CIFS name of machines on other networks. You can set up FreeNAS to use a WINS server somewhere else on the network by simply pointing it to the IP address of the WINS server.
	If you are using FreeNAS just for machines on the local LAN, then you can leave this empty.

CIFS Advanced Settings

These are advanced parameters and you should only change them if you know what you are doing and why you would want to change them. For 99.9% of all cases, these parameters can be left alone.

Parameter	Meaning
Create mask	Every data file created on the FreeNAS has some default read and write permissions. Use this option to override the file creation permissions. (0666 by default).
	See the tip below for more information.
Directory mask	All directories that are created on the FreeNAS server have default read and write permissions. Use this option to override the directory creation permissions (0777 by default).
	See the tip below for more information.
Send Buffer Size	Size of send buffer (16384 by default). For Windows 95/98, you have to use a 8192 buffer size.
Receive Buffer Size	Size of receive buffer (16384 by default). For Windows 95/98, you have to use a 8192 buffer size.
Large read/write	Use the new 64k streaming read and write variant SMB requests introduced with Windows 2000.
EA support	Extended attribute support. Allow clients to attempt to store OS/2 style extended attributes on a share.

Create Mask

In FreeBSD (and most UNIX operating systems), each file or directory has 3 levels of read/write permissions. User, Group, and World. The permission to read, write or execute a file can be set at each level.

When FreeNAS creates files that have been copied over the network, a default set of file permissions is set for that file. This is determined by the default create and directory masks (see above).

Using a numbering scheme, the create or directory mask has four number places starting always with 0, for example 0744, representing the three levels. The first number on the left side is for "user", the middle one is for "group", and the right-hand one for "world." Here is what each number means:

0 = no access, 1 = execute only, 2 = write only, 3 = write and execute, 4 = read only, 5 = read and execute, 6 = read and write, 7 = read, write and execute (full access).

Options when Adding Shares

Like the general CIF settings, there are several different options available when you add a share on the **Services: CIFS/SMB: Share: Add page**. Here is a brief look at those options and what they do.

Parameter	Meaning
Browseable	This controls whether this share is seen in the list of available shares in a net view and in the browse list. If it is not browseable, the share is still accessible but only when the address is specified directly.
Inherit permissions	The permissions on new files and directories are normally governed by create mask and directory mask, but the inherit permissions parameter overrides this. This can be particularly useful on systems with many users to allow a single share to be used flexibly by each user.
Recycle bin	This will create a recycle bin on the share. If you create the recycle bin, you have to empty it manually.
Hosts allow	This parameter is a comma, space, or tab delimited set of hosts that are permitted to access this share. Use the keyword ALL to permit access for everyone. Leave this field empty to disable this setting.
Hosts deny	This parameter is a comma, space, or tab delimited set of host that are NOT permitted to access this share. Where the lists conflict, the allow list takes precedence. In the event that it is necessary to deny all by default, use the keyword ALL (or the netmask 0.0.0.0/0) and then explicitly specify to the host's allow parameter those hosts that should be permitted access. Leave this field empty to disable this setting.

What does It Mean to Map a Network Drive?

When accessing files over the network, there are two ways to find the data. One is to browse to it using the *My Network Places* (or similar depending on your version of Windows). Here, you can find a machine and then drill down until you find the folder you want. The other option is to mount the remote shared folder as a drive on your machine. This *network drive* always takes you to the right place where the data is on the remote server. You can also configure it to be mounted every time you start windows. This is particularly useful for something like the FreeNAS server as the storage space made available is always available on your PC.

Connecting with CIFS via Windows Millennium

Double click on **My Network Places**. Here, you can browse the local network and see recently accessed network resources.

1. Double clicking on **Entire Network** will take you to a list of the workgroups and domains on your local network. On a small network, this may well just be one workgroup, mostly likely **WORKGROUP** or **MSHOME**.

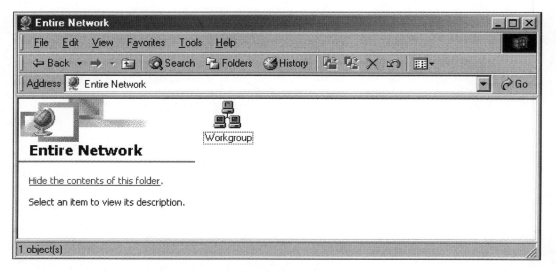

2. Double click on **Workgroup** and you will see a list of machines in that workgroup.
3. Find the FreeNAS server, it is probably called **Freenas**. Now double click on it and you will see a list of available shares on the FreeNAS server.
4. If you are using a test FreeNAS server setup according to the quick installation guide in chapter 2 then you will only see one share called *store*. If you double click on *store*, you will have access to that storage space on the FreeNAS server. You can try copying some files to *store* and see the FreeNAS server in action.

[

To save time finding the FreeNAS server, you can just enter its address directly in the Address bar in *My Network Places*. The address is in the form **\\server\share** so in our example we would use **\\freenas\store**.

Now just hit *Enter* and you will have access to the FreeNAS server.
]

5. There are a couple of ways to map a network drive in Windows Millennium. One is that when you have the FreeNAS machine open in My Network Places. Rather than double clicking on store, you can right-hand click on it instead. This will produce a small menu. Now click on **Map Network Drive...**

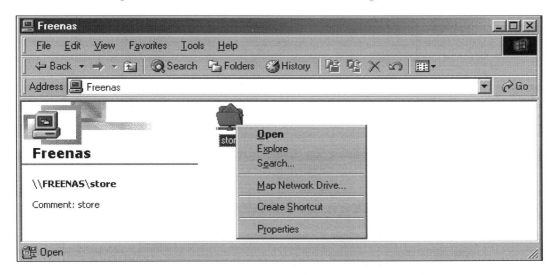

Now, choose the drive letter you wish to map to this network share and tick **Reconnect at logon** if you want the drive to be automatically mounted when you start Windows.

Once you have done this, the network drive will appear in *My Computer* and you can use it much like you would any other hard drive on your machine.

Using CIFS with Windows XP

Assuming your FreeNAS and your Windows XP machine are in the same workgroup, when you open *My Network Places*, the *store* share on the *Freenas* server should appear automatically. If it doesn't, wait a few moments (as sometimes it takes Windows a few minutes to collate the list of all available resources in the workgroup) and press *F5* to refresh the display.

Another way to get to the FreeNAS server is to click on **View workgroup computers** in the **Network Task** panel which is on the left side of the window. This will show you all the computers in your workgroup that should include the FreeNAS server. From here, you can drill down and find the network share *store*.

Like Windows Millennium and Windows Vista, you can enter the address of the FreeNAS server directly in the address bar of the *My Network Places* window.

To map a drive from *My Network Places* to the FreeNAS server, find the *Freenas* machine either through the workgroup or by entering its name in the address bar.

1. Right-click the shared folder that you want to map, and then click **Map Network Drive**.
2. Click the drive letter that you want to use, and then specify whether you want to reconnect every time that you log on to your computer.

[Network drives are mapped by using letters starting from the letter Z. This is the default drive letter for the first mapped drive you create. However, you can select another letter if you want to use a letter other than Z.]

3. Click **Finish**.
4. A window opens that displays the contents of the *store* share that you have mapped and the drive letter (for example Z) will be available in **My Computer**.

FreeNAS, CIFS, and Windows Vista

Accessing the FreeNAS server via CIFS in Windows Vista is very similar to the previous versions of Windows and was also covered in chapter 2. In summary, open the Network and Sharing Center by clicking **Network** on the Start menu. When the window appears, Vista will automatically scan the network for any shared network resources. When it has finished, you will see the available machines on the network including FREENAS.

Also, to access the FreeNAS server without using the Network and Sharing Center, click **Start**, and type **\\freenas** and then press *Enter*. This will bring up the shares available on the FreeNAS server directly.

To map a network drive, click **Start**, and type **\\freenas,** and then press *Enter*. Right-hand click the shares you wish to map (e.g. *store*) and click on the **Map Network Drive...** item that appears in the menu. Like XP, network drives are mapped by using letters starting from the letter Z. This is the default drive letter for the first mapped drive you create. However, you can select another letter if you want to use a letter other than Z. Click **Finish** and the drive will be mapped.

Accessing the FreeNAS via CIFS from Linux

All the popular Linux distributions support the CIFS protocol using a piece of software called Samba. Samba is an open source suite that allows users of non-Windows operating systems, like Linux, to interoperate with Windows machines and servers. The goal behind the Samba project is one of removing barriers to interoperability.

Using the client aspects of Samba (as Samba is also a server) in Linux is easy. For example in Kubuntu, to get a listing similar to My Network Places in Windows, open Konqueror and enter **smb:/** in the address bar. This will then show you the workgroups available. From here, you can drill down to the FreeNAS server and the *store* share. This should work for all KDE-based distributions like Mandriva and SuSE. Alternatively, you use the **Remote Places** icon that you will find on the System Menu (which isn't to be confused with the K Menu). Here, you can click on **Samba Shares**, which will take you to the smb:/ listing.

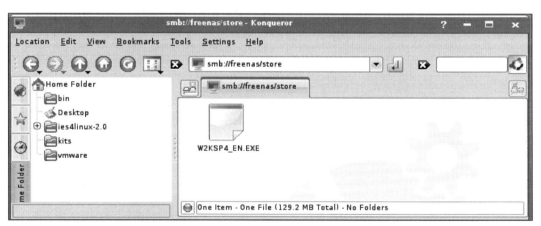

A CIFS Connection from OS X

Apple's OS X operating system has full Windows connectivity. With the release of OS X 10.5 Leopard, it's easy of use has also been improved. Leopard will automatically detect the available CIFS shared resources available on the local area network. They appear in the Finder window on the left-hand-side under SHARED. Click on the resource you want to use (in case of FreeNAS, it will say "freenas SMB Service") and from there, you just access them as you would any other folder.

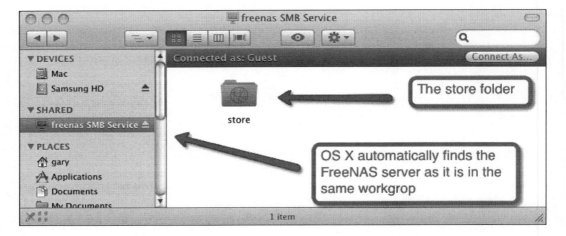

FTP

While CIFS and NFS are file system protocols, which means that whole file systems can be shared on the network and other computers can uses those file systems as if they were attached locally, FTP is more limited in that it is designed just to for the transfer of files from one computer to another. In CIFS and NFS, when you read or write to files, they remain on the remote server, whereas with FTP, files are transferred from the server to the local machine or vice-versa. Any changes you make to the files once downloaded to your computer, will not be reflected in the files on the server.

The main use of the FTP protocol is for downloading files from the server onto the local computer. Files can be uploaded once to the server (also by FTP) and then downloaded many times by those who need the files. This can be useful in one of two ways:

- For the small office or home environment, it is perfect as a repository for downloaded software and drivers. As all web browsers have support for FTP, it means that files can be downloaded on to the local machine with just a standard web browser, or more complex FTP clients can be used.

- In the business environment, if there is a company Intranet, then links from the various internal websites can link to files on the FreeNAS server via FTP. This is particularly useful if there are large files to be downloaded that don't need to reside on the web server.

FTP also supports the uploading of files to the server. Here, those responsible for the Intranet or file repository upload the files to the FreeNAS server and then those needing the files can download them as described above.

To configure the FTP service, go to **Services: FTP** and tick the **Enable** box. Click **Save and Restart** and FTP is configured. The rest of the settings can be left as they are. But should you consider changing any of them, below is a table of what each parameter means.

Parameter	Meaning
TCP port	If, for networking reasons, you need to change the port for FTP, you can change it here. The default is port 21.
Number of clients	Maximum number of simultaneous clients.
Max. conn. per IP	Maximum number of connections per IP address (0 = unlimited).
Timeout	Maximum idle time in minutes.
Permit root login	Specifies whether connecting user is allowed to log in as superuser (root) directly. Use this option with care as enabling it can be a security risk.
Anonymous login	Enable anonymous login.
Local User	Enable local user login.
Banner	Greeting banner displayed by FTP when a connection first comes in.

There are also several advanced FTP options. The table below describes them:

Parameter	Meaning
Create mask	Use this option to set a new default file creation mask (077 is the initial default).
Directory mask	Use this option to set a new default directory creation mask (022 is the initial default).
FXP	Enable FXP protocol. FXP allows transfers between two remote servers without any file data going to the client asking for the transfer (insecure!).
NAT mode	Force NAT mode. Enable this if your FTP server is behind a NAT box that doesn't support applicative FTP proxying.

Parameter	Meaning
Keep all files	Allow users to resume and upload files, but NOT to delete or rename them. Directories can be removed, but only if they are empty. However, overwriting existing files is still allowed.
chroot everyone	chroot() everyone, but root.
Passive IP address	Force the specified IP address in reply to a PASV/EPSV/SPSV command. If the server is behind a masquerading (NAT) box that doesn't properly handle stateful FTP masquerading, put the IP address of that box here. If you have a dynamic IP address, you can put the public host name of your gateway, which will be resolved every time a new client will connect.
pasv_min_port	The minimum port to allocate for PASV style data connections (0 = use any port).
pasv_max_port	The maximum port to allocate for PASV style data connections (0 = use any port).

Using the Command Line FTP Client

In chapter 2, we saw how to use the free FTP client, CoreFTP, to connect from a Windows machine to the FreeNAS server, and we also mentioned the built-in FTP client that comes with Windows Explorer. All the major operating systems (including Windows also) include a built in command line FTP program. They are all essentially the same regardless of operating system so if you know how to use the command line FTP program on OS X, you will be able to manage on Linux and so on. For this example we will use Apple's OS X.

To start, you need to open a terminal window (on OS X or Linux) or a command prompt (on Windows). To connect to the FreeNAS server you type:

`ftp 192.168.1.250`

Where `192.168.1.250` is the IP address of the FreeNAS server, you will need to enter the IP address of the FreeNAS if yours is different.

The first thing you need to enter is a user name, for now we will use anonymous FTP, which means that anyone can access the FTP. The next chapter we will look at user management and authentication. So enter:

`anonymous`

Now, you will need to enter a password. As we are doing an anonymous login, any password will do, including just pressing *ENTER*.

You will then be in the FTP program and you will see the prompt **ftp>**.

To see a listing of what is in the directory, we use the `ls` command. So type `ls` and then press *ENTER*. The result will be something similar to this:

```
ftp> ls
227 Entering Passive Mode (192,168,1,250,112,201)
150 Accepted data connection
drwxrwxrwx    3 0           0              512 Jan 22 11:59 store
226-Options: -l
226 1 matches total
ftp>
```

The important line amongst all this information is the line starting with `drwxrwxrwx`. You will see on the right-hand-side the word *store*. This is the disk called store that was added, formated, and mounted in the quick start guide of chapter 2. The `drwxrwxrwx` shows us that it is a directory (because of the leading d) and that everyone has read, write, and execute permissions.

We now want to change directory to *store,* to do this we use the `cd` command:

```
ftp> cd store
250 OK. Current directory is /store
ftp>
```

Doing a directory listing of the store folder reveals:

```
-rwx------    1 21          0        135477136 Jan 22 12:45 W2KSP4_EN.EXE
```

This is Service Pack 4 for Windows 2000. I have copied to my FreeNAS server as an example. If I have one or more Windows 2000 machines on my network, which need to be upgraded to service pack 4, I can download the file from the FreeNAS server and run it on each machine.

To get the file and download it on to my machine, I use the `get` command:

```
ftp> get W2KSP4_EN.EXE
```

The transfer will start and will finish with a summary like this:

```
135477136 bytes received in 00:15 (8.50 MB/s)
```

To exit the FTP program, just type `quit`.

Connecting to the FreeNAS

Here are a few more FTP commands to help you on your way:

Command	Description
Delete	Deletes a file in the current remote directory.
lcd	Changes directory on your local machine.
mkdir	Makes a new directory within the current remote directory.
mget	Copies multiple files from the remote machine to the local machine; you are prompted for a y/n answer before transferring each file unless you use the prompt off command before hand.
mput	Copies multiple files from the local machine to the remote machine; you are prompted for a y/n answer before transferring each file, unless you use the prompt off command before hand.
put	Copies a file from the local machine to the remote machine.
pwd	Displays the current working directory on the remote machine.
rmdir	Deletes a directory in the current remote directory.

Using a Web Browser for FTP

All web browsers contain a simple FTP client and it is possible to browse the FTP areas and download files. Start your web browser and then in the address bar, enter:

`ftp://192.168.1.250/`

Notice that the address starts with `ftp://` and NOT `http://`.

The web browser will show something like this:

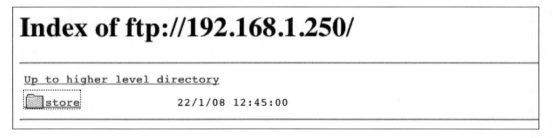

Here, the web browser shows *store*, the disk that was previously configured. Unlike CIFS, you don't need to add each disk individually; all the disks mounted are available.

Chapter 4

If you click **store**, you will be taken into the **store** folder and you will see something like this:

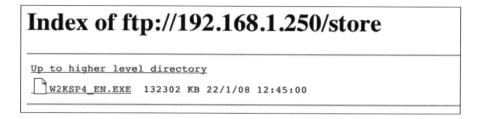

From here, you can click on the Service Pack and the web browser will start to download it for you.

NFS

The Network Filing System is the UNIX equivalent to the CIFS protocol. Although there are 3rd party packages to allow Windows machines to use NFS resources, NFS has remained most dominant on the UNIX/Linux operating systems.

To configure the NFS service, go to the **Services: NFS** page. As with all the other services, to enable it you need to tick the Enable box.

There are few parameters for NFS, but they are important.

> The following instructions are for the 0.68 series of FreeNAS releases. The 0.69 and 0.7 versions of FreeNAS treat NFS slightly differently but essentially the ideas are the same.
>
> In 0.69 and 0.7 please note the following differences:
>
> The Services: NFS settings page now has two tabs; *Settings* and *Shares*.
>
> The Settings tab has a new parameter: *Number of servers* that specifies how many NFS processes to create. There needs to be enough processes to handle the maximum level of concurrency from NFS clients on the network. A typical figure would be four to six.
>
> The NFS set-up now has the concept of shares (very similar to that of CIFS), to make a folder or disk available on the network a 'share' must be created for it. To do this you click on the *Shares* tab and click the Add circle.
>
> The rest of the parameters described below are now set on a per share basis and not for the whole server.

The first parameter is *Map all users to root*. This means that on the FreeNAS machine remote users will have root privilege (or administrator right in Windows terminology) while accessing the disks over NFS. This is generally a bad idea and while the default is *yes*, it is best to change it to *no*. Also, any OS X clients connecting to the FreeNAS via NFS will issue a few warnings about needing usernames and passwords. When *Map all users to root* is set to *no*, this doesn't happen.

The second parameter is the list of authorized networks that are allowed to connect to the FreeNAS server via NFS. This list of authorized networks is defined by setting which group of addresses can access the server.

If your FreeNAS server has a netmask of 255.255.255.0 (which is most probably the case) then:

Click the add circle and enter the first 3 numbers of the IP address of the FreeNAS server (with . in between) and then finish it with dot zero (.0). For example, if the IP address of the FreeNAS server is 192.168.1.250, then you would enter 192.168.1.0 for the authorized network. Finally, select 24 (in other words 255.255.255.0) in the drop down box.

If you are using a netmask of 255.255.0.0, then you need to enter the first 2 numbers of the IP address and end with dot zero dot zero (.0.0), for example 192.168.0.0. Set the drop down box to 16.

If you are using a netmask of 255.0.0.0, then you need to enter just the first number of the IP address and end with dot zero dot zero dot zero (.0.0.0), e.g. 192.0.0.0. The drop down box needs to be set to 8.

If you are unsure what the value of the netmask is, then go to Interfaces: LAN and see the IP Address field. You need to set the drop down box in the Services: NFS page to that of the value of the drop down box in the IP Address field.

Using NFS from OS X

At the core of Apple's OS X, is the open source UNIX operating system called Darwin. As a result, OS X natively understands the NFS protocol. To connect to the FreeNAS server from OS X, open the Finder and the Go->Connect to Server... (Or Apple-K as a shortcut)

In the Server Address field enter:

```
nfs://192.168.1.250/mnt/store
```

The address is made up of 3 parts. First is `nfs://`, which tells OS X that we want to talk via NFS. Then comes the address of the FreeNAS server (192.168.1.250, change this accordingly) and finally, the resource to which we want to connect. All the disks are exported as /mnt/name. In this case, the name is store as we previously defined *store* in Disks: Mount Point: Management. Once mounted, it will appear under SHARED in the Finder on the left-hand side.

Mount FreeNAS via NFS on Linux

The particular Linux distribution you are using may have a graphical to mount NFS shares, but the lowest common denominator that works for all Linux versions is to use the command line.

To mount the FreeNAS server via NFS is easy and also mostly the same as in OS X, but rather than entering the command in the GUI, it is entered at the command line. In Linux, to mount any type of device, remote or local, you need to have a mount point, a place to peg the mounted resource. So open a terminal window and become root (usually with the *su* command, or alternatively you can prefix *sudo* in front of the following commands).

First, you need to change directory to the /mnt directory:

```
# cd /mnt
```

Now create a directory to peg the FreeNAS server to:

```
# mkdir freenas
```

And now mount the FreeNAS server:

```
# mount 192.168.1.250:/mnt/store /mnt/freenas
```

Once completed, all the files and folders on the disk *store* on the FreeNAS server will appear under `/mnt/freenas`. So using earlier examples, you will find the Windows 2000 Service Pack 4 at `/mnt/freenas/W2KSP4_EN.EXE`, not that it would be much good here!

RSYNCD, Unison, AFP, and UPnP

CIFS, NFS, and FTP are the 3 main file access protocols for FreeNAS, however, FreeNAS doesn't stop there, it has another 4 protocols for different specialized tasks including backups and streaming multimedia.

Using RSYNC for Backups

RSYNC copies files between machines in an efficient manner and is therefore excellent for making backups. The RSYNC protocol allows RSYNC to transfer just the differences between two sets of files across the network connection, using an efficient algorithm. RSYNC is a client/server system meaning that a server is running to receive the backup file and a client sends the files from the local machine. For FreeNAS, this means that the RSYNC service can be configured and computers on your network can be backed up to it using an RSYNC client.

To enable the RSYNC service, tick the Enable box on the Services: **RSYNCD: Server** page. The other parameters you can leave at their defaults.

RSYNC is essentially a command line tool with a Linux/UNIX background, however, there are some Windows programs for handling backups via RSYNC. For more information, visit the websites:

- DeltaCopy (http://www.aboutmyip.com/AboutMyXApp/DeltaCopy.jsp)
- NasBackup (http://www.nasbackup.com)

Both of these tools are open source and free to download and use without restriction.

From the Linux (or OS X) command line, you can start a backup of files on the local machine like this:

```
rsync -a /home/user/backup rsync://192.168.1.250/store
```

This will backup the directory /home/user/backup to the FreeNAS onto the *store* disk. The -a parameter put RSYNC into archive mode, which means that any subdirectories will also be copied while preserving time stamps.

As before, you need to change the IP address (192.168.1.250) to the IP address of your FreeNAS server.

> FreeNAS can also act as a RSYNC client, which means it send files from the server to another server and so, allowing the FreeNAS server to be backed up. We will look at this in more detail in chapter 7.

Using Unison for Backups and Synchronization

Unison is a file-synchronization tool for UNIX and Windows. It allows two replicas of a collection of files and directories to be stored on different hosts (or different disks on the same host), modified separately, and then brought up-to-date by propagating the changes in each replica to the other. It is similar to RSYNC in that it can perform mirroring/synchronization of two directories, but unlike RSYNC, Unison can deal with updates to both copies of a distributed directory structure. Updates that do not conflict are propagated automatically. Conflicting updates are detected and displayed. Unison is open source and is published under the GNU Public License.

To enable the Unison service, go to **Services: Unison** and tick the Enable box. You need to choose which share the unison service will use and you can probably leave the other settings to their defaults.

For Unison to work, the Secure Shell (SSH) must be enabled (Services: SSH) and the user must have shell access enabled (Access: Users).

SSH and user administration are covered in detail in the next chapter.

Connecting to FreeNAS via AFP

Like CIFS for Windows and NFS for UNIX, Apple also have a file system protocol called AFP (Apple Filing Protocol). It allows Apple Macs to connect natively to the FreeNAS server. As with CIFS, the Mac will automatically discover any AFP services offered on the local area network. The AFP service will appear in the **SHARED** section in the Finder.

Connecting to the FreeNAS

To enable AFP, go to the **Services: AFP** page, and tick the Enable box. Now tick the **Enable guest access** box and click **Save and Restart**. The local authentication method will be looked at in the next chapter along with all other user management issues. AFP will now be running. Go to your Mac and you will find the server as described above.

There are a few options available when configuring AFP, here is a brief look at them:

Parameter	Meaning
Server Name	Name of the server. If this field is left empty, the default server is specified.
Authentication	Guest access or local user authentication. You must select one of these, select guest access for the anonymous access.

Streaming Media with UPnP

UPnP (Universal Plug and Play) is a set of network protocols that allow devices to connect seamlessly and to simplify the implementation of networks in the home. It is popular for easily enabling the streaming of multimedia data from a server to a client. In the FreeNAS context, UPnP allows a previously configured directory to be made available to a UPnP multimedia client such as a wireless media center that attaches to your TV. The UPnP client will find the FreeNAS server via the UPnP protocols and play (via a selection menu) the multimedia files stored in the FreeNAS server.

To enable UPnP, go to the **Services: UPnP** page and tick the Enable box.

You can leave the name and the network interface at their defaults.

Now, you need to add which disks you would like to share on the FreeNAS server. Clicking the add circle will bring up the familiar window for selecting which disks to share. In our test setup, we need to share **/mnt/store**. Enter this and the click **Add**.

Finally, click **Save and Restart**.

There are also a few parameters that can be changed:

Parameter	Meaning
Port	Enter a custom port number for the HTTP server if you want to override the default (49152). Only dynamic or private ports can be used (from 49152 through 65535).
Profile	Compliant profile to be used. UPnP has several profiles and you need to adjust this according to which device you are streaming to. If you are using a Microsoft's Xbox 360 then select Xbox 360, if you are using a Digital Living Network Alliance (formerly Digital Home Working Group) compliant device then select DLNA.
Control web page	Enable control web page. Accessible through http://ip_address:port/web/ushare.html. This is a rudimentary web page that allows you to add more shares. It is also the page Windows will show as you double click on the FreeNAS UPnP icon.

As a test client, we can use the GeexBox Linux distribution (http://geexbox.org). GeeXboX is a free Linux distribution that turns a computer into a Home Theater PC or Media Center. It is a standalone LiveCD-based distribution, meaning it boots from the CD and runs out of the box on any modern PC. It can even be used on a diskless computer, as the whole system is loaded in RAM. Much like FreeNAS, you need to download the .iso image file and burn it onto a CD and then boot the PC from the CD.

Once booted, you can select **Open** from the main menu followed by **Open File...** and then choose the UPNP option and finally, the FreeNAS server. If you have copied any multimedia files on to the FreeNAS server, you can play them.

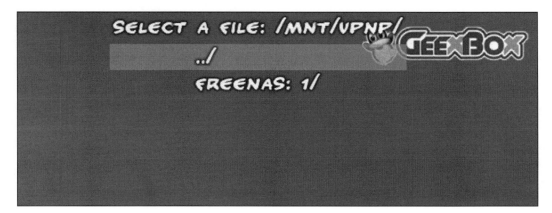

iSCSI Target

iSCSI is an evolution of the SCSI protocol, which allows SCSI commands to be sent over a network. It allows two hosts to negotiate and then exchange SCSI commands using IP networks. The result is that a remote device with iSCSI capabilities can be seen to be a local disk drive but the commands and data for that device are being sent over the network rather than down a cable in the machine.

FreeNAS can be configured to be an iSCSI target, this means it acts as a remote SCSI disk and it can receive SCSI commands and apply them to a local disk. Once configured, an iSCSI initiator can connect to the FreeNAS iSCSI target and use the designated disk as a local disk.

To use the iSCSI functionality of FreeNAS, your server needs to have a minimum of 256MB of RAM.

iSCSI configuration starts on the **Services: iSCSI Target** page. An iSCSI target is formed from one of two things: an extent (the actual storage file or hard disk) or a device (a combination of other extents or devices in a RAID 0 or RAID 1 configuration). Therefore, there are a few steps to configuring a iSCSI target:

1. First, an extent needs to be created or defined.
2. Optionally, a device can be configured.
3. Finally, the target needs to be defined using information about the extent or device.

Extent in this context means the device or file that will ultimately act as the iSCSI device. From the iSCSI Target page, click the add circle for extent section. Here, you need to enter two things: the name which by default is **extent0**, and then the path to the extent. Here, you can choose a device like **/dev/ad0** or a file. For this example I will choose a file as this offers the greatest flexibility in that the same physical disk can be used to host several iSCSI targets (note however, that you get greater performance when using a whole device). The name for the file is in the format **/mnt/sharename/extentname** so in this example it will be **/mnt/store/extent0**. Finally, put in a size, in megabytes, for example 2048 for 2 gigabytes.

If you wish to combine several extents or devices, then next, you can create a device. This is an optional step and isn't required if you are using a single extent (whether a file or hard disk). Click the add circle for the device section. You need to enter a device name which by default is **device0**. Next, select how you want to combine the extents (either with RAID 0 or RAID 1, see chapter 3 for more information on RAID).

Finally, you need to define the iSCSI target itself. Click on the add circle for the target section. Enter a target name, the default is **target0**. Then tick the extent that makes up the target, in this case **extent0**. You also need to configure the authorized networks that can access this iSCSI target. This is similar to the way in which NFS networks are authorized.

iSCSI disks behave in exactly the same way as local disks in that you can only have one computer controlling that disk. Therefore, it is important to ensure that only one iSCSI initiator uses any particular iSCSI target. If two (or more) iSCSI initiators use an iSCSI target, there will be data corruption.

One way to ensure that only one iSCSI initiator is using the iSCSI target is to limit the authorized network to just one IP address. If my iSCSI initiator has an IP address of 192.168.1.100, then entering that address along with 32 from the drop down box will limit iSCSI connections to just that IP address.

However, if your iSCSI initiator doesn't have a fixed IP address (and is using DHCP), then you won't be able to permanently set the IP address. In this case, you can only limit the IP address to a range of addresses on your network. Assuming your FreeNAS server has a netmask of 255.255.255.0, enter the first 3 numbers of the IP address of the FreeNAS server (with . in between) and then finish it with dot zero (.0). For example, if the IP address of the FreeNAS server is 192.168.1.250, then you would enter 192.168.1.0 for the authorized network. Finally, select 24 (in other words 255.255.255.0) in the drop down box.

Once you have done this, apply the changes. The FreeNAS server will now create the 2GB file **extent0 in /mnt/store** and make the iSCSI target available on the network.

You will need to note the target name that is displayed as you will need this for the iSCSI initiator.

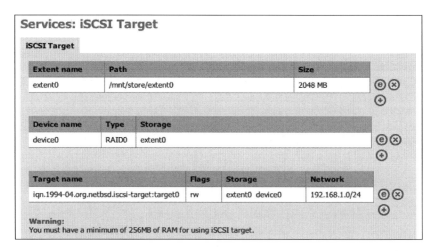

Testing the iSCSI Target with Another FreeNAS Server

To test the iSCSI target, we can get another FreeNAS server and connect it to the iSCSI disk on the iSCSI target FreeNAS server and see how the disk is used. To avoid confusion, I shall refer to the FreeNAS server where the iSCSI target is defined as the FreeNAS target server, and the server that will mount the remote iSCSI disk as the FreeNAS initiator server.

Only One FreeNAS Server Available

If you only have access to one FreeNAS server, you can still perform this test by using the same FreeNAS server. Here, the iSCSI initiator will loop back to the same FreeNAS server and use the defined iSCSI target. This isn't very practical but it proves that you have iSCSI working.

1. On the FreeNAS initiator server, go to the **Disks: Management** page and click on the iSCSI Initiator tab. Now click the add circle.

2. Enter a name for the iSCSI disk, say iSCSI0. It isn't too important as it for information only (it is not using during iSCSI negotiation).

3. For the initiator name, enter: **iqn.1994-04.org.netbsd.iscsi-initiator:freenas**.

   These names do have a special format (see below) but the most important aspect is that they are unique. For uniqueness, you can vary the part after the last colon, **freenas2** etc.

4. For the target name, enter: **iqn.1994-04.org.netbsd.iscsi-target:target0**, which should be the target name you noted down on the FreeNAS target server.

5. Finally, enter the IP address of the FreeNAS target server. And then click **Add**.

> iSCSI names may seem long and complicated but it is possible to understand them. They are technically called iSCSI Qualified Names or IQNs for short and they all start with the letters iqn.
>
> Here is a reminder of the target name:
>
> **iqn.1994-04.org.netbsd.iscsi-initiator:freenas**
>
> After **iqn.** comes a date code specifying the year and month in which the organization registered the domain, here it is April 1994.
>
> Then comes the domain name which is backwards: **iscsi-initiator.netbsd. org**
>
> NetBSD is a sister project to FreeBSD, and the iSCSI parts of FreeBSD come from NetBSD, so their domain name is used.
>
> Finally, there is a **:** and a local defined string to make sure the address is unique, in this case, **freenas**, which was the name of the target server.
>
> If you have many iSCSI targets and initiators, you might consider using the last number of the IP address along with the word freenas to make unique names, e.g. freenas-250.

If you get any errors, try looking at the logs pages for clues to what went wrong:

- **Diagnostics: Logs: System**
- **Diagnostics: Information: Disks**
- **Diagnostics: Information: iSCSI Initiator**

Also, there is more help in tracking down iSCSI problems in Chapter 9.

1. Now back to the **Disks: Management** page. Click the add circle and select the iSCSI device from the Disk drop down menu. It should read something like:

   ```
   da0: 2048MB (NetBSD NetBSD iSCSI 0)
   ```

2. Add the disk in the normal way and apply the changes.
3. Now the disk can be formatted from the **Disks: Format** page and mounted on the **Disks: Mount Point: Management** page exactly as we have done previously in the quick start guide in chapter 2.

After that, you will be able to use the disk via any of the protocols of your choosing including CIFS, NFS, AFP, and FTP.

> Did you notice that the iSCSI disk needs to be formatted and mounted just like a physical disk? This is because iSCSI disks are low level devices and the operating system that initiated the connection sees the iSCSI as if it were a normal hard disk in the system. This means it can be partitioned, formatted, and used like any local other disk.

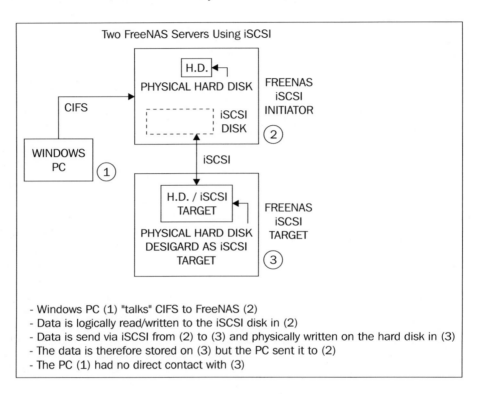

Testing the iSCSI Target with Windows Vista

Microsoft Windows Vista comes with some built-in iSCSI initiator software (and it is also available as a separate download for Windows XP from the Microsoft website). This allows Windows to connect to an iSCSI device and use it as a local hard disk.

1. Having defined an iSCSI target on your FreeNAS server, go to the Windows machine and launch the iSCSI Initiator tool. It can be found in the Administrative Tools area of the Control Panel. Specifically: **Control Panel | System and Maintenance | Administrative Tools | iSCSI Initiator**.

2. Click on the **Discovery** tab and then click **Add Portal...** Enter the IP address of your FreeNAS sever in the **IP address or DNS name** field and leave the

Port at the default of 3260. Click **OK**. If the iSCSI component of the FreeNAS server is running correctly, you will be returned quickly to the **Discovery** tab. However, if a connection cannot be made to the iSCSI target, then an error dialog will appear. In the case of an error, go back and verify the FreeNAS iSCSI target.

3. Now click the **Targets** tab. The FreeNAS iSCSI target will be listed as something like: **iqn.1994-04.org.netbsd.iscsi-target:target0**. Click it and then click on **Log on...**

4. In the next dialog box, you have the chance to configure Windows to **automatically restore this connection when the computer starts**, which is useful if this is going to be a permanent storage option for this PC. Click **OK**. Windows will now connect to the iSCSI target and its **Status** will change to **Connected**. You can now click on **OK** to close the iSCSI initiator tool.

5. If you now open **Computer** you will see that **nothing** has changed. But don't be alarmed, this is as expected. The iSCSI connection is at the lowest level and it is similar to adding a new hard drive to your machine. Before that hard drive can be used, it needs to be formatted.

6. To initialize and format the drive, you need to use the Computer Management tool. To start it click the **Start** button, click **Control Panel**, **click System and Maintenance**, click **Administrative Tools**, and then double-click **Computer Management**. (If you are prompted for an administrator password or confirmation, type the password or provide confirmation). Finally, in the Navigation pane, under Storage, click **Disk Management**.

7. The iSCSI disk will be listed as a disk and it will be marked as **Not Initialized**. To initialize the disk, right-click on the disk label (where it says **Not Initialized**) and click **Initialize Disk**. Accept the defaults on the dialog that appears and click **OK**. The status of the disk will now change from **Not Initialized** to **Online**.

8. To format the drive, you need to create a partition and then format it. To do this, right-click on an unallocated region of the hard disk and then click **New Simple Volume**. In the **New Simple Volume** Wizard, click **Next**. Type the size of the volume you want to create in megabytes (the default is the maximum size) and then click **Next**. Choose a drive letter to identify the partition and then click **Next**. To format the volume with the default settings, click **Next**. Review your choices, and then click **Finish**.

9. You will now have a new hard disk on your computer. Whenever you use this hard disk, the commands to control, read and write to the disk will be sent using iSCSI to the FreeNAS server.

Accessing Your Files Using HTTP and the Built-In Web Server

The web browser has become a ubiquitous tool on the desktop, and as such the ability to access files on the FreeNAS server while using a web browser has become an important file access method. Also, the protocol behind the web, HTTP (Hyper Text Transfer Protocol) is well understood by firewall devices. As such, using HTTP can mean that firewalls can be passed through, (of course, in a controlled manner and when desired) allowing you access to your firewalls when you find yourself on the other side of the firewall.

 To use the built-in web server, you will need to use FreeNAS v0.69 or greater.

Having enabled a general-purpose web server in the FreeNAS server, the developers also added the ability to use PHP as well as HTML. However, the FreeNAS web server isn't intended to be a comprehensive web server. It does not support any type of database connectivity nor does it have advanced features such as URL re-writing or bandwidth quotas.

To enable the built-in web server, go to **Services: Webserver** and tick the enable box. The web server has 5 parameters:

Parameter	Meaning
Protocol	Choose HTTP or HTTPS as the connection protocol. If you choose HTTPS you will need to paste an X.509 certificate in the Certificate field.
Port	TCP port for the server. Port 80 is the default for HTTP but it is used for the web administration interface. You need to choose another port here or move the web interface to another port (on the System: General Setup page) and use 80 here. Standard alternative ports include 81 and 8080.
Document root	Document root of the web server. This is where the web server will look for the web pages and files it is asked to serve.
Authentication	Give only local users access to the web server. You can define which directories need authorization to access them. Any locally defined user can then have access to that page.
Directory listing	A directory listing is generated if a directory is requested and no index-file (index.php, index.html, index.htm or default.htm) was found in that directory. This is useful if you just want to give access to some files without having to generate HTML or PHP files.

Once you have entered the parameters, you need to click **Save and Restart**. Some parameter changes will require the server to be rebooted before they take effect.

The simplest parameter set to test the web server is to use HTTP on port 8080 with a document root of /mnt and with the directory listings enabled. To test the web server, enter the following URL in your web browser:

`http://192.168.1.250:8080`

Where 192.168.1.250 is the IP address of your FreeNAS.

You will see a simple listing:

Index of /

Name	Last Modified	Size	Type
Parent Directory/		-	Directory
store/	2008-May-27 12:00:52	-	Directory

lighttpd/1.4.19

Summary

In this chapter, we have looked at the different protocols that can be used to connect to the FreeNAS server from a variety of operating systems including Windows, Linux, and OS X.

We have seen that CIFS is available across the board and NFS is useful for Linux or OS X networks. Also, we looked at specialized protocols like RSYNC and UPnP, which allow the FreeNAS server to be used as a backup server or as a multimedia streaming server respectively.

In the next chapter, we shall look at the various user and system administration tasks.

5
User and System Administration

In this chapter, we will look at the different system administration tasks for the FreeNAS server as well as user administration. Areas covered include:

- Adding new users
- Using local user authentication with CIFS, FTP, AFP, and SSH
- Rebooting and shutting down the server
- Simple network management including configuring FreeNAS to use DNS and setting the default gateway
- Getting status information about the server

Introduction

In general, once the FreeNAS server is configured and running, it doesn't really need much attention, it should just work. However, there are lots of different features which can be configured. This chapter will look at some of the common administration tasks for setting up your FreeNAS server.

Local User Management

Until now, we have only used the FreeNAS server in an "anonymous" mode, meaning that anyone can connect to the server and read, create, and delete files. This isn't always what you want, so FreeNAS has some user management features that change the way CIFS, FTP, and AFP allow users to connect to the server.

User and System Administration

The 0.6 series of FreeNAS releases has rather blunt user management. The defined users have access or they don't have access, period. There is no granularity; for example being able to give some users read access while others have read/write access.

The roadmap for the 0.7 releases promises the ability to create a share (meaning a folder on a selected disk), with user/group/quota property on this share. This implies a greater level of control.

The first step to creating a user is in fact to create a group. Each user must belong to a group. Groups are sets of users who are associated with one another. So in your business, you might have a *sales* group and a *engineering* group. At home, you probably only want one group, for example *home*.

1. To create a group, go to **Access: Users and Groups** and click on the **Group** tab.
2. Now click on the add circle.
3. The form is very simple; you need to add a name and a description. For example sales and "The sales people".
4. Now click **Add** and then apply the changes.

Only a-z, A-Z, and 0-9 are supported in the group name. _ (underscores) and spaces are not supported, neither are punctuation characters like $%&* etc.

Now that you have a group created, you can create a user.

1. Click on the **Users** tab.
2. And then on the add circle.

There are four mandatory fields:

- **Login**: This is the unique login name of user. If the user already has a login name on other servers or workstations, like a Windows user name or a Linux user name, it is best to keep it the same here. This way the user doesn't need to try an remember an extra username and also some programs (particularly Windows) try and log in with the Windows user name before asking which name it should use. Keeping them the same will ease integration.
- **Full Name**: The user's full name. Often, the login name is an abbreviation or short name for the user like john, gary. Here you need to enter the full name so that it is easy to tell which login name belongs to which person.
- **Password**: Their password (with confirmation). The colon ':' character isn't allowed in the password.

[102]

- **Primary Group**: The group to which they belong, for example sales.

Login	john
	Unique login name of user.
Full Name	John Smith
	User full name.
Password	****
	**** (Confirmation)
	User password.
Primary Group	sales
Home directory	
	Enter the path to the home directory of that user. Make sure that this path exists and is always mounted at startup. Leave this field empty to use default path /mnt.
Full Shell	☐ Give full shell to user
Administrator	☐ Put user in the administrator group
	Add

3. To finish, you need to click **Add** and apply the changes.

You now have a user added to your FreeNAS server.

There are three more optional fields when adding a user: Home Directory, Full Shell, and Administrator, and we shall look at these in a moment, but first let's look at what effect adding a user has on the rest of the FreeNAS server.

Using CIFS with Local Users

To use the users you have defined with Windows networking, you need to go to the **Services: CIFS/SMB** page and change the **Authentication** field to **Local User**. Then click **Save and Restart** to apply your changes.

What this means is that only authenticated users can now access the FreeNAS shares via CIFS.

 In version 0.6, this user authentication is for all the shares, the user has access to everything or nothing. This should change with 0.7.

When trying to connect now from a Windows Vista machine, a window pops up asking for a user name and password.

Once authenticated, the user has access to all the user shares on the FreeNAS server.

FTP and User Login

On the **Services: FTP**, there are two fields that control how users log in to the FreeNAS server:

- **Anonymous login**: This allows you to enable anonymous login. This means the user connects with the user name **anonymous** and any password.
- **Local User**: This enables a local user login. Users log in using the user name and passwords defined in the Access: Users and Groups page.

The two can be used together; however, they do negate one another in terms of security. It is best to run the FTP with either anonymous logins enabled and local user logins disabled or vice versa. If you run with both enabled, then people can still log in using the anonymous method even if they don't have a user account and so, it diminishes the benefits of having the user accounts enabled.

Other than the security benefits, another advantage of local user login with FTP is that you can define a home directory for the user and when the user logs in, they will be taken to that directory and only they have access to that directory and those below it. This effectively offers each user their own space on the server and other users cannot interfere with their files.

To get this working, you need to create a directory on your shared disk. You can do this with any of the access protocols CIFS, NFS, FTP, and AFS. You need to connect to the shared disk and create a new folder.

Then, in **Access: Users,** either create a new user or edit an existing one (by clicking on the 'e' in a circle). In the **Home directory**, you need to enter the directory for that user. For example for the user john, you might create a directory cunningly named *john*. Assuming the disk is named *store* (as per the quick start guide) then the path for the home directory would be: /mnt/store/john.

Click **Save** and apply the changes. Now when John logs in using the user name *john* he will be taken directly to the *john* directory. He doesn't have access to other files or folders on the *store* disk, only those in *john* and any sub folder.

> **chroot() Everyone, but Root**
>
> In the advanced settings section of the Services: FTP page, there is a field called **chroot() everyone, but root**. What this means is that when a user logs in via FTP, the root directory (top or start directory) for them will be the directory set in the **Home directory** field. Without this set, the user will log in to the server at the physical / and will see the server in its entirety including the FreeNAS and FreeBSD system files. It is much safer to have this box checked. The exception to this is the user root (which in FreeBSD terms is the system administer account). If **Permit root login** is enabled, then the user root can log in and they will be taken to the root of the actual server. This can be useful if you ever need to alter any of the system files on the FreeNAS, but this isn't recommend unless you absolutely know what you are doing!

Authenticating AFP Users

Like CIFS and FTP, the Apple Filing Protocol (AFP) can also use the local user authentication features of FreeNAS.

In the **Services: AFP** page, there are two options for controlling access to the server via AFP:

- **Enable guest access**, meaning that anyone can connect without giving a username or password. The users have full read and write access.
- **Enable local user authentication**, meaning that only users defined on the FreeNAS server (on the **Access: Users** page) can access the server. The user name and password set in the FreeNAS server need to be given to authenticate.

User and System Administration

Like FTP, the two can be used together, however, they do negate one another in terms of security. It is best to run the AFP service with either guest logins enabled and local user logins disabled or vice versa. If you run with both enabled then people can still log in using the guest account even if they don't have a user account and so it reduces the benefits of having the user accounts enabled.

With just local user authentication enabled, initial connections from an Apple Macintosh will fail. In the top right-hand corner of the Finder window, there is a button labeled **Connect As...**. Use that to enter a user name and password.

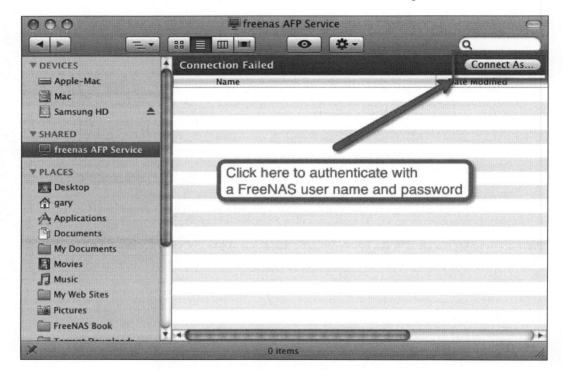

Connect to the FreeNAS Server via SSH

One of the services that hasn't been mentioned much in this book so far is Secure Shell access or SSH for short. It is really for advanced users and it will be used to connect to the server in Chapter 10, when we look at FreeBSD and command line tools available.

However, SSH depends heavily on the local users defined on the server and as such it is worth looking at now.

SSH is a network protocol that allows data to be exchanged over an encrypted (secure) channel between two computers. It is commonly used as a secure command line interface to a remote computer. This means that you can access the command line interface of the FreeNAS server from a remote computer without having to access the keyboard the and monitor of the FreeNAS server. On the FreeNAS server, it is also used in conjunction with the Unison suite of programs. Unison uses SSH to log in to the server and start the synchronization process.

On the **Access: Users: Add** page, there is a field called **Full Shell**, which when enabled, gives that user access to the FreeNAS server via SSH.

To test SSH connectivity:

1. Create a user and make sure that **Full Shell** is enabled.
2. Go to the **Services: SSHD** and enable the service.
3. Make sure that Password authentication is ticked.
4. Click **Save and Restart**.
5. Connect to the FreeNAS server using a SSH client (see below).

Password Authentication

It is possible to connect to the FreeNAS server without giving a user name and password but by relying on an exchange of encryption keys that verify that you are who you claim to be. With Password Authentication enabled, you are able to log in just using a username and password.

You can connect to the FreeNAS server via the command line program *ssh* using Linux and Mac OS X. For Windows, you will need a SSH client, the best one is called Putty (http://www.chiark.greenend.org.uk/~sgtatham/putty/). We will look in more detail at Putty in Chapter 10.

From a Linux or OS X command line type:

`ssh -l john 192.168.1.250`

Don't forget to change the address to that of your FreeNAS if you aren't using the default.

The -l tells the SSH program which user you want to use as the login name, in this case, I have chosen john.

The first time you log in, you may be asked if you trust the remote machine as you are about to enter into encrypted communications with it. It should read some thing like this:

```
The authenticity of host '192.168.1.250 (192.168.1.250)' can't be
established.
DSA key fingerprint is b2:d0:99:cb:6e:b2:53:95:4d:f6:b3:02:1d:bc:36:db.
Are you sure you want to continue connecting (yes/no)? yes
Warning: Permanently added '192.168.1.250' (DSA) to the list of known
hosts
```

Answer yes and then type in the password for the user. You are now connected to the FreeNAS server via SSH. From here, you can access the command line tools of the FreeNAS server. See chapter 10 for more details.

Services that Don't Use Local User Accounts

Not all services provided by FreeNAS use local accounts for authentication, most notably NFS. This requires a note of caution. If you have NFS enabled, and are using local user authentication for CIFS, FTP, and AFP be aware that users can still connect to the FreeNAS server using NFS without any username and password. This is an easy way for people to circumvent the local user authentication process.

Using FreeNAS with the Microsoft Active Directory

Until now, we have defined all the user information locally on the FreeNAS server. This is fine for small networks but if you have a large business network, you may already have Microsoft's Active Directory deployed. FreeNAS can use the user database of a Microsoft Active Directory (Windows 2000/2003) to authenticate user names and passwords and therefore, remove the need to define users locally.

When Active Directory is being used, the FreeNAS server will authenticate users using the directory for the following services: CIFS, FTP, SSH, and Unison.

[**Pre-Windows 2000**
FreeNAS is considered as a pre-Windows 2000 client and as such the Active Directory must be configured with pre-Windows 2000 compatibility.]

Assuming the Active Directory is installed and running:

1. Go to **Access: Active Directory**.
2. Tick the Enable check box in the title bar of the table.
3. Enter the Active Directory server name in the **AD server name** field. For example the Windows Server 2003 server on my test network is called WS2003, so I entered WS2003.
4. Enter the IP address of the Active Directory server in the **AD server IP** field.
5. Enter the domain name for Active Directory. This is in pre-Windows 2000 format.
6. Enter the domain administrator account user name (probably Administrator) and the password.
7. Finally, click **Save**.

To check if the FreeNAS is able to communicate with the Active Directory correctly:

1. Go to **Diagnostics: Information**
2. Click the **MS Domain** tab.

This will test the connecting to the Active Directory.

A successful test will look like this:

```
Accessibility test to MS domain:
Results for net rpc testjoin:
Join to 'FREENAS' is OK
Ping winbindd to see if it is alive:
Ping to winbindd succeeded on fd 4
Check shared secret:
Checking the trust secret via RPC calls succeeded
```

After the Active Directory is configured, CIFS, FTP, SSH, and Unison authentication will rely **only** on account information in the Active Directory.

The authentication method for CIFS/SMB is automatically changed to *Domain* when the Active Directory is configured for use.

To check this, go to **Services: CIFS/SMB** and notice that **Authentication** is now set to **Domain**.

To test the use of Active Directory, try connecting to the FreeNAS server via CIFS, FTP or SSH and use account information from the Active Directory.

User and System Administration

System Admin

Some of the common administration tasks for the system admin:

How to Change the Web GUI User Name and Password

When you first install or boot-up the FreeNAS server it has a default username and password for accessing the web GUI. These are *admin* and *freenas* respectively. If your FreeNAS is in an environment where others could potentially access the FreeNAS server and change settings, either maliciously or by accident/curiosity, it is advisable that you change the password and possibly even the username for access to the web GUI.

To change the password, go to **System: General** and click on the **Password** tab. Enter the current web GUI password (which is probably *freenas*) and then enter the new desired password twice, the second time for confirmation to make sure you entered the right characters. Now click on **Save**.

Once saved, you will automatically asked to log in again. So enter the username (probably *admin*) and then the new password you entered.

> **Choosing a Good Password**
>
> You need to choose a strong password, which means one that is difficult to guess.
>
> It is best to choose a password that you will remember, that way you don't have to write it down or leave it in the open.
>
> But avoid using a complete word from a dictionary or a name.
>
> The more characters your password contains, the harder it is for someone to guess it. Often a longer but simple password can be safer than a short, complex one; it also has the benefit that it is easier to remember.
>
> Use a combination of capital and lowercase letters, numbers, and standard symbols (! @ # $ % ^ & *). The FreeNAS web GUI password is case-sensitive, which means that a capital letter Z is different from a lowercase z.
>
> Don't use your birthday, your child or pet's name, your phone number etc. Personal information can be easy for someone to figure out.
>
> Avoid the obvious password like "123456", "test" or "password."

It is also possible to change the default username from *admin* to another name of your choosing. To change it, go to **System: General** and enter a new username in **username** field. Click Save to apply the changes. You will be asked to log in again, this time you will need to enter the new username.

Rebooting and Shutting Down

It is possible to shutdown and reboot the FreeNAS server from the web interface. In the web interface, rebooting and shutting down work in very similar fashions. To reboot, you need to go to **System: Reboot** and to shutdown go to **System: Shutdown**.

There are two types of reboot/shutdown, immediate (now) or scheduled. To reboot or shutdown immediately, go to the respective page and click on **Yes** in answer to the question **Are you sure?** Once you have clicked on **Yes**, the system will start to shutdown/reboot.

For scheduled reboots or shutdowns, click on the **Scheduled** tab.

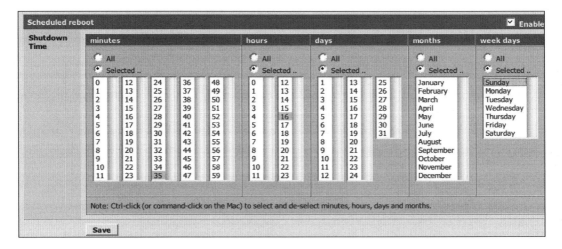

Reboots and shutdowns are scheduled by selecting which minute, hour, day, and month you want the reboot or shutdown or occur. This is a re-occurring event and as such you can also choose a day of the week rather than day of the month for the reboot.

To enable the scheduled reboot or shutdown, tick the enable tick box and then select the time you want for the reboot or shutdown. For example, to reboot the server **every** Sunday at 4:35PM you would select:

- 35 from the minutes section
- 16 from the hours (remember it is a 24 hour clock)
- Sunday from the week days
- Days and months would remain empty

How to Set the Hostname of the Server

Your FreeNAS server has a name, known as the hostname. This name uniquely identifies the server. If you have more than one FreeNAS server on your network, you need to change the hostnames so that each one is unique.

To change the hostname, go to **System: General** and enter a new hostname in the **Hostname** field. If you are deploying your FreeNAS in a network environment, which also uses Internet domains names for identification, then you can also enter a domain name (e.g. yourcompany.com) in the **Domain** field.

Configuring the Web Interface to use HTTPS

HTTPS (Hypertext Transfer Protocol over Secure Socket Layer) is a way for your web browser to connect to the FreeNAS server over a secure encrypted connection. If your FreeNAS server is in an environment where people can "snoop" on the network to discover the passwords being used, it is best to use HTTPS. This is also true if you have configured your network in such a way that your FreeNAS can be administered from the Internet (probably through a firewall). This can be useful when the FreeNAS server is in a different location than the person responsible for administering it.

To enable HTTPS, go to **System: General** and check the HTTPS checkbox in the **WebGUI protocol** field. After you have clicked **Save**, you will need to reboot the server for the changes to be applied.

Once rebooted, you now connect to the web GUI with:

```
https://192.168.1.250
```

Notice that the URL starts with `https` and not `http` as before. Once you connect to the server, your browser will almost certainly tell you that the certificate for this secure connection is signed by an unknown authority. It will question if you can trust server or not. Don't be alarmed, this isn't a problem. Accept the certificate and proceed. Depending on your browser, you may be able to accept this certificate permanently so as to not receive the warning in future. You can now log in as usual.

> When a web browser makes a connection to a secure site using HTTPS, the web server presents the browser with a certificate identifying itself. This certificate contains unique, authenticated information about the certificate owner. To be sure that this information is correct, a 3rd party needs to vouch for the certificate and say it is trustworthy. This 3rd party is called a Certificate Authority (CA) and they verify the identity of the certificate owner. They establish a level of trust. If *they* say this certificate is valid then I *trust* them.
>
> Web browsers are preprogrammed with an accepted list of Certificate Authorities and when they see a CA that isn't on that list, the web browser will question if this is a trustworthy certificate.
>
> FreeNAS uses a self-signed certificate, which means it vouches for itself. This would be a problem for a major website that accepts online payments but for FreeNAS it is acceptable as it isn't the trust of the server that is required but rather the ability to talk securely. Once you accept the certificate, the secure communications will begin with the FreeNAS server based on some of the information in the certificate.

Changing the Web Interface Port

Sometimes, it can be useful to change the web server port from the default value of 80 (443 for HTTPS) to something else. For example if you want to administer your FreeNAS server from the Internet and you need to configure your firewall with a forwarding rule, then it can be helpful to put the web server on a different port.

To change the port number, go to **System: General** and enter the new port number in **WebGUI port** field. When you change the port number, you need to reboot the server for the settings to take effect. Once rebooted, you need to use a new URL:

```
http ://192.168.1.250:8080
```

Where 8080 is the new port number you choose and of course 192.168.1.250 is the IP address of your FreeNAS server, you will need to change this accordingly.

How to Set a DNS Server

Several of the services on the FreeNAS server like the Network Time Protocol service and the sending of email status reports require the FreeNAS to use DNS. DNS is an Internet service that translates domain names into IP addresses. Each time you use a domain name (in your web browser for example), DNS is used to translate the name into the corresponding IP address. To find different servers on the Internet, like an email server, FreeNAS also needs to use DNS.

Your can ascertain the DNS servers you need to use from one of several sources:

- If you are using the FreeNAS on your company network, you may well have DNS servers on your LAN. You need to speak to your network administrator to get the correct information.
- If you are using the FreeNAS server at home, then your DNS could be the address of your ADSL/DSL modem.
- Alternatively, for the home user, the DNS servers could be those of your ISP. You need to contact your ISP (or search their website) to find out what DNS servers you should use.

If you can't find which DNS servers to use, then copy the settings from an existing machine on your network. For example, to find out what your DNS settings are in Windows XP, Windows Server 2003, and Vista, click on **Start** then **Run...** and type **cmd** and press *ENTER*. A command prompt will appear. Now type:

`C:\>ipconfig /all`

The result will list various bits of information about your network connection. In the **Ethernet adapter Local Area Connection**: section, there will be information about the DNS servers.

```
C:\WINDOWS\system32\cmd.exe

C:\>ipconfig/all

Windows IP Configuration

        Host Name . . . . . . . . . . . . : vmware-xp
        Primary Dns Suffix  . . . . . . . :
        Node Type . . . . . . . . . . . . : Unknown
        IP Routing Enabled. . . . . . . . : No
        WINS Proxy Enabled. . . . . . . . : No
        DNS Suffix Search List. . . . . . : lan

Ethernet adapter Local Area Connection:

        Connection-specific DNS Suffix  . : lan
        Description . . . . . . . . . . . : VMware Accelerated AMD PCNet Adapter
        Physical Address. . . . . . . . . : 00-0C-29-EF-24-3C
        Dhcp Enabled. . . . . . . . . . . : Yes
        Autoconfiguration Enabled . . . . : Yes
        IP Address. . . . . . . . . . . . : 192.168.1.249
        Subnet Mask . . . . . . . . . . . : 255.255.255.0
        Default Gateway . . . . . . . . . : 192.168.1.254
        DHCP Server . . . . . . . . . . . : 192.168.1.254
        DNS Servers . . . . . . . . . . . : 192.168.1.254
        Lease Obtained. . . . . . . . . . : Friday, February 01, 2008 6:28:58 PM
        Lease Expires . . . . . . . . . . : Saturday, February 02, 2008 6:28:58 PM

C:\>
```

How to Set the Language for the Web Interface

Along with English, the FreeNAS web interface comes in several different languages including: Bulgarian, Chinese, Dutch, French, German, Greek, Hungarian, Italian. Japanese, Norwegian, Polish, Portuguese, Romanian, Russian, Slovenian, Spanish, and Swedish.

To change the language of the web interface, go to **System: General Setup** and select the desired language from the **Language** drop down box. Once you click **Save,** the language should change straight away, however, sometimes because of browser caching you might need to click to another section of the web interface before you see the language change.

Date and Time Configuration

All PCs have a clock and can keep a track of the date and time. Keeping the date and time correct is important for several reasons including:

- Files will be marked with the correct creation and modification time stamps.
- The scheduled reboots and shutdowns will occur at the right time.
- The FreeNAS server can act as a time server to Windows machines.
- Scheduled status reports sent by email will be sent at the right time and will have the correct time and date on them.
- Log files will have the right time stamps, which aids any diagnostics.

The date and time can be set in one of three ways:

- Set it in the computers BIOS
- Set it via the web GUI
- Configure automatic time adjustment via NTP

The time and date configurations are made on the **System: General** page.

The first thing to set is your time zone, this is done by selecting it from the **time zone** drop down box. You need to select the nearest location to you (normally, the capital city of the country you are in or a state capital), for example **America/New York**. You can also select the time zone in a more manual fashion, for example **Etc/GMT-1**. Use the **Save** button to apply the changes.

If you need to set the date and time, you can choose to set the date and time by entering them into the **System time** field. The format is mm/dd/yyyy hh:mm. You can also use the icon to select the date and time from a simple calendar widget. It is worth noting that the seconds cannot be set using this method. Use the **Save** button to apply the changes.

You can choose to configure the date and time automatically using the Network Time Protocol (NTP). NTP is a way of synchronizing computer clocks over the Internet. The time server normally has a very accurate atomic clock attached to it, and other computers ask it the time and set their clocks accordingly. The protocol has special algorithms to allow for the delays in sending and receiving requests over the Internet. With this, protocol clocks can be accurate within a fraction of a second.

To enable NTP, tick the **Enable NTP** field. Next, you need to enter which time server you want to use, `pool.ntp.org` is the default and should be just fine for your usage. If your FreeNAS doesn't have access to the Internet, then you will need to find an NTP server on your local network. Although using one NTP server is sufficient, the recommendation from the NTP people is to specify 3 servers:

- `0.pool.ntp.org`
- `1.pool.ntp.org`
- `2.pool.ntp.org`

Use a space to separate the hosts.

> The `pool.ntp.org` project is a big virtual cluster of timeservers striving to provide reliably easy to use NTP service for millions of clients without putting a strain on the big popular timeservers.
>
> To spread the load and handle the occasional down server, the NTP project have created random sets of servers using the 0, 1, and 2.pool.ntp.org names. The servers in each set randomly change every hour.

The last thing to set is the interval, in minutes, between network time syncs. The default is 300, which is every 5 hours. This should be sufficient for most needs.

For the NTP protocol to work correctly, you need to make sure you have defined at least one DNS server for name resolution. See the *How to set a DNS server* section for more details.

How to Disable Console Menu

Beyond initial network settings, the FreeNAS server uses the web interface for the majority of its configuration. However, the console menu remains active even when you don't need it anymore. This can be a security risk as anyone with access to the keyboard and monitor attached to the server can change settings either deliberately or by accident.

To disable the console menu, go to **System: Advanced** and check the **Disable console menu** checkbox. Once you click **Save**, you will need to reboot for the console to be disabled.

How to Stop the Startup and Shutdown Beeps

When FreeNAS starts up and shuts down, it plays a few melodious beeps to indicate that it has started. If you want to disable them, then go to the **System: Advanced Setup** page and tick **the System Beep** box, this will disable the speaker beep on startup and shutdown.

Adding Predefined Network Hosts

In the rare case that you don't have access to a DNS server but yet you still want to use the NTP protocol or email status reports, you will need to define the NTP server or the email (SMTP) server manually. You can do that on the System: Hosts page.

To add, say an NTP server, with the address 86.125.34.112, click the add circle and then enter the host name of the server and its IP address. You can also add a description.

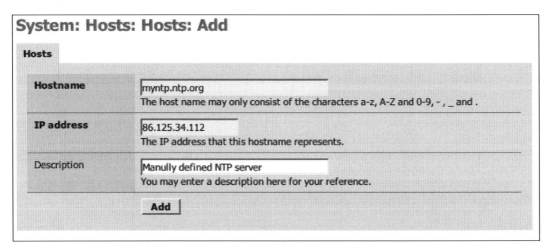

Reset the Server to the Factory Defaults

If you want to reset the FreeNAS server back to its original installation state (or Live CD boot state), which is often known as the factory settings (metaphorically: the settings it had when it left the factory) then you can do this on the **System: Factory** defaults.

If you click **Yes**,, the FreeNAS server will be reset to factory defaults and will reboot immediately. The entire system configuration will be overwritten. The LAN IP address will be reset to 192.168.1.250 and the password will be set to 'freenas'.

> It is worth noting that when you reset the server to the factory defaults, the data on the disks won't be touched. This means that you can reset the server and then reconfigure it to find your data. But be VERY CAREFUL, if during the re-configuration phase you reformat a disk or apply a different configuration than before, you are likely to lose data.

Simple Network Administration

On the **Interfaces: LAN** page, you can perform some limited network administration tasks such as defining a new IP address for the FreeNAS server and defining a default gateway for the server.

The default gateway is the IP address of another device on the network that will accept network traffic for forwarding on to another network. The most common default type of default gateway in the home situation is the ADSL/DSL modem/router that is provided by your Internet Service Provider (ISP). The modem's job is to route traffic from your home network on to the Internet and the reverse.

In a business environment, the setup may be same or if you have a comprehensive network infrastructure, the default gateway will be a network device that connects your segment of the network to the rest of the corporate network.

You will almost certainly need to set your default gateway to give the FreeNAS server access to the Internet ,which you will especially need if you are using an Internet NTP service.

You need to ask your network administer or ISP for the details of the default gateway. Another way to ascertain the default gateway settings is to see what they are on another machine on your network.

For example, to find out what your default gateway is in Windows XP, Windows Server 2003, and Vista, click on **Start** then **Run...** and type **cmd** and press *ENTER*. A command prompt will appear. Now type:

`C:\>ipconfig /all`

The result will list various bits of information about your network connection. In the **Ethernet adapter Local Area Connection**: section, there will be information about the Default Gateway.

```
C:\Windows\system32\cmd.exe
   NetBIOS over Tcpip. . . . . . . . : Enabled
Ethernet adapter Local Area Connection:

   Connection-specific DNS Suffix  . : lan
   Description . . . . . . . . . . . : Realtek RTL8139/810x Family Fast Ethernet
 NIC
   Physical Address. . . . . . . . . : 00-1A-92-AA-EB-0F
   DHCP Enabled. . . . . . . . . . . : Yes
   Autoconfiguration Enabled . . . . : Yes
   Link-local IPv6 Address . . . . . : fe80::c0f7:aed6:d93e:51af%9(Preferred)
   IPv4 Address. . . . . . . . . . . : 192.168.1.245(Preferred)
   Subnet Mask . . . . . . . . . . . : 255.255.255.0
   Lease Obtained. . . . . . . . . . : 04 February 2008 07:31:31
   Lease Expires . . . . . . . . . . : 05 February 2008 07:31:30
   Default Gateway . . . . . . . . . : 192.168.1.254
   DHCP Server . . . . . . . . . . . : 192.168.1.254
   DHCPv6 IAID . . . . . . . . . . . : 218110610
   DNS Servers . . . . . . . . . . . : 192.168.1.254
   NetBIOS over Tcpip. . . . . . . . : Enabled

Tunnel adapter Local Area Connection* 7:

   Connection-specific DNS Suffix  . :
   Description . . . . . . . . . . . : Teredo Tunneling Pseudo-Interface
```

Disabling Bonjour/ZeroConf

By default, FreeNAS will announce which services it provides (CIFS, AFP etc) with the Zeroconf protocol. This will permit other computers on the LAN to detect that there is a server that provides network services. Zeroconf/Bonjour is used by Apple OS X operating system and recent Linux distributions.

If you wish to disable this feature, then remove the tick from the **Zeroconf** field on the **System: Advanced Setup** page.

Getting Status Information About the Server

FreeNAS comes with some excellent tools to monitor the status of your server. These are all grouped together under the heading **Status** in the left-hand menu column.

User and System Administration

The different status categories are:

- **System**: This is the summary page that is displayed when you first connect to the web interface. It will tell you, among other things, which version of FreeNAS you are running, how long the server has been up and running, the amount of the memory being used, and the disk space usage.
- **Process**: This will show you some summary information about the processes running on your FreeNAS server and a list of the top processes.
- **Interfaces**: This displays a summary of the network interfaces in the server and some simple statics about their traffic loads.
- **Disks**: Here you can see a list of disks currently configured on your system including each disks size, description, and status.
- **Wireless**: This displays a summary of the wireless network interfaces in the server and some simple statics about their traffic loads.
- **Graph**: This page is divided into 2 sections, Traffic graph and CPU load. The first is a real time graph showing the amount of traffic on the network card and the second the amount of CPU usage. Both work in a 2 minute window.

FreeBSD is able to run many programs at the same time and FreeNAS uses this multitasking ability of FreeBSD to run the web server, the CIFS server, the FTP etc simultaneously.

Each of these programs or services runs as a separate **process**. Each process uses time on a system's CPU, as well as other system resources such as memory and disk space.

The various status pages help you keep a eye on those process and the resources being used by the FreeNAS server.

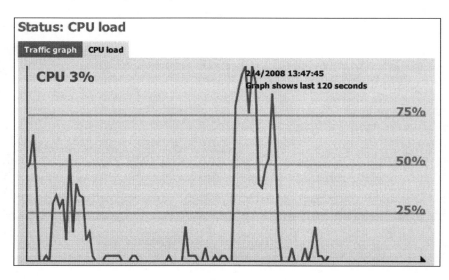

> The output from the processes status page can seem a bit strange if you are not used to UNIX-type systems, here is a quick guide:
>
> **PID**: Each process has a unique process ID called the PID.
>
> **SIZE**: SIZE is the total amount of memory used, in kilobytes, by the process.
>
> **RES**: Is the actual amount of physical memory being used by the process. This can different from SIZE as FreeBSD shares regions of memory (called pages) between processes that have the same values and have not been changed.
>
> **STATE**: This is the current state of the process (one of sleep, wait, run, idl, zomb or stop).
>
> **TIME**: This is the number of system and user CPU seconds that the process has used.
>
> **WCPU**: This is percentage of the CPU being used at that moment.
>
> **COMMAND**: Is the command line which started the process.

Sending Status Report by Email

FreeNAS has the ability to send status reports by email at pre-programmed times. To configure these reports, go to **Status: Email Report**. FreeNAS doesn't include an email server (SMTP server), so you need to tell it which server to use. If you are a home user then this will be the SMTP server provided by your ISP. For business environments, you will need to ask your network administrator where is the address of the SMTP server on your network. If you are addressing the SMTP server by its domain name (e.g. mail.myisp.com) then you need to be sure that DNS is configured so FreeNAS can look up the IP address of the mail server. You could also predefine the server in System: Hosts.

If your SMTP server requites authentication (which is almost certainly found to be true if you are using the SMTP server provided by your ISP) then tick the **Authentication** box and enter the appropriate user name and password.

Next, you need to set who the email is from and where you want it to go. The **To email** needs to be the address where you want to receive the email and the **From email** the sender of the email. For the **From email,** you need to enter a valid address as any notifications of failure to deliver the email will be sent there. Also, you want the **From email** address to be valid so as not to antagonize any spam filtering that your email system may have.

You can fill in the desired subject line of the email and also fine tune what is included in the email report.

Finally, you need to define the time when these status messages will be sent. The table is exactly the same as the one used for scheduled reboots/shutdowns. Messages scheduled by selecting which minute, hour, day, and month you want the messages to be sent. This is a re-occurring event and as such you can also choose a day of the week rather than day of the month for the messages. For example, to send a status message on the 1st of every month at 9:00AM you would select:

- 0 from the minutes section.
- 9 from the hours.
- 1 from the days.
- Select *All* for the months.
- The week days would remain unused.

Summary

In this chapter, we have looked at the different administration tasks for setting up your FreeNAS server including user management and its effects on the access protocols like CIFS and FTP. We have also looked at some of the system administration options as well as simple administration tasks like shutting down and rebooting.

In the next chapter, we shall take a more in depth look at configuring disks on the FreeNAS server including setting up software RAID.

6
Configuring Storage

In this chapter, we will look how to manage hard disks in the FreeNAS server and how to configure them to form RAID sets that improve fault tolerance and increase drive performance.

Introduction

The essence of the FreeNAS server is to provide storage that is easily accessible from the network. To this end, it is important to understand how FreeNAS handles the storage or more specifically hard disks and how they can be configured and used to provide the best and most reliable storage for your network. In this chapter, we shall use the words storage and hard disk almost interchangeably. Technically, a hard disk is a type of storage and there are many other types of storage besides hard disks, but as FreeNAS is primarily concerned with using hard disks as storage, the two terms will at times seem like one. The only exception to this will be when we look at iSCSI, as iSCSI allows remote storage to be added to the FreeNAS server as if it was a local hard disk. Of course, ultimately the remote storage is also a hard disk!

How FreeNAS Handles Data Disks

As mentioned in Chapter 2, adding storage to the FreeNAS server is done in 4 steps:

1. The FreeNAS server is "told" about a physical hard disk.
2. This disk is formatted.
3. The resulting storage space is mounted and made available internally.
4. The mounted storage space is made available on the network via services like CIFS and NFS.

Configuring Storage

Step one, telling the FreeNAS server about the disks at its disposal is handled in Disks: Management. On opening this page, you will see a list of disks that are already configured and using the add circle you have the possibility to add more. To add a disk, click the add circle and you will be taken to the **Disks: Management: Disk: Add** page.

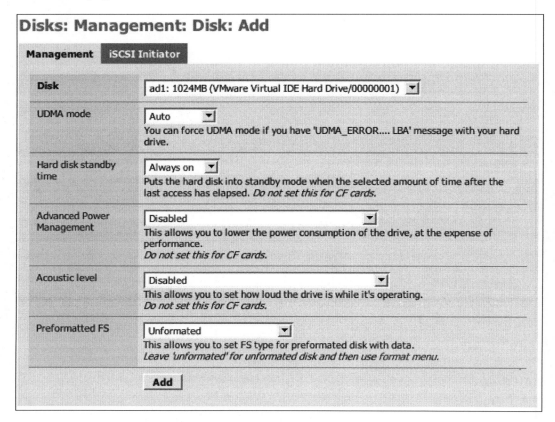

The most important field on this page is the **Disk** field where you select which disk you want to add to the FreeNAS configuration. You can select the disk using a drop down box.

UNIX Device Names

In a UNIX type operating systems, including FreeBSD, devices like hard disks are usually referred to by a slightly cryptic name which looks something like this:

```
/dev/ad0
```

It isn't actually all that difficult once you understand how the name is made up. The first bit /dev is easy. It is a special directory on the server that holds information about all the devices on the system, where dev is short for device. Therefore, all devices start with /dev.

The second part is the device itself. Here, it can be a bit more complicated, but ad0 means disk 0, or the first hard disk as listed in the BIOS. Here is a table with some common device names:

Free BSD device name	Description
/dev/ad*	ATA and SATA hard disks
/dev/da*	SCSI and USB flash storage
/dev/acd*	IDE CD drives
/dev/cd*	SCSI CD drives
/dev/fd*	Floppy disks

The * is a wild card, which in the real world is a number starting from 0. So /dev/da2 is the 3rd (as it starts from 0) SCSI hard disk in the system.

RAID Controllers

If you are using a hardware RAID controller, for the disks attached it, don't use the standard device names for each disk. Instead, these RAID controllers present a virtual disk for each RAID set, using a device named after the RAID controller driver. For example, the *amr* driver (which supports controllers by MegaRAID and some Dell and Intel cards) presents its virtual disks as /dev/amrd*. Also, some RAID cards present their hard drives as /dev/da* devices.

Adding the Disk

Once you have selected the right disk from the drop down box, you can normally just go ahead and click **Add**. However, there are some parameters that you can tweak and the final field **Preformatted FS** needs to be set correctly if this disk is already formatted and has data on it.

Configuring Storage

Disk parameter	Description
UDMA mode	Normally, the interface speed of you hard disk is automatically detected. You can force interface speed (called the UDMA mode) if you have 'UDMA_ERROR.... LBA' message with your hard drive.
Hard disk standby time	Puts the hard disk into standby mode when the selected amount of time after the last access has elapsed. Do not use this with flash memory devices.
Advanced Power Management	This allows you to lower the power consumption of the drive, at the expense of performance. Success will vary depending on your BIOS and hard disk. Do not use this with flash memory devices.
Acoustic level	This allows you to set how loud the drive is while it's operating. Success will vary depending on your BIOS and hard disk. Do not use this with flash memory devices.
Pre-formatted FS	This allows you to set the file system type for pre-formatted disk with data. Leave 'unformatted' for an unformatted disk and then use format menu for format it.

Don't Erase Existing Data by Mistake

If you have converted an existing server into a FreeNAS server or you have put disks in your FreeNAS server with data already on them, then you need to be sure you set the **Preformatted FS** field correctly. Apart from the native UFS format of the FreeBSD, FreeNAS supports FAT32, NTFS, and EXT2.

Once you have selected the disk from the drop down menu and set any of the optional parameters, you can click the **Add** button. Don't forget you also need to apply the changes.

The **Disks: Management** page will now show your disk(s) in a table including information about the disk name, size, and file system.

The next step is to format the disk.

Formatting a Newly Added Disk

Once the disk has been *added* to the FreeNAS server, it needs to be formatted.

1. Go to the **Disks: Format** page.

2. Select which disk you wish to format. Only the disks you have added in the **Disks: Management** page are available to be formatted. If the disk you want to format doesn't appear in the drop down list, then go back to the **Disks: Management** page and check that your disk has been added correctly.

3. Next, you must choose the file system you want to use on this disk. The default will be UFS and unless you specifically need FAT32 or EXT2, it is best to format the disk with UFS.

> **UFS is Best**
>
> UFS is the NATIVE file format for FreeBSD (the underlying OS of FreeNAS). Attempting to use other file formats such as FAT, FAT32, EXT2, EXT3, or NTFS can result in unpredictable results, file corruption, and loss of data!

4. You can also enter an optional volume label for the disk, but it isn't very useful as it isn't used in the FreeNAS web interface.

5. Leave the minimum free space percentage at its default 8% as lowering the threshold can adversely affect performance and auto-defragmentation.

6. The final option allows you to tweak the way the disk is formatted, specifically to not replace the Mater Boot Record (MBR) with a new one during the format process. Normally, this shouldn't be needed but some hardware RAID cards store information in the MBR. If you find that the drive doesn't format correctly and you are using a hardware RAID card, you can try formatting the disk with the option enabled.

7. Once you click **Format Disk**, you will asked if you are sure that you wish to format the disk. Click **OK** to proceed.

The output of formatting the disk will look something like this:

```
Erasing MBR and all partitions.
Creating partition:
/dev/da0p1 added
Creating filesystem with 'Soft Updates':
/dev/da0p1: 5120.0MB (10485692 sectors) block size 16384, fragment size 2048
        using 28 cylinder groups of 183.77MB, 11761 blks, 23552 inodes.
        with soft updates
super-block backups (for fsck -b #) at:
 160, 376512, 752864, 1129216, 1505568, 1881920, 2258272, 2634624, 3010976,
 3387328, 3763680, 4140032, 4516384, 4892736, 5269088, 5645440, 6021792,
 6398144, 6774496, 7150848, 7527200, 7903552, 8279904, 8656256, 9032608,
 9408960, 9785312, 10161664
Done!
```

Configuring Storage

The key is to look for the **Done!** comment at the end and the long list of superblock numbers before it. If you see that, then everything is OK. If the formatting failed for some reason then before the **Done!,** you will see an error message. For example if spaces aren't permitted in the volume label, trying to format a disk like this will result in the last lines of the output reading:

```
newfs: bad volume label. Valid characters are alphanumerics.
Done!
```

Mounting Your Newly Formatted Disks

Once you have formatted the disk, you need to make it available internally in the FreeNAS server. This processing is called *mounting* the disk and is a term left over from the early days of computing when an operator had to mount a magnetic tape or hard disk on a spindle before using it. Mounting a disk makes it available for use within the server and only previously *added* and *formatted* disks can be mounted.

1. To mount a disk go to **Disks: Mount Point** and click the add circle.

There are five important fields to fill in here: **Type**, **Disk**, **Partition**, **File System**, and **Name**.

> **Partitions**
>
> To partition a disk means to divide it into parts. All disks need at least one partition and having a single partition means using the whole disk. It is also possible to partition a disk into many parts. Under FreeNAS, if you install the server software on a hard disk, then two partitions are created, the first for the operating system software and the second for data. When mounting disks, you need to know which partitions you wish to mount.
>
> By default, FreeNAS doesn't use the legacy method to partition disks, which involved storing the partition data in the Mater Boot Record (MBR); instead it used the GUID Partition Table (GPT) which is part of the Extensible Firmware Interface (EFI) standard proposed by Intel as a replacement for the soon to be obsolescent PC BIOS.

- **Type**: Here, you can select if you want to mount a disk or an ISO file. For new physical disks, you need to select disk. The ISO option is useful if you have an .iso file and you wish to make its contents available on your network.
- **Disk**: Select the disk which you wish to mount. This will be the same disk as you used in the **Disks: Management** (to add the disk) and **Disks: Format** (to format it).

- **Partition**: If you have just formatted this disk using FreeNAS, then you will need to select EFI GPT here. If your disk has previous data on it then you need to select which partition the data is on. If you have installed FreeNAS on a disk and you want to use the rest of the disk for data then select 2.
- **File System**: For disks that have been formatted using FreeNAS, you need to select UFS. If you have chosen to use another file system format or the disk already had data on it, you need to select the appropriate file system type (one of FAT, NTFS, EXT2).
- **Name**: Each mounted disk needs a name to distinguish it from other disks. It does seem possible to use spaces in the name but for safety I would recommend using a simple single word mount point name. The name specified will used to mount the disk under the **/mnt** directory on the FreeNAS server, so if we used *store2* then the disk will be mounted on **/mnt/store2** and that would be the name used to share the disk on the network using CIFS etc.
- **Description**: You can fill in an optional description for this mount point.
- **Read only**: Tick this to mount the file system as read-only, even the Administrator account (super user/root) may not write it.

> **Using Disks Formatted under Older Versions of FreeNAS**
>
> If your disks were configured using a version of FreeNAS prior to version 0.683b then you need to manually select partition 1 for a UFS formatted drive or software RAID volume. The *File System* type should be set to UFS.

2. Once you have filled in all the data, click the **Add** button.
3. You will be shown a table with a list of the mounted drives on the FreeNAS server. Their status will be listed as **Configuring**.
4. You now need to click **Apply changes**. Once the changes have been applied, the newly displayed table should include the new mount point with the status of OK.

Making the New Disk Available on the Network

Now that the new disk is formatted and mounted, it can be made available on the network. To do this, enable the appropriate network services like CIFS, NFS, and AFP and if necessary, (for example with CIFS) add the new disk as a shared resource. For NFS and AFP, all mounted drives are automatically shared. See chapter 4 for more details.

Configuring Software RAID on FreeNAS

FreeNAS has the ability to combine disks and either use them in a concatenated manner (meaning they are added together and will appear as one large disk) or use them together for redundancy and improved performance (by spreading the data across several disks). Using many disks in a set like this is called a RAID (Redundant Arrays of Inexpensive Disks) configuration. We looked at RAID in some detail in Chapter 3 but to save you from turning there again, here is a summary (you will need to go back to Chapter 3 if you need more details).

RAID is a system that divides and duplicates data across several hard disks. Depending on which scheme you use, your data is copied, in full or in part, across other disks in the RAID set, and if one of those disks fails, the other disks (with the copy of the data) continue to work and the data as a whole remains intact.

FreeNAS supports several different RAID configurations that are called RAID levels:

JBOD (Just a Bunch of Disks): This is simple form of disk concatenation, the resulting disk appears as one large disk and there is no attempt to spread the data across the two disks. Data that falls in the first half of the RAID disk is written to disk 1, and data in second half to disk 2. There is **no fault tolerance**.

RAID 0 (Striped set without redundancy): RAID 0 is a way of joining two disks together to create one big disk. The data is interleaved between the two disks and so it improves performance but there is **no fault tolerance**.

RAID 1 (mirroring): Here, two disks are used with one disk mirroring the contents of the other disk. If either of the disks fails, the RAID continues using the remaining disk. When the faulty disk is replaced, the new disk will be synchronized with the good disk and the mirroring will continue as before.

RAID 5 (striped set with distributed parity): This is one of the most popular and arguable one of the most useful RAID levels. It allows you to combine a larger number of physical disks, and still maintain some redundancy. RAID 5 can be used on three or more disks. If one disk fails, the data remains intact. RAID 5 can survive one disk failure.

RAID All Starts with Adding the Disks

The first step in configuring a RAID set is in the adding of disks on the **Disks: Management** page. Click the add circle and select the first disk you wish to make part of a RAID set. You do this by selecting it from the drop down box of available disks. You can't use a disk that is already mounted.

The trick now is to set the **Preformatted FS** field to **Software RAID**. This isn't instantly obvious as the disk isn't pre-formatted and in fact, it will be formatted later, but in essence what is happening is that this disk is being marked as a disk available for software RAID. Then, in the next step, when the RAID set is defined, it will appear in the list of disks available for RAID.

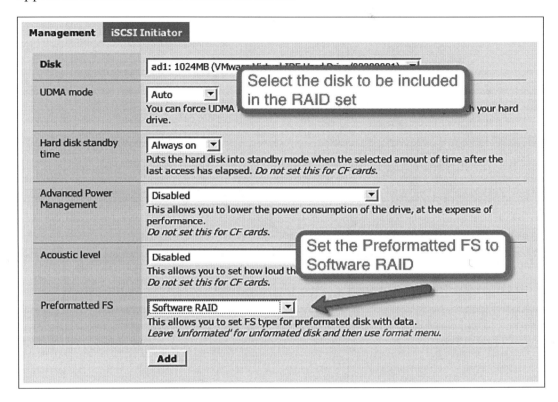

Click on **Add,** and then on **Apply changes**. The list of disks will now show the disk added but notice now that the File system column says, SoftRaid and not UFS.

You need to add at least two disks to use JBOD, RAID 0, and RAID 1. For RAID 5, you need at least 3 disks. Repeat the above procedure to add the other disks.

The next step is to add the disk together to make a RAID set (sometimes referred to as a RAID array). The process is almost identical for all the RAID levels.

Configuring RAID 1

To define a RAID 1 set, go to the **Disks: Software RAID** page. The title of the initial page will read **Disks: Geom Mirror: Manage RAID**. At the top, there is a series of tabs to select other RAID pages including JBOD, RAID 0, RAID 1, and RAID 5.

> **GEOM**
>
> GEOM is FreeBSD's disk management system. GEOM provides an infrastructure system that allows the FreeBSD developers to easily write modules for different types of disk functionality. The RAID capabilities of the FreeNAS server come from Geom Concat, Geom Stripe, Geom Mirror, and Geom Raid5 modules.

To set up mirroring, you need two disks where one will be the mirror of the other i.e. if one fails then the other disk works in its place. During read operations from the disk set, either disk can be used to fetch the data and so read performance is significantly improved.

To create a RAID array, click on the add circle. In essence, to get the RAID1 array working, you need to enter an array name of your choosing and then tick the disks that are part of the array. Finally, click **Add**.

The array name should be descriptive and you should consider using useful information in the name like the type of raid and the size of the disks, so a mirror of two 80GB disks could be called *mirror80gb* or *80gbraid1* etc.

The **Members of this volume** field offers a list of disks that have been previously added to the system with the **Preformatted FS** field set to **Software RAID**. Tick each disk you want to include in the RAID array.

> **Mixing Your Buses**
>
> It is possible to uses IDE, SCSI, and SATA disks in RAID arrays and mix and match them. On a "professional" server, there are often several SCSI cards and disks, used from different SCSI cards to make the array. The reason for this is to limit the load on any one part of the system. So, you might find that performance increases by say using SATA and SCSI together. Of course, any performance benefit will be nulled if one of the disks is physically significantly slower that the other. Here, the bottleneck becomes the disk itself and not the interface servicing it. This might be the case if you have fast, expensive SCSI drives but only "consumer" level SATA drives, mixing the disks here won't improve you overall system speed.

With RAID1, there is one other option that isn't available in the other RAID configurations and that is the **Balance algorithm**. FreeBSD offers 3 different algorithms for controlling how data is read from the mirror set.

- **Round-robin read**: Here, the disks are used in turn to read data from the RAID array and hence the load is equally split over the two.
- **Split request**: Here, larger read requests are split into two requests and one sent to disk1 and the other to disk2.
- **Read from lowest load**: This attempts to read from this disk with the lowest load.

It is generally considered that the round-robin balance algorithm is the best. You can of course, try the other settings and see if you get any performance increases.

Once you click on **Add**, the RAID array will start to be formed. Creating a RAID array isn't an instant thing and sometimes several minutes (or even hours) can pass before the array is set up. Don't forget also to apply the changes. The **Disks: Software RAID** page will keep you up-to-date on the status of the array. When the array is forming, the status of the array will be listed as **Configuring** and when the array is ready it will read **COMPLETE**. You will need to keep going back to the **Disks: Software RAID** page to check the progress.

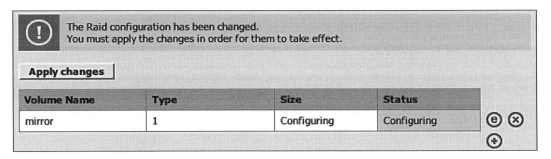

From here, this RAID set is considered by FreeNAS as a single disk. Of course, it is made up of two disks, but logically, it is now one disk. It can be formatted, mounted, and shared on the network just like any other disk.

So, once the array is ready, the next step is to format it. **Don't try and format the array before it is ready.**

Go to the **Disks: Format** page. Find the RAID set in the drop down disk menu. It will be named according to the name you gave the mirror when you created the array followed by its size and finally, by **Software gmirror RAID 1**.

Make sure the **File system** is set to UFS, enter the optional volume name and click **Format disk**. Confirm that you want to format the mirror and just like formatting a single drive, you will see the output of the commands used to format the RAID set and it should end with list of super block numbers and the reassuring **Done!**

Now, the disk can be mounted exactly like any other disk. To mount the disk, go to **Disks: Mount Point** and click the add circle. Select the disk from the drop down menu. On the format page, it will be named according to the name you gave the mirror when you created the array followed by its size and finally, by **Software gmirror RAID 1**. Make sure that the **Type** is **Disk**, **Partition** is **EFI GPT** and the **File system** is **UFS**. Enter the name for the mount point and click **Add**. Apply the changes and your disk is now ready and mounted. It can now be exported to the network using CIFS, NFS and AFP as before.

Configuring RAID 5

RAID 5 uses the striping of RAID 0 but now with three disks in the array parity data is also stored. If one disk fails, the data remains intact. Configuring a RAID 5 set is very similar to that of a RAID 1, except that a RAID 5 array must have at least 3 disks.

To define a RAID 5 set, go to the **Disks: Software RAID** page, and click on the **RAID 5** tab. Now click the add circle. The page to define the RAID array is very similar to that of RAID 1. Enter a name for the array (remembering to be descriptive) and then tick the disks that you want to include in the array (with a minimum of 3).

Click on **Add the RAID array** to start off the formation of the array. Apply the changes and wait for the array to become ready. Revisit the RAID 5 page until the status reads **COMPLETE**.

Go to the **Disks: Format** page. Find the RAID set in the drop down disk menu. It will be named according to the name you gave the RAID 5 set when you created the array followed by its size and finally by **Software graid5 RAID 5**.

Make sure the **File system** is set to **UFS**, enter the optional volume name and click **Format disk**. Confirm that you want to format the logical disk and just like formatting a single drive, you will see the output of the commands used to format the RAID set and it should end with list of super block numbers and the reassuring **Done!**

Now the disk can be mounted exactly like any other disk. To mount the disk, go to **Disks: Mount Point** and click the add circle. Select the disk from the drop down menu. As on the format page, it will be named according to the name you gave the RAID 5 set when you created the array followed by its size and finally, by **Software graid5 RAID 5**. Make sure that the **Type** is **Disk**, **Partition** is **EFI GPT** and the **File system** is **UFS**. Enter the name for the mount point and click **Add**. Apply the changes and your disk is now ready and mounted. It can now be exported to the network using CIFS, NFS and AFP as before.

Configuring JBOD or RAID 0

JBOD (Just a Bunch of Disks) and RAID 0 (Stripe set) are configured in a very similar way to RAID 1. Go to the **Disks: Software RAID** page, and click on the **JBOD** or **RAID 0** tab as required. Now click the add circle. The page to define the RAID array is very similar to that of RAID 1. Enter a name for the array (remembering to be descriptive) and then tick the disks that you want to include in the array.

Click on **Add the RAID array** to start off the formation of the array. Apply the changes and wait for the array to become ready. Revisit the page until the status reads **COMPLETE**.

Go to the **Disks: Format** page. Find the RAID set in the drop down disk menu. It will be named according to the name you gave the RAID set when you created the array followed by its size and finally, by **Software gconcat JBOD** or **Software gstripe RAID 0** for JBOD and RAID 0 respectively.

Now the logical RAID disk can be mounted exactly like any other disk. To mount the disk go to **Disks: Mount Point** and click the add circle. Select the disk from the drop down menu. It will be named as it was in the format page. Make sure that the **Type** is **Disk**, **Partition** is **EFI GPT** and the **File system** is **UFS**. Enter the name for the mount point and click **Add**. Apply the changes and your disk is now ready and mounted. It can now be exported to the network using CIFS, NFS and AFP as before.

Nested RAID Configurations

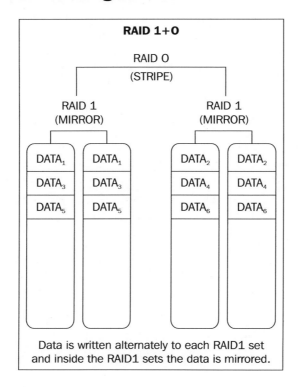

As well as the standard RAID levels, it is possible to create hybrid levels by combining one logical RAID disk with another logical RAID disk in a new RAID array. This is sometimes called nesting RAID levels.

For example you can configure two disks to be a RAID 1 mirror and then another two disks to be a second RAID 1 mirror. These two mirror sets can be combined with RAID 0 to make a new striped RAID set.

There are many possible combination of RAID levels, of which some of the most popular are RAID 1+0, RAID 0+1, RAID 5+0, and RAID 5+1.

Sometimes, these hybrid RAID level are named without the plus sign, so RAID 1+0 becomes RAID 10, RAID 5+1 becomes RAID 51, and so on.

> **Read the RAID Levels Backwards**
>
> The simplest way to understand what each RAID level means is to read the RAID levels backwards, so RAID 1+0 is a RAID 0 array at the highest level made up of RAID 1 sets beneath it. Alternatively, it might help you picture it by understanding that as you read from left to right you are going up the nested RAID tree with the first RAID level being at the bottom, working with the actual hard disks.

Configuring RAID 1+0

RAID 1+0 is a stripe of mirrors meaning the there are two (or more) RAID 1 (mirror) arrays and these are combined in a RAID 0 stripe set.

1. To create a RAID 1+0 set with FreeNAS, you will need at least 4 hard disks. Create two RAID 1 mirrors sets (which I will refer to as mirror1 and mirror2) as described in the *Configuring RAID 1* section above **but** do not format or mount the RAID arrays.

2. Go to the **Disks: Format** page and select **mirror1**. Change the **File system** to **Software RAID** and format the disk. The output will be short and simple:

   ```
   Erasing MBR and all partitions.
   Formating disk.
   Done!
   ```

What has happened is that the RAID 1 mirror set, mirror1, as of now has itself been marked as a disk (albeit a logical disk) for software RAID.

3. Repeat the process for mirror2.
4. Now, go back to the **Disks: Software RAID** page. On the **RAID 1** tab, the two mirror sets will be listed. Click on the **RAID 0** tab and then click the add circle.

The first thing to notice is that in the **Members of this volume** field, there are now two additional disks listed:

```
mirror1 (, Software gmirror RAID 1)
mirror2 (, Software gmirror RAID 1)
```

Above them, will be the other 4 drives that you have used to create these two mirror sets. Also, notice that they are grayed out and you can't tick them for inclusion in another RAID set, which is of course correct as they are already in use for mirror1 and mirror2.

Configuring Storage

5. Enter the name for the RAID set, let's say **raid10** and then tick **mirror1** and **mirror2** to include them in the RAID array. Click **Add** and apply the changes.
6. Once the RAID is formed, its status will read **UP**. Once the RAID 1+0 is **UP**, it can be formatted and mounted just like any other disk.
7. Go to the **Disks: Format** page. Find the RAID 1+0 set in the drop down disk menu. It will be named according to the name you gave the raid set when you created the array (**raid10**) followed by its size and finally by **Software gstripe RAID 0**.
8. Now the logical RAID 1+0 disk can be mounted exactly like any other disk. To mount the disk, go to **Disks: Mount Point** and click the add circle. Select the disk from the drop down menu. It will be named as it was in the format page. Make sure that the **Type** is **Disk**, Partition is **EFI GPT** and the **File system** is **UFS**. Enter the name for the mount point and click **Add**. Apply the changes and your disk is now ready and mounted. It can now be exported to the network using CIFS, NFS, and AFP as before.

Configuring RAID 0+1

RAID 0+1 is a mirror of two stripe sets. The key difference from RAID 1+0 is that RAID 0+1 creates a secondary stripe set to mirror the first striped set. A RAID 1+0 setup can cope with two disk failures as long as they are in the same stripe set or in other words, one whole side of the mirrored configuration can fail and the mirror will keep on working.

Creating a RAID 0+1 configuration is similar to that of a RAID 1+0 set and it is best that you have read that section before you proceed here.

1. To create a RAID 0+1 set, two RAID 0 sets need to be created as described in the **Configuring JBOD or RAID 0** section. Let's call these **raid0a** and **raid0b** After the sets have been created, they need to formatted as Software RAID on the **Disks: Format** page.
2. Now, go back to the **Disks: Software RAID** page. On the **RAID 0** tab, the two **raid0** sets will be listed. On the **RAID 1** tab, click the add circle.

Listed in the *Members of this volume* field will be the two RAID 0 sets, **raid0a** and **raid0b**.

3. Enter the name for the RAID set, let's say **raid01** and then tick **raid0a** and **raid0b** to include them in the RAID array. Click **Add** and apply the changes.

Once the RAID is formed, its status will read **COMPLETED**. It can now be formatted and mounted just like any other disk.

4. Go to the **Disks: Format** page. Find the RAID 0+1 set in the drop down disk menu. It will be named according to the name you gave the RAID set when you created the array (**raid01**) followed by its size and finally, by **Software gmirror RAID 1**.

5. Now the logical RAID 0+1 disk can be mounted exactly like any other disk. To mount the disk, go to **Disks: Mount Point** and click the add circle. Select the disk from the drop down menu. It will be named as it was in the format page. Make sure that the **Type** is **Disk**, **Partition** is **EFI GPT** and the **File system** is **UFS**. Enter the name for the mount point and click **Add**. Apply the changes and your disk is now ready and mounted. It can now be exported to the network using CIFS, NFS and AFP as before.

Configuring RAID 5+0

RAID 5+0 is a stripe of RAID 5 sets meaning that there are two (or more) RAID 5 (stripes with parity) arrays and these are combined in a RAID 0 stripe set. You need a minimum of 6 disks to build a RAID 5+0 array.

1. To create a RAID 5+0 array, you must first create two RAID 5 sets called (for example) **raid5a** and **raid5b**. This is described in the *Configuring RAID 5* section. Do **not** format them as UFS disks.

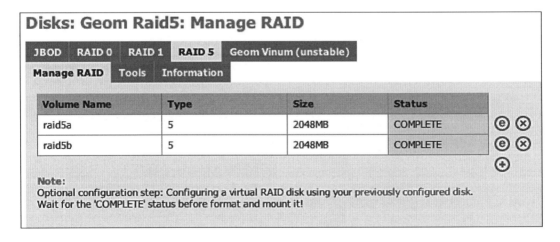

2. Go to the **Disks: Format** page and select **raid5a**. Change the **File system** to **Software RAID** and format the disk. The output will be short and simple:

    ```
    Erasing MBR and all partitions.
    Formating disk.
    Done!
    ```

The RAID 5 set, **raid5a** is now marked as a disk (albeit a logical disk) ready for use in a software RAID set.

3. Repeat the process for raid5b.
4. Now, go back to the **Disks: Software RAID** page. On the **RAID 5** tab, the two RAID sets will be listed. Now click on the **RAID 0** tab and then click the add circle.

Notice that in the **Members of this volume** field there are now two additional disks listed:

```
raid5a (, Software graid5 RAID 5)
raid5b (, Software graid5 RAID 5)
```

Above them will be the other 6 drives that you have used to create these two RAID 5 sets.

5. Enter the name for the raid set, let's say **raid50** and then tick **raid5a** and **raid5b** to include them in the RAID array. Click **Add** and apply the changes.
6. Once the RAID is formed, its status will read **UP**. Once the RAID 5+0 is **UP** it can be formatted and mounted just like any other disk.
7. Go to the **Disks: Format** page. Find the RAID 5+0 set in the drop down disk menu. It will be named according to the name you gave the RAID set when you created the array (**raid50**) followed by its size and finally, by **Software gstripe RAID 0**.
8. Now the logical RAID 5+0 disk can be mounted exactly like any other disk. To mount the disk, go to **Disks: Mount Point** and click the add circle. Select the disk from the drop down menu. It will be named as it was in the format page. Make sure that the **Type** is **Disk**, **Partition** is **EFI GPT** and the File system is **UFS**. Enter the name for the mount point and click **Add**. Apply the changes and your disk is now ready and mounted. It can now be exported to the network using CIFS, NFS, and AFP as before.

Configuring RAID 5+1

A RAID 5+1 array is a mirror of two RAID 5 sets. Such a configuration can handle the failure of two disks as long as each disk is in a different RAID 5 set and multiple disk failures are inside the same RAID 5 set.

Configuration of a RAID 5+1 is very similar to that of a RAID 5+0 set and you should familiarize yourself with the *Configuring RAID 5+0* section before proceeding.

1. As with RAID 5+0, you must first create two RAID 5 sets called (for example) **raid5a** and **raid5b**. This is described in the **Configuring RAID 5** section. Do not format them as UFS disks.
2. Go to the **Disks: Format** page and select **raid5a**. Change the **File system** to **Software RAID** and format the disk. The RAID 5 set, **raid5a** is now marked as a disk (albeit a logical disk) ready for use in a software RAID set. Repeat the process for **raid5b**.
3. Now go back to the **Disks: Software RAID** page. On the **RAID 5** tab, the two RAID sets will be listed. Now click on the **RAID 1** tab and then click the add circle.

Notice that in the **Members of this volume** field there are now two additional disks listed:

```
raid5a (, Software graid5 RAID 5)
raid5b (, Software graid5 RAID 5)
```

Above them will be the other 6 drives which you have used to create these two RAID 5 sets.

4. Enter the name for the RAID set, let's say **raid51** and then tick **raid5a** and **raid5b** to include them in the RAID array. Click **Add** and apply the changes.
5. Once the RAID is formed, its status will read **UP**. Once the RAID 5+1 is **UP**, it can be formatted and mounted just like any other disk.
6. Go to the **Disks: Format** page. Find the RAID 5+1 set in the drop down disk menu. It will be named according to the name you gave the RAID set when you created the array (**raid51**) followed by its size and finally by **Software gmirror RAID 1**.
7. Now the logical RAID 5+1 disk can be mounted exactly like any other disk. To mount the disk, go to **Disks: Mount Point** and click the add circle. Select the disk from the drop down menu. It will be named as it was in the format page. Make sure that the **Type** is **Disk**, **Partition** is **EFI GPT** and the **File system** is **UFS**. Enter the name for the mount point and click **Add**. Apply the changes and your disk is now ready and mounted. It can now be exported to the network using CIFS, NFS, and AFP as before.

RAID 10+0 and Beyond

As any RAID array can be formatted as **Software RAID** and then that logical disk used inside another RAID array, the number of permutations of nested RAID levels is endless, if not always useful. It is technically possible to create a mirror of a mirror (a RAID 1+1) or a RAID 5 of three mirror sets (a RAID 15) or a stripe of two RAID 15 arrays (a RAID 150—two RAID 5 sets of three mirrors sets) and so on.

Another popular RAID format is the so called RAID 10+0 or RAID 100. A RAID 10+0 is a stripe of two RAID 10 sets. It is generally implemented using software RAID 0 over hardware RAID 10. With FreeNAS, it is possible to implement it with just software.

For complicated RAID sets, the combination of hardware RAID and software RAID can be very powerful, along with the spreading of the load over different interface cards. Whatever your RAID needs, FreeNAS can almost certainly do it!

iSCSI Initiator

Another way to add storage to a FreeNAS server is via iSCSI. In Chapter 4, we looked at how the FreeNAS server can act as an iSCSI target, that is a remote hard disk that can be accessed by an iSCSI initiator (a client). We also saw how one FreeNAS server can initiate an iSCSI connection to another FreeNAS server and use the storage of the target server as if it was local storage.

The iSCSI technology in FreeNAS isn't only limited to working between FreeNAS servers. The FreeNAS server can also connect to Windows, Linux, and Solaris iSCSI targets. This way, it is possible to extend the storage capacity of your FreeNAS server using SCSI over IP.

To demonstrate the FreeNAS server using iSCSI to a different platform, we shall look at using Windows.

There are several different iSCSI solutions for Windows including a special version of the Windows server called the Windows Storage Server. However, the Windows Storage Server is an OEM version of Windows and isn't available for consumer purchase. But there are other iSCSI solutions for Windows. A company called Rocket Division Software (http://www.rocketdivision.com) has a free (for personal use) iSCSI target solution called StarWind. It allows you to create RAM disks and images files and serve them as iSCSI targets.

To test FreeNAS with StarWind on Windows, you need to download and install the StarWind software. Use the documentation to familiarize yourself with the StarWind software and then create an iSCSI target called *istore*. This can be a RAM disk or an image file.

One thing to watch when using iSCSI software on Windows is that you may need to explicitly open port 3260 in the Windows firewall for the connections to work.

To configure the iSCSI initiator on FreeNAS, you need to:

1. On the FreeNAS initiator server, go to the **Disks: Management** page and click on the **iSCSI Initiator** tab. Now click the add circle.
2. Enter a name for the iSCSI disk, say **iSCSI0**. It isn't too important as it for information only (it is not using during iSCSI negotiation).
3. For the initiator name, enter: **iqn.1994-04.org.netbsd.iscsi-initiator:freenas.**
4. For the target name, enter: **istore**, which is the target name your created in StarWind.
5. Enter the IP address of the Windows target server. And then click **Add**.
6. Now back to the **Disks: Management** page. Click the add circle and select the iSCSI device from the Disk drop down menu. It should read something like:

   da0: 16MB (ROCKET RAM DISK 16 MB 0001)

   or

   da0: 2048MB (ROCKET IMAGEFILE 0001)

7. Add the disk in the normal way and apply the changes.
8. Now the disk can be formatted from the **Disks: Format** page and mounted on the **Disks: Mount Point: Management** page exactly as we have done previously in the quick start guide in Chapter 2.

After that, you will be able to use the disk via any of the protocols of your choosing including CIFS, NFS, AFP, and FTP.

Summary

In this chapter, we have looked how FreeNAS handles disks and how these disks can be used in combination to create RAID sets that provide fault tolerance and improved performance compared to disks used in isolation.

In the next chapter, we shall look at the different backup strategies that can be used with the FreeNAS server.

7
Backup Strategies

Now that you have data on your FreeNAS server and you can access it from your PC, Mac, Linux or UPnP device, it is time to think about backup. In this chapter, we shall explore the different options that exist to back up the data on the FreeNAS server including using RSYNC to a second local disk as well as to a remote machine.

From one point of view, the fact that the FreeNAS server has no support for tape or optical disk (DVD or Blu-ray) backup is a weakness. But from another point of view, this is normal as the nature of Network Attached Storage is that it is accessible from the network. All operations including configuration, management, and data access occur over the network. As such, backup is also performed over the network.

There are two mains strategies for performing a network-based backup. The first is to initiate a backup directly to tape, compressed file archive (like ZIP or compressed tar) or even optical disk from a remote server or workstation. Here, the data is pulled from the FreeNAS server (via CIFS, NFS or AFP) and written to the backup store (tape, hard drive or optical store). The second option is to copy the data, internally, inside the FreeNAS server. Here, the data remains on the FreeNAS server but is stored on a second disk or RAID set.

Backup Your FreeNAS Using Windows XP's Built-In Backup Utility

Windows XP includes its own backup program and to start it click **Start**, point to **All Programs**, point to **Accessories**, point to **System Tools**, and then click **Backup**.

Backup Strategies

> **Windows XP Home**
>
> If you are using Windows XP Professional, the Windows Backup utility should be ready for use. If you use Windows XP Home Edition, you'll need to follow these steps to install the utility:
>
> 1. Insert your Windows XP CD into the drive and, if necessary, double-click the CD icon in **My Computer**.
> 2. On the Welcome to Microsoft Windows XP screen, click **Perform Additional Tasks**.
> 3. Click **Browse this CD**.
> 4. In Windows Explorer, double-click **the ValueAdd** folder, then **Msft**, and then **Ntbackup**.
> 5. Double-click **Ntbackup.msi** to install the Backup utility.

1. By default, the Backup utility starts in Wizard mode, you can opt to go to advanced mode if you feel confident of configuring the backup manually. Here, we will use the Wizard mode for ease of use.
2. The first Wizard question is **What do you want to do?** referring to doing a backup or restoring files. The default should be **Back up files and settings**, which is what you want, so just click **Next**.
3. You can now choose what you want to back up. The backup program is orientated to backing up the local machine, however, it can be used to back up a network share. Select the last option **Let me choose what to back up** and click **Next**.

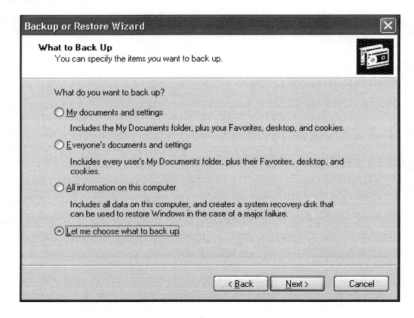

4. The next step is to choose which items to back up. In the left hand pane, you can select files from **My Computer, My Documents,** and also from **My Network Places**, which is what you need to back up your FreeNAS server. Click on the small plus sign **+** next to **My Network Places** and this will expand the **My Network Places** tree. Under this, the available shares on FreeNAS server will be listed. Tick each share that you wish to back up. Using the sample configuration from the quick start guide in chapter 2, there is a share called store. Tick the box next to store to make a backup of it.

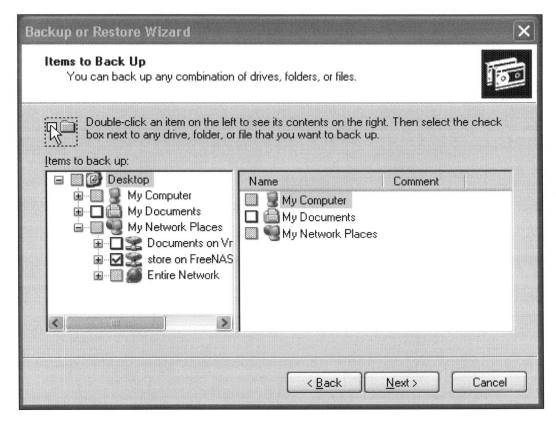

5. Click **Next** to move on to **Backup Type, Destination,** and **Name** page. Here, you can specify a location for the backup data. If you want to use a tape drive then Backup utility gives you a choice of options in the **Select the backup type** box. If you don't have a tape drive then the default backup type will be **File**. By default, Backup proposes saving everything to the floppy drive. This clearly isn't a sane option so instead click **Browse** and choose where you would like to save the backup.

Backup Strategies

There are a number of places you put your backup:

- The computer's hard disk. You need to be sure that the local hard disk is big enough for the backup.
- A shared network drive. You can back up the FreeNAS server to another network server, even another FreeNAS server. One thing to note is that this might not be the most efficient method as it is most likely that this middle Windows XP machine could be taken out of the equation and the two remaining machines (the FreeNAS server and the other network server) can talk directly to make the backup.
- An external hard disk drive. USB 2.0 and FireWire drives have become very cheap and drives space is now measured in terabytes. Adding an external hard drive and using it as backup solution is both practical and inexpensive.

> The built-in backup program in Windows XP doesn't support backing up to an optical drive like a DVD or Blu-ray disk. To get these features, you will need to explore some of the other freeware and commercial backup programs.

6. The final step is to enter a name for the backup. As always, be descriptive. Click **Next** to display the wizard's final page and then click **Finish** to begin backing up immediately.

Setting Scheduled Backups with XP's Built-In Backup Utility

XP's built-in backup utility also has some advanced options including the ability to schedule regular backups.

1. To schedule a backup, start making a backup as described above BUT when you get to the final page of the Backup Wizard, don't click **Finish**, instead, click the **Advanced** button.
2. The first page of the Advanced options is the **Type of Backup** page. Here you can choose what type of backup you wish to make including Full (**Normal**) or **Differential**. If you are unsure. leave it at **Normal** (but note this will create a full backup of all the data on the FreeNAS every time the schedule backup runs). If you want to back up only the files created or changed since the last normal backup, choose **Differential**.
3. Click **Next** to move on to to the **How to Back Up** page.

> **Types of Backups**
>
> Following are the different kinds of backups:
>
> **Normal Backup**—A normal backup copies all selected files and marks each file as having been backed up (in other words, the archive attribute is cleared). With normal backups, you need only the most recent copy of the backup file or tape to restore all of thefiles. You usually perform a normal backup the first time you create a backup set.
>
> **Differential Backup**—A differential backup copies files created or changed since the last normal or incremental backup. It does not mark files as having been backed up (in other words, the archive attribute is not cleared). If you are performing a combination of normal and differential backups, restoring files and folders requires that you have the last normal as well as the last differential backup. The Differential Backup, used in combination with the Normal Backup, is the easiest way to create backups without having to create a full backup of all the data every time the backup is performed.
>
>
>
> **Copy Backup**—A copy backup copies all selected files but does not mark each file as having been backed up (in other words, the archive attribute is not cleared). Copying is useful if you want to back up files between normal and incremental backups because copying does not affect these other backup operations.
>
> **Daily Backup**—A daily backup copies all selected files that have been modified the day the daily backup is performed. The backed-up files are not marked as having been backed up (in other words, the archive attribute is not cleared).
>
> **Incremental Backup**—An incremental backup backs up only those files created or changed since the last normal or incremental backup. It marks files as having been backed up (in other words, the archive attribute is cleared). If you use a combination of normal and incremental backups, you will need to have the last normal backup set as well as all incremental backup sets in order to restore your data.

4. On this page, you can tick the box to have your backup data verified after the backup has occurred. Verifying the backup gives you that extra assurance that the backup worked correctly, but it will lengthen the time needed to make the backup. Tick **Verify data after back up** if required and click **Next**. On the **Backup Options** page, leave the **Append this backup to existing backups** selected and click **Next**. It is not advisable to use the **Replace existing backups** option when using any kind of incremental or differential backup, as the previous backups are essential for restoring the files, should that be necessary later on.

Backup Strategies

5. On the **When to Back Up** page, choose **Later** rather than **Now**. Enter a name for this backup job (for example FreeNAS nightly backup) and then click **Set Schedule...**

6. Now, you can set different time intervals for the backups including daily, weekly, and monthly. The screenshot below shows the settings for a 12:05AM backup every day of the week except the weekends.

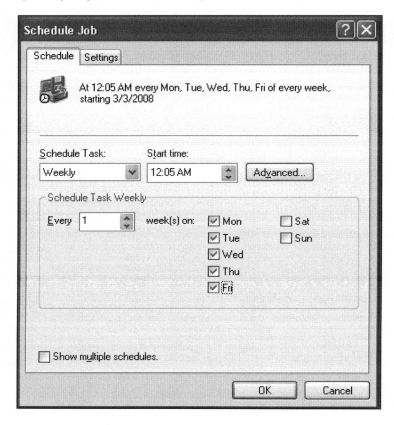

7. Click on **OK** to exit from the scheduling page and click **Next**. You may be asked to enter a username and password for the user who will run this job. It is best to enter the Administrator username and password.

8. On the final summary page, click **Finish** to program the scheduled backup.

Removing scheduled backups

If you wish to remove a previously scheduled backup job, then go to **Control Panel** and double click on **Scheduled Tasks**. From there, you can delete the backup job.

Restoring a FreeNAS Backup Made with XP's Built-In Backup Utility

Once you have your backup, it is important to know how to restore it if the worst has happened.

1. Start the Backup program and choose **Restore files and settings** from the first page of the wizard.
2. Click **Next** and then double click on the name of the backup file that will be listed in the right-hand pane.
3. To do a full restore, then tick all the backup sets listed and click **Next**.
4. To selectively restore certain files, then expand the different backup sets and find the files you want to restore. Tick the small box next to the file or folder and click **Next**.

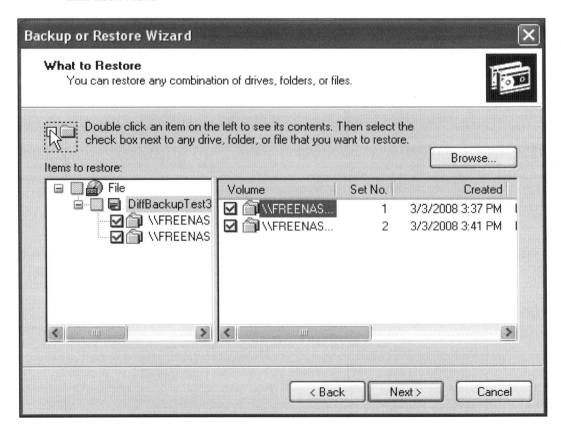

5. On the summary page, click **Finish** and the restore will start.

By default, the files will be restored to their original locations, which in this case is the FreeNAS server. If you want the files to be restored to another location, then before clicking **Finish** on the summary page click on **Advanced**. There you will be able to specify a different restore location and also control how the restore is performed (for example should files be overwritten and so on).

Backing Up the FreeNAS Configuration Files

While talking about backup, it is useful to also mention backing up the configuration files. This is important for 2 reasons:

- When performing an upgrade, it is always advisable to back up your configuration information in case something goes wrong during the upgrade and you wish to return to a previously good known state.
- If you need to perform a reinstall of the FreeNAS software (for whatever reason including failed hardware) then the new installation can be configured exactly like the old installation in a matter of seconds by restoring the configuration files.

Backup Configuration

To backup your configuration, go to the **System: Backup/Restore** page. This page is in two sections: one for backup and another for restore. To backup the configuration, click on **Download configuration**. The FreeNAS server will then send the configuration file to your web browser. Your web browser will then ask you if you would like to save the file. You should save the file on your hard disk. The filename for the configuration file is in the format *config-<hostname>-<year><month><day><hour><minute>.xml* for example: *config-f6862a.local-20080304150414.xml*.

What is XML?

XML stands for eXtensible Markup Language and it is a general-purpose specification for creating simple, very flexible text files that describe different types of data. It is called extensible because it allows its users to define their own elements. In FreeNAS, it is used to store all the information about your system.

A snippet from the FreeNAS configuration file would look like this:

```xml
<interfaces>
    <lan>
        <ipaddr>192.168.1.251</ipaddr>
        <subnet>24</subnet>
        <gateway>192.168.1.254</gateway>
    </lan>
</interfaces>
```

Since XML is relatively human-legible, we can see that this sample is about the networking components of the FreeNAS server, and we can find the IP address, the subnet mask, and the default gateway with relative ease.

Restore Configuration

To restore a configuration file, click on the **Browse...** button and find the configuration .xml file you wish to restore. Now, click on **Restore configuration**. The FreeNAS configuration file will be restored and then the FreeNAS server will be rebooted.

Using Another FreeNAS Server as a Backup Server

Clearly, one very useful option is to use a second FreeNAS server as the backup for your primary FreeNAS server. There are two possible ways to do this:

- Using the built-in Windows backup software
- Interfacing two FreeNAS servers

The first method has been covered in the previous section where we create a backup of the FreeNAS primary server on a FreeNAS backup server.

The second method has the added benefit that if the hardware fails on the first machine, the second machine will be ready quite quickly to take the failed machine's place. To transfer the data between the primary server and the backup machine, we shall use RSYNC.

RSYNC is a network protocol, specifically designed for performing network backups. RSYNC creates an exact copy of your data over the network, but to save network bandwidth, it has a built-in algorithm that only copies the parts of files which are different from the original. This makes it efficient and effective.

Before you start, you need to set up a second FreeNAS server. You need to follow the normal steps for settings up a FreeNAS server:

- Burn a CD and boot from it (and optionally install to a hard disk)
- Configure the networking
- Configure storage (either RAID or simply disks)

Now, on the primary FreeNAS server, you need to configure the RSYNC server.

1. Go to **Services: RSYNCD** and enable the RSYNC Daemon. You can leave the rest of the settings as they are.
2. Click on the **Modules** tab.
3. In RSYNC, talk modules are like shares in CIFS. To give others access to a particular area on your FreeNAS server, you need to create a module for it. Click on the add circle to add a new module.

There are 3 mandatory fields; name, comment, and path:

- **Name** — This is a label for the module and it will be used by the RSYNC client to identify this particular shared resource.
- **Comment** — This is a description of the module, for example: Sales Material. Having a good comment here is essential for debugging and problem solving.
- **Path** — This is the path to the storage that is to be shared using RSYNC. The format of this is */mnt/storagename* where storage name is the mount point name of the disk or RAID set you configured in the **Disks** section. Click on ... at the end of the Path section. This will bring up a simple file system browser. Click the desired mount point (for example store) and click **OK** and you will be taken back to the RSYNC modules page. Now, the mount point (e.g. */mnt/store/*) has been added as the path.

4. For extra safety, you can set the **Access mode** to **Read only**, which will ensure that this module can't be written to by other RSYNC clients. Once the RSYNC server is configured, any RSYNC client on the network can access these files. To stop mishaps and accidents, it is best to limit it to read only.
5. The rest of the options can be left at their defaults.

6. Click **Add** and apply the changes.

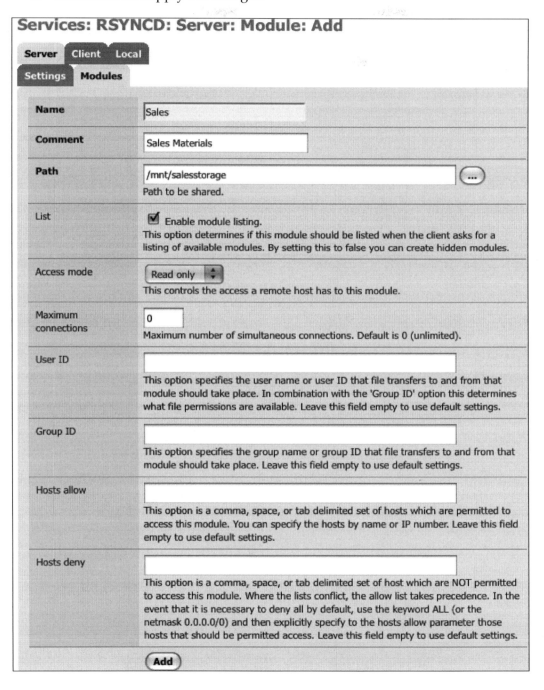

Now on the FreeNAS backup server, we need to create an RSYNC client. The client will connect to the server and copy the files in its local storage. Every time the RSYNC client runs, it will back up the data on the primary server to the backup server. Because of the nature of the RSYNC algorithms, only data that has changed will be copied over and so reduce the overheads in copying the files.

1. To create the RSYNC client go to **Services: RSYNCD** on the backup server.
2. Click on the **Client** tab.
3. Click on the add circle to create a new client.

On the **Client: Add** page there are 4 obligatory fields; Local share, Remote RSYNC Server, Remote module name, and Synchronization Time:

- **Local share** — This is the local storage where the file from the primary FreeNAS server will be copied. It needs to be big enough to hold all the files that will be copied over from the primary server. The format of this is **/mnt/storagename** where storage name is the mount point name of the disk or RAID set you configured in the **Disks** section. Click on ... at the end of the Path section. This will bring up a simple file system browser. Click the desired mount point (for example backup) and click **OK** and you will be taken back to the RSYNC modules page. Now the mount point (e.g. */mnt/backup*) has been added as the path.

- **Remote RSYNC Server** — This is the IP address of the primary FreeNAS server. The address will be in dot notation, for example 192.168.1.250.

- **Remote module name** — This is the label or module name you configured in the Modules page of the RSYNC server on the primary FreeNAS machine. You need to enter it exactly here as you entered it there.

- **Synchronization Time** — The client runs to synchronize the backup server with primary server at scheduled times. These synchronizations are scheduled by selecting which minute, hour, day, and month you want them to occur. As this is a re-occurring event, you can choose which time, date, and day of the week the backup will be made. To schedule the backup, select the time you want by selecting the appropriate minute, hour, day, month, and week day. For example, to back up every morning at 12:05 AM, Monday to Friday you would select:

    ○ 5 from the minutes section
    ○ 0 from the hours (remember it is a 24 hour clock)
    ○ Monday through to Friday from the week days
    ○ Days and months would remain as ALL

Use *CTRL*-click (or Command-click on the Mac) to select and de-select minutes, hours, days, months, and week days.

4. You can also set the optional parameter **Delete files that don't exist on sender**. Ticking this means that if a file is deleted on the primary FreeNAS server, it will also be deleted on the backup server when the synchronization occurs. The negative side of this is that when a file is deleted on the primary server, it is effectively lost forever (unless you are also using some other type of backup system) as it will be deleted on the backup server as well. The other thing to note is that if files are not deleted, then the size of the backup data will keep increasing and never go down even when files are deleted from the primary server.
5. Now click **Save** and apply the changes.

That is it, when the next synchronization interval comes around, the two servers should synchronize automatically.

Debugging Your RSYNC Setup

If your backups are scheduled to happen once a day, it can be a long process to verify that the backups are occurring. For every simple typing mistake, you have to wait 24 hours to see if the backups happened. This can be very frustrating. There are a few things you can do to ensure that your RSYNC configuring is correct.

One thing you can do to shorten the wait is to temporarily schedule the backup for a few minutes from now. Then, when you know the backup is working correctly, you can schedule your desired backup time.

On the backup server, it is possible to check that the RSYNC client can communicate with the RSYNC server on the primary FreeNAS server and that the module is visible. Go to **Diagnostics: Information** and click on the **RSYNC Client** tab. Here, each configured RSYNC client will be listed along with its configuration parameters. The most useful information is the **Detected shares on this server** section. Here, the RSYNC client has contacted the server and asked for a list of modules. The modules available are listed.

Backup Strategies

If the modules are listed and specifically the one needed by the backup server to perform its backup, then you know that the configuration is on the right track.

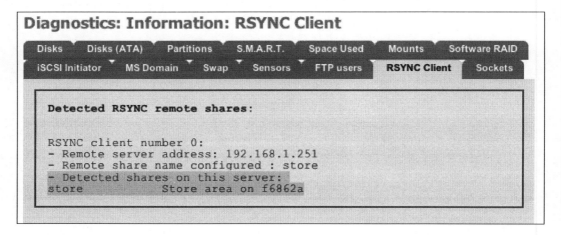

On the primary server, there is a log file of RSYNC activity. This will allow you to check that the backups are occurring. Go to **Diagnostics: Logs** and click on the **RSYNCD** tab. By default, the latest entries are shown at the bottom on the log. You are looking for something similar to this:

Mar 4 12:35:00 rsyncd[3545]: connect from UNKNOWN (192.168.1.252)

Mar 4 12:35:00 rsyncd[3545]: rsync on store from UNKNOWN (192.168.1.252)

Mar 4 12:35:00 rsyncd[3545]: building file list

Mar 4 12:35:00 rsyncd[3545]: sent 673 bytes received 70 bytes total size 3998023

This shows that a connection was made (in this example from my backup server) and that synchronization was started for the *store* module. The last line shows the amount of network traffic, which in this case was low as there were no changes to synchronize.

RSYNC Internal Backup

In a similar way that two FreeNAS servers can use RSYNC to synchronize data, FreeNAS has an option to use RSYNC to synchronize data from one hard disk to another inside the same FreeNAS server. This is known as local RSYNC synchronization and to use it, you need at least two hard disks or RAID sets (the source and the destination), which are both configured and mounted.

To enable this feature, go to **Services: RSYNCD** and click on the **Local** tab. Now click on the add circle to configure a new local synchronization. You need to complete three fields to configure the synchronization: **Source share**, **Destination share**, and **Synchronization Time**:

- **Source share** — This is the mount point of the data that needs backing up. The format of this is */mnt/storagename* where storage name is the mount point name of the disk or RAID set you configured in the **Disks** section. Click on ... at the end of the Path section. This will bring up a simple file system browser. Click the desired mount point (for example store) and click **OK**. You will be taken back to the RSYNC modules page. Now, the mount point (e.g. /mnt/store/) has been added as the path.
- **Destination share** — This is the mount point where you want the data to be copied. The format of this is /mnt/storagename where storage name is the mount point name of the disk or RAID set you configured in the Disks section. Click on "..." at the end of the Path section. This will bring up a simple file system browser. Click the desired mount point (for example backup) and click OK and you will be taken back to the RSYNC modules page. Now the mount point (e.g. /mnt/backup/) has been added as the path.
- **Synchronization time** — The program runs to synchronize the two storage areas at scheduled times. These synchronizations are scheduled by selecting which minute, hour, day and month you want them occur. As this is a re-occurring event, you can choose which time, date, and day of the week the backup will be made.

Debugging Your Internal RSYNC Setup

As with network-based RSYNC processes, if you backups are scheduled to happen once a day, it can be a long process to verify that the backups are occurring. There are a couple of things you can do to ensure that your RSYNC configuring is correct.

Making sure the backup works correctly is to schedule the first backup for a few minutes from now. Then, when you know the backup is working correctly, you can schedule your desired backup time.

You can also check the RSYNC activity in a log file. To do this, go to **Diagnostics: Logs** and click on the **RSYNCD** tab. By default, the latest entries are shown at the bottom on the log. Look for something similar to this:

Mar 4 14:48:00   **root: Start of local RSYNC from /mnt/store2/ to /mnt/backup/**

Mar 4 14:48:00   **root: End of local RSYNC synchronization from /mnt/store2/ to /mnt/backup/**

To distinguish this from network-based RSYNC activity, notice that the first line says **Start of local RSYNC** and then lists the source and destination. Unfortunately, there isn't much more information, but you can see at what time the synchronization finished. In this particular example, it was in under 1 second, but there wasn't any synchronization to perform and it had a limited number of files.

Mirroring vs Conventional Backups

If you use RSYNC (or RAID), do you need to make other types of backup? This is an important question and the simple answer is yes, you do. The primary gain of using RAID or mirrored backups (via RSYNC) is that you are protected from hardware failure. In the RAID scenario, if a disk fails, the server continues and after the disk is replaced, the system continues as before and no data is lost. When mirroring the data on another server, if the primary server fails, the data is intact on the other server.

However, RAID and RSYNC don't protect you from human error. The scenario goes like this: you have an important document that someone manages to delete. The only copy of that document was on the FreeNAS server. If you are using RAID, then the file has been deleted on all the disks in the RAID set at the moment it was deleted. If you are using mirroring, then you have a small window until the mirrored copy will also be deleted. There is no history with these types of backups, no way to go back in time to find a certain version of a file or a file that was deleted.

An offline backup to a tape or optical disk has the advantage that once the backup is made, the tape or disk can be stored on a shelf (or better still in a safe) and when you need that backup in 1 month or 1 years time, it will still be there along with the data on it (assuming you verified the backup when it was made).

Along with RAID and RSYNC mirroring, you should consider making other types of offline backup to tape or disk similar to the procedure described in the section *Backup your FreeNAS using Windows XP's built-in Backup utility* earlier in this chapter. There are many commercial and freeware programs that can help you do this.

Summary

In this chapter, we have looked at the different backup strategies that exist for your FreeNAS server. Being network orientated, backups must also be performed over the network. We looked at how Windows XP can be used to back up the server along with using RSYNC to create copies of the data on a remote server and on another hard drive.

In the next chapter, we shall look at advanced system configuration.

8
Advanced System Configuration

If you have followed everything in this book until now, you are almost an expert in all things FreeNAS. There are just a few more things to learn and your training will be complete. This chapter looks at Advanced System Configuration like disk encryption, adding a swap space, and tweaking FreeBSD.

Disk Encryption

If the data you are storing on your FreeNAS server is of a sensitive nature (for example military, medical, financial or other confidential data) then it is worth considering using encryption to protect your data should the server fall into the wrong hands.

If security is a top priority for you, then encrypting the data on the disk is only one of several measures you should take to safe guard your data. For example if your building or the people in your building (for example employees) aren't subject to stringent security measures then having your hard disk encrypted is of minimal value. Someone (from within or without) could access your data over the network and copy the sensitive data and then email it to almost anywhere. Having your hard disk encrypted won't stop that from happening.

FreeNAS offers the ability to encrypt an entire disk with a strong level of encryption. If the server should be stolen, then the perpetrators will have a tough time accessing the data on the disk.

Normally, to add a new disk to your FreeNAS server you need to:

1. Add the disk in **Disks: Add**.
2. Format the disk in **Disks: Format**.
3. Add a mount point in **Disks: Mount Point**.

Advanced System Configuration

To add a new encrypted disk, almost the same procedure is used except that there is a new step to create an encrypted volume between step 1 and step 2. The new sequence of events becomes:

1. Add the disk in **Disks: Add**.
2. Create an encrypted volume using the previously added disk in **Disks: Encryption**.
3. Format the disk in **Disks: Format**.
4. Add a mount point in **Disks: Mount Point**.

Notice that the creation of the encrypted volumes occurs before the disk is formatted. This is because the encryption used by FreeNAS is at a very low level. It is not file-based (meaning that each file is individually encrypted) but rather it is sector-based, which means that each piece of information that is written to the hard disk (including directory names etc) is encrypted.

Do You Really Need Encryption?

Encrypting your data actually increases the chances of data loss. Your data is actually more likely to be lost to encryption misconfiguration or lost keys than to theft. **There is no password recovery system for an encrypted hard drive**. If the password is lost, misplaced, forgotten or the holder becomes unavailable then the data is in actuality lost.

Encrypting a Disk in FreeNAS

If you are encrypting a disk that has previously had data on it, it is important to completely erase all the old data before using the disk for encryption. This is because when the disk is initialized for encryption, the old data is not physically overwritten and as such, this old data would still be accessible at the sector level of the hard disk should the disk be stolen and analyzed. Unfortunately, FreeNAS doesn't provide a way to do this and you will need to remove the disk from the FreeNAS server and security wipe it in another machine.

To encrypt a disk, first of all, make sure it has been added to the system using the **Disks: Add page**. Then, go to **Disks: Encryption**.

Click on the add circle to add a new encrypted disk. There are four parameters for adding an encrypted disk:

- **Disk**—Select the disk you want to encrypt. It has to be a whole disk and can not be a partition of a disk. This means that you can't encrypt the second partition of a disk where you have installed FreeNAS on the first partition. Also, the disk must have been previously added in **Disks: Add**.

- **Encryption algorithm** – You can choose between three different encryption algorithms with which to encrypt your data. If you are unsure, stick with AES as it is the standard encryption method used by the U.S. government, it has been analyzed extensively and is now used worldwide.
- **Passphrase** – The password. Whenever the disk is mounted on the FreeNAS server (generally after a reboot), then the password needs to be entered to unlock the encrypted drive. Using a good, solid password is essential for the disk encryption to be worthwhile. Don't use your birthday or your daughter's name!
- **Initialize** – If this disk has never been used as an encrypted disk before, it needs to be initialized and made ready for the encryption process. You need to tick this box unless this is a previously a encrypted disk that you are adding back into the FreeNAS server.

 Initializing the disk will cause all data to be lost on this disk.

Having selected the disk from the drop down box as well as picking an algorithm, you need to enter a good unguessable password and tick the **initialize** box. Now click **Add**. The disk will now be prepared and encrypted. The output will look something like this:

```
Encrypting '/dev/ad1'... Please wait!
Calculating number of iterations...
Done, using 38638 iterations.
Metadata value stored on /dev/ad1.
Done.
Attaching provider '/dev/ad1'.
Attached to /dev/ad1.
Done.
```

The reassuring **Done**. lets you know that all went well. It is always best to double check the output for any errors.

Now that the disk has been set up for encryption, it can be used just like any other disk. You can format it or mount it and also share it on the networking using CIFS, NFS, and AFP etc.

Entering the Password When You Reboot

Because the volume is encrypted, it needs a password to unlock it and allow it to be accessed. Whenever the FreeNAS server is rebooted, the encrypted volume will not be accessible until you have entered the password.

Once the system is booted, go **to Disk: Mount Point**. You will see an error because FreeNAS can't mount the encrypted volume without the password.

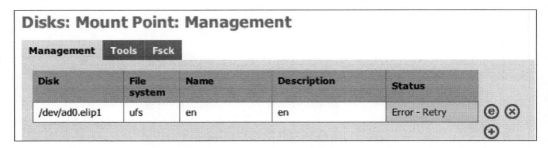

Now go to **Disk: Encryption**. The encrypted volume has the status **Not attached**. To enter the password, click on the **Tools** tab. Choose the encrypted disk from *Encrypted disk name* drop down list and select the command **attach** (which should be the default). Now enter the password and click on **Send Command!** The output should be something like this:

```
Attached to /dev/ad0.
Done.
Mounting device.
Successful.
```

If you mistyped the password, then the output would be something like this:

```
Wrong key for ad0.
```

Click on the **Management** tab and the disk status will now be shown as **Attached**. Finally, go back to **Disk: Mount Point** and check that the mount point status is **OK**. If it isn't, click on **Retry** (which forces FreeNAS to mount the disk again) and then it should show **OK**.

Encryption Tools

When the FreeNAS server is rebooted, the password needs to be entered to unlock the volume. To do this, you use **Tools** tab in **Disk: Encryption** (see *Entering the password when you reboot* above). Here is an overview of the other actions that can be performed on an encrypted disk.

How to Unlock an Encrypted Disk—Attach and Detach

Attach and detach are technical FreeBSD words for unlock and lock. Attach means that the password supplied will be used to open up the disk and set up the necessary decryption parameters. Once successfully attached, the disk is able to be used like any other hard disk.Detach is the opposite. Here, the disk is locked and the data is inaccessible without the correct password. To detach an already attached disk, choose the attached, encrypted disk from *Encrypted disk name* drop down list and select the command **detach** and click on **Send Command!**

How to Change the Password on an Encrypted Disk—setkey

Remaining on the **Tools** tab in the **Disk: Encryption** page, you can change the password of an encrypted disk by using the setkey command. Choose the encrypted disk from *Encrypted disk name* drop down list and select the command *setkey*. Now enter the old password along with the new password and click on **Send Command!** The output is just a simple **Done**.

[You are not asked to confirm the new password. If you make a mistake in typing in the new password, all your data will be lost as you can not unlock the disk.]

Checking the Status of an Encrypted Disk—list and status

To get some simple status information about your encrypted drives, you can use the `status` and `list` commands.

`status` simply lists which drives are encrypted and in fact, might not even tell you their status! Here is an example output:

```
Name      Status    Components
ad0.eli   N/A       ad0
```

The list command is a bit more verbose. An example out would be:

```
Geom name: ad0.eli
EncryptionAlgorithm: AES-CBC
KeyLength: 128
Crypto: software
UsedKey: 0
```

```
    Flags: NONE
    Providers:
    1. Name: ad0.eli
       Mediasize: 10262568448 (9.6G)
       Sectorsize: 512
       Mode: r1w1e2
    Consumers:
    1. Name: ad0
       Mediasize: 10262568960 (9.6G)
       Sectorsize: 512
       Mode: r1w1e1
```

The `Geom name:` tells you the name of the encrypted disk. It will be the name of the disk device (say ad0 for the first IDE hard disk) followed by `.eli`, in our example it was: `ad0.eli`. The `EncryptionAlgorithm:` tells you which algorithm is being used (which in this case was AES) and the `KeyLength:` tells you the strength of the encryption.

The provider and consumer are the two ends of the encryption process. In FreeBSD terms, this means the physical hard disk (ad0) and the pseudo device (ad0.eli) which is the hard disk after encryption. As FreeBSD writes to the pseudo version of the hard disk, (ad0.eli) the encryption software applies its algorithms and the encrypted data is written to the real hard disk (ad0). The opposite happens during a read; the encrypted data is read from the hard disk and passed to the decryption software before being passed on higher up.

Advanced Hard Drive Parameters (S.M.A.R.T)

Self-Monitoring, Analysis, and Reporting Technology, or S.M.A.R.T, is a system for monitoring hard disks to report on a variety of characteristics that pertain to the reliability of the disk. Monitoring these characteristics should (in theory) help anticipate drive failures. According to Seagate, the hard disk manufacturer, mechanical failures (that are usually predictable failures) account for 60 percent of drive failure.

Not all hard drives have S.M.A.R.T capabilities and different manufacturers measure different characteristics and define different thresholds of failure. Essentially each hard disk model defines its health according to the rules set down by its manufacturer. Therefore one model of hard disk may have a different value for a certain characteristic than another model of hard drive and yet both be defined as acceptable by the manufacturer.

The characteristics or attributes of each drive has two values: one is the raw value whose meaning is defined by the drive manufacturer. The other is a normalized value that ranges from 1 to 253 (where 1 is the worst case and 253 the best).

Enabling and using S.M.A.R.T of the FreeNAS

Before you can use S.M.A.R.T on your FreeNAS server, you need to check if your hard disk supports S.M.A.R.T. Go to **Diagnostics: Information** and click on the **S.M.A.R.T.** tab. The output will show a list of disks (IDE, SATA, SCSI, and even flash disks) along with any S.M.A.R.T information available.

If a particular device doesn't support S.M.A.R.T, the output will simply say:

```
Device does not support SMART
```

If the device supports S.M.A.R.T, it will report more information about the drive including the model number. Here is an example for an aging 10GB Quantum Fireball disk:

```
Device Model:       QUANTUM FIREBALLlct10 10
Serial Number:      872001057089
Firmware Version:   A03.0900
User Capacity:      10,262,568,960 bytes
Device is:          Not in smartctl database [for details use: -P
showall]
ATA Version is:     4
ATA Standard is:    ATA/ATAPI-4 T13 1153D revision 15
Local Time is:      Tue Mar 18 21:22:34 2008 UTC
SMART support is: Available - device has SMART capability.
SMART support is: Disabled
```

The key thing to note here is that *SMART support is: Available – device has SMART capability*. But that *SMART support is: Disabled*.

To enable S.M.A.R.T monitoring for this disk, go to **System: Advanced** and tick the **S.M.A.R.T Daemon** box. This will enable the S.M.A.R.T daemon (monitoring process) and log the status to the log file.

Now, if you return to the **Diagnostics: Information** page and again click on the **S.M.A.R.T.** tab, you will see that the output has changed significantly. The first difference is that *SMART support is: Enabled*. Below the initial summary is now a comprehensive list of different drive attributes pertaining to the reliability of the hard disk.

Advanced System Configuration

The first line is normally a report on the overall health of the disk. If it is healthy, it should read something like this:

```
SMART overall-health self-assessment test result: PASSED
```

If the overall health is listed as FAILED, then you need to back up the hard disk immediately and replace it with another one.

Below the overall health check is a list of hard disk-specific information that culminates in a list of *Vendor Specific SMART Attributes with Thresholds*. This list shows each attribute along with its normalized value, the worst value that this attribute has had in the life time of the drive, and the thresholds of the value. When reading these values, you need to remember that 1 is the worst case and 253 the best. For example:

```
Vendor Specific SMART Attributes with Thresholds:
ATTRIBUTE_NAME           FLAG     VALUE WORST THRESH RAW_VALUE
Raw_Read_Error_Rate      0x0029   100   253   020    0
Spin_Up_Time             0x0027   083   081   020    2195
Start_Stop_Count         0x0032   093   093   008    5025
Reallocated_Sector_Ct    0x0033   100   100   020    0
Seek_Error_Rate          0x000b   100   100   023    0
Power_On_Hours           0x0012   090   090   001    6675
Calibration_Retry_Count  0x0013   100   100   020    0
Power_Cycle_Count        0x0032   093   093   008    4740
Read_Soft_Error_Rate     0x000b   100   100   023    0
UDMA_CRC_Error_Count     0x001a   116   116   000    84
Reallocated_Event_Count  0x0010   100   100   020    0
Current_Pending_Sector   0x0032   100   100   020    0
Offline_Uncorrectable    0x0010   100   253   000    0
```

Looking at the `Raw_Read_Error_Rate`, you can see that its normalized value is `100` but that the raw value is `0`. This means that there have been no read errors on this hard disk that the disk manufacturer has normalized to the value `100`. However, what is important is that the threshold is `20`. So IF read errors started to appear on this drive, then the normalized value would start to shrink until it reached `20`. At which point, the overall health of the drive would be reported as FAILED.

An attribute from a failing hard disk might look like this:

```
ATTRIBUTE_NAME                   VALUE WORST THRESH   WHEN_FAILED
Reallocated_Sector_Ct    136     136   140            FAILING_NOW
```

Notice here that the `when_failing` column reports the drive in the process of failing. Looking at the normalized value, we read `136` and the threshold is `140`. Remembering that the lower the number the worse the situation, we see that this particular attribute has just recently gone passed its threshold and as such triggered the failure warnings.

On the FreeNAS server, when an attribute passes its threshold it will be reported in the SMARTD log on the **Diagnostics: Logs** page.

Here is a list of some key S.M.A.R.T attributes that if they pass their threshold, the disk is in a critical state:

Attributes	Meaning
Read Error Rate	Measures the rate of read errors that occurred when reading data in the disk.
Reallocated Sectors Count	The number of reallocated sectors. When the hard drive finds a sector with an error it marks this sector as "reallocated" and transfers data to a special reserved area. If the number reallocated sectors increases too much, the disk is starting to fail.
Spin Retry Count	Number of retries of spin start attempts. This is the total number of the spin retries. An increase of this number is a sign of a mechanical problem.
Uncorrectable Sector Count	This is total number of uncorrectable errors when reading or writing to a sector. If this number starts to increase, it can mean that there is a problem with the hard disk's magnetic surface.

File System Consistency Check—FSCK

The FreeNAS server has a tool to verify if the file system on a disk is healthy. This is different than checking the S.M.A.R.T status of the disk in that S.M.A.R.T is at the hardware level and support for it is provided by the disk manufacturer. However, FreeBSD/FreeNAS writes data to the disk in a certain order and using a special structure that enables it to find files and folders. This special structure is called a file system and it is important to verify (from time to time) that the file system is intact and doesn't contain any errors. File system errors most often occur when the FreeNAS server is switched off without a proper shutdown. This can mean that the file system is left in a state where write operations were queued or cached and they were never actually completed. What remains therefore is a file system inconsistency. The FreeBSD tool for checking the file system consistency is called fsck (File System Consistency checK).

Advanced System Configuration

To run a file system consistency check, go to **Disks: Mount Point** and click on the **Fsck** tab. First, you need to select the disk to check from the drop down box. Next, you need to decide how you want to run the file system check.

If the **Unmount disk/partition** is not ticked then fsck is run in read-only mode. Here the file system is checked for errors but any errors are reported but **not** corrected. Running a file system check on a busy disk can reduce performance.

If **Unmount disk/partition** is ticked then the disk will first be unmounted and all errors will be fixed automatically. During the file system check, the data on the disk won't be available to the network users.

The output for fsck will look something like this:

```
** /dev/ad0p1 (NO WRITE)
** Last Mounted on /mnt/store
** Phase 1 - Check Blocks and Sizes
** Phase 2 - Check Pathnames
** Phase 3 - Check Connectivity
** Phase 4 - Check Reference Counts
** Phase 5 - Check Cyl groups
317 files, 17249 used, 4833873 free (121 frags, 604219 blocks, 0.0% fragmentation)
Successful
```

> **Large Disks and fsck**
>
> Depending on the hard disk size, running fsck can take from minutes to hours. Therefore, on large hard disks, running fsck from the web interface can give you a time-out. fsck will fix all errors on the file system but you will not see the output on web interface.
>
> Also, note that fsck requires a large amount of RAM to run. For large volumes (2TB or greater), you should have a minimum 512MB RAM.

It is also possible to run the fsck tool from the command line. This might be useful for large hard disks if the web interface times out while waiting for the command to complete. Please see chapter 10 for more details.

Advanced OS Tweaking

The underlying operating system of FreeNAS is FreeBSD. Like all complex systems, FreeBSD has a number of configuration parameters that can change its behavior. At the heart of the FreeBSD system, is its kernel and the kernel can be 'tweaked' to perform better under certain situations. The FreeNAS developers have defined a set of kernel parameters that can be tweaked at the click of the mouse. These parameters are as follows:

Parameter	Normal value	Tweaked value	Meaning
`net.inet.tcp.delayed_ack:`	1	0	This tells FreeBSD to attempt to include TCP ACK information on a data packet instead of sending additional packets to signal the end of a connection.
`net.inet.tcp.sendspace:`	32768	65536	This along with `net.inet.udp.recvspace` define the maximum network packet size. Increasing the packet size can increase network performance, but it also increases memory usage.
`net.inet.udp.recvspace:`	42080	65536	See above.
`net.inet.udp.maxdgram:`	9216	57344	This is the maximum outgoing UDP datagram size. Increasing it can improve network performance but also increased memory usage.
`net.local.stream.recvspace:`	8192	65535	This and the .sendspace below are further buffer tweaks for networking. Performance can increase but so will memory usage.
`net.local.stream.sendspace :`	8192	65535	See above.
`kern.ipc.maxsockbuf:`	262144	2097152	This is the maximum combined buffer size for both sides of a TCP socket. It is increased along with the other network related parameters to boost network performance.
`kern.ipc.somaxconn:`	128	8192	This controls how many simultaneous connection attempts the system will try to handle.
`kern.ipc.maxsockets:`	3072	16424	This is the total number of sockets available on the system. You need one socket for every network connection.

Parameter	Normal value	Tweaked value	Meaning
`kern.ipc.nmbclusters:`	3072	60000	This controls the number of *mbufs* allocated by the system An *mbuf* is a chunk of kernel memory used for networking. This is increased in line with other network buffer increases.
`kern.maxfiles:`	1064	65536	The maximum number of files that the system can have open for reading or writing at any one time.
`kern.maxfilesperproc:`	957	32768	This is the maximum number of files a single process can open.

Enabling Kernel Tuning will result in two things. First, a probable increase in the performance of the FreeNAS server and second, an increase in the amount of memory used by the FreeNAS server. If your system has sufficient memory (256MB or more) and your server experiences heavy network traffic, try enabling Kernel Tuning.

To enable it, go to **System: Advanced** and tick the **Tuning** box. Click **Save** to apply the changes.

Tweaking the Network Settings

The FreeNAS server has a couple of advanced sections for controlling the network. The first is the global network configurations for each network installed in the machine and the second is the ability to add static routes to the network routing table.

MTU, Device Polling, Speed, and Duplex

On the **Interfaces: LAN** page (where LAN represents the default network card), there are four parameters that can be changed to increase the performance of your network.

Parameters	Meaning
MTU	The Maximum Transmission Unit (MTU) is the size (in bytes) of the largest packet that can be sent on your network. A higher MTU means higher bandwidth efficiency. For an 10/100 Ethernet network, 1500 is the largest allowed MTU. For a Gigabit Ethernet network (with Jumbo Frame support), 9000 is best (and maximum) option.
Device polling	Device polling is a technique that lets the system periodically poll network devices for new data instead of relying on interrupts. This can reduce CPU load and therefore increase throughput, at the expense of a slightly higher forwarding delay (the devices are polled 1000 times per second). Not all network cards support polling.
Speed	The speed of your network card should be automatically selected (autoselect) but if you find that it is not selected, then you can manually select from: 10baseT/UTP, 100baseTX, 1000baseTX, and 1000baseSX.
Duplex	If your network card and the switch to which it is connected are capable of supporting full duplex communications (meaning the card and switch can send while receiving and visa-versa) then you can set it here.

Avoid Duplex Mismatch.

Duplex mismatch occurs when two connected devices operate in different duplex modes (one in half duplex while the other is in full duplex). The result of a duplex mismatch is a network that is not completely 'broken' but is incredibly slow. Duplex mismatch may occur from wrongly manually setting two connected network interfaces at different duplex modes, and also from connecting a device that performs auto-negotiation to one that is manually set to a full duplex mode. The auto-negotiating device will assume half duplex if it fails to negotiate.

Adding a Static Route

If you are using two or more network cards, it can sometimes be of benefit to add a static route to the networking routing table. The network routing table defines to who each network connection is routed, or in other words which path it takes across the network. A default route is defined when you configure the default gateway in either the console menu or the Interfaces section of the web interface. By defining the default gateway, you are creating a default path for all traffic that is not destined for the local network. It is assumed that the router (which can be another PC or a DSL modem as well as a network router) can correctly direct the traffic to its destination. If you have more than one network card or you have a second router that handles traffic for a particular part of your network, it can be beneficial to add a static route telling the FreeNAS server to direct all traffic for that particular network to the second router rather than to the default gateway.

Advanced System Configuration

To add a static route, go to **System: Static routes** and click on the add circle. There are three mandatory fields to complete:

Parameter	Meaning
Interface	Specify which interface this route applies to.
Destination network	Destination network for this static route.
Gateway	Gateway to be used to reach the destination network.

The destination network takes the form of an IP address in dot notation (or more specifically a subnet address in that the ending digits will be 0 depending on the network mask) followed by a network mask specified as with 8, 16 or 24 for 255.0.0.0, 255.255.0.0 or 255.255.255.0, respectively.

For example, if the IP address of my FreeNAS server is 192.168.1.250 and there is a router other than the default gateway that can router traffic to the network 192.168.99.0 (meaning all machines with the IP address from 192.168.99.1 to 192.168.99.254), and that this router has an IP address of 192.168.1.123 then the settings would be:

  Destination network: 192.168.99.0/24

  Gateway: 192.168.1.123

Click **Add** and apply the changes to add the static route.

System: Static routes

Static routes

Interface	Network	Gateway	Description	
LAN	192.168.99.0/24	192.168.1.123	Router to the 192.168.99.0 network	⊚ ⊗
				⊕

Using Wireless

If you have a wireless network card that is supported by FreeNAS, then you can configure it to offer wireless access to the FreeNAS server.

To configure the wireless card, go to the **Interfaces: Management** page. Here, you will be able to configure the card and set the various wireless parameters like the Service Set Identifier (SSID) and the channel number. You can also configure the wireless security with Wired Equivalent Privacy (WEP).

Adding a Swap File

Some operations on the FreeNAS server, most notably using the iSCSI target and running fsck for big hard disks, require a minimum of 256MB of RAM (Random Access Memory). If your system does not have 256MB of RAM, you can use a swap file to temporarily extend the system's memory.

FreeBSD divides its physical RAM into chucks of memory called pages. Swapping is the process whereby a page of memory is copied to a swap file, to free up that page of memory. The combined sizes of the physical memory and the swap file is the amount of virtual memory available.

Swapping is necessary when the system requires more memory than is physically available; the kernel (the core of FreeBSD) swaps out less used pages and gives memory to the current application (process) that needs the memory immediately.

However, swapping does have a downside. Compared to memory, disks are very slow. Accessing the disk can be tens of thousands times slower than accessing physical memory. The more swapping that occurs, the slower your system will be.

Before adding a swap file, it is best to consider the option of adding more memory to your system.

To add a swap file go to **System: Advanced** and click on the **Swap** tab. To enable the use of a swap file, tick the **Enable** box in the title bar. Select the disk you wish to use to host the swap file, it will be listed by mount point name in the **Mount to use for swap** drop down box. Now, enter the amount of swap space you require. 256MB will be more than enough (note that you don't need to enter the MB part, just 256).

Once you click on **save**, a file called `swap_file` will be created on the specified disk and it will be used for swapping.

To double check that your swap file is configured correctly go to **Diagnostics: Information** and click on the **Swap** tab. The output should look something this:

```
Swap Status:
Device           512-blocks      Used     Avail Capacity
/dev/md0             524288         0    524288     0%
```

This shows that there is a 256MB swap file in use (524288 divided by 2 as it is shown in 512 byte blocks not in Kilobytes). Currently, all the swap space is available as none of it is being used.

Advanced System Configuration

Enabling Secure Shell Connections (SSH)

In chapters 9 and 10, it may be necessary to make a connection to the FreeNAS server and use the command line of FreeBSD. The command line is often referred to as a terminal or a shell (name after the command line interpreter of the same name). Secure SHell (SSH) is a way to use the command line on the FreeNAS via an encrypted connection and so allows you to use the FreeNAS server without the danger of others, who are snooping around on your network, discovering your passwords.

By default, SSH access is disabled to enable it go to **Services: SSHD** and enable the **SSH Daemon** (server) by ticking **Enable** in the title of the configuration data table. Click **Save and Restart** to finish start the SSH server.

By default, SSH only allows local FreeNAS users to log in if they have been granted **Full Shell** access. Go to **Access: Users and Groups**. If you don't have any users created, then create one (after first creating a group). When you create the user, make sure the **Full Shell** box is ticked. This tells FreeNAS that this user is allowed to connect to the server via SSH and have access to the command line. For more details on user management, see chapter 5.

If you already have a user created who you wish to grant **Full Shell** access, then click the **edit** button next to the user name (an 'e' in a circle) and tick the **Full Shell** attribute. Click **Save** to store the new settings and apply the changes.

In FreeBSD, there are two categories of users, one is the normal user who has limited privileges (for example they can't stop or start services) and the other is the administrator or in FreeBSD terms is know as **root**. Root is a superuser who can do anything on the server.

Allow Root Login

For troubleshooting and using FreeBSD, the most useful user is root. By default, root is not allowed to log in to the FreeNAS server via SSH as it can pose a security risk. To allow root to log in go to **Services: SSHD** and tick **Permit root login**. Then click **Save and Restart** to finish start the SSH server.

> **Root Password**
>
> The root password is the same as the web interface password, which by default is *freenas*. If the web interface password is changed, so does the root password.

Types of SSH Authentication

SSH has two types of authentication method. The first is what it calls *keyboard-interactive authentication*, which in normal English—means you type in a username and password to log in. The second type is known as *public key authentication* Here, a system known as public-key cryptography is used to enable a remote SSH client to log in to the FreeNAS without a password.

In public key cryptography, there are two keys called a private key and a public key. The magic behind public key cryptography is that you are free (in fact, encouraged) to give out your public key to anyone who wants it. Then that person can encrypt some information using the public key and once encrypted, only the private key can unlock it. Someone with your public key cannot unlock a message created with your public key.

What this means for SSH is that if the FreeNAS has a copy of your public key, it can correctly authenticate you as the holder of the private key. Thus, a secure connection is made between you and the FreeNAS server and you can use the command line knowing that your passwords and commands cannot be seen.

To get this working with the FreeNAS server, a few simple steps need to occur:

1. A public and private key need to be generated.
2. The public key needs to be copied to the FreeNAS server.
3. You connect to the FreeNAS server and by exchanging of data encrypted using your public key and decrypted using your private key, secure communications are established.

The following example is for Apple OS X and Linux. If you are using Linux, you need to be sure that the OpenSSH package is installed (which it will be by default on most Linux distributions).

First, a public and private key pair need to be generated. This is done with the *ssh-keygen* command:

```
ssh-keygen
```

Advanced System Configuration

The output will look something like this:

```
Generating public/private rsa key pair.
Enter file in which to save the key (/Users/gary/.ssh/id_rsa):
Enter passphrase (empty for no passphrase):
Enter same passphrase again:
Your identification has been saved in /Users/gary/.ssh/id_rsa.
Your public key has been saved in /Users/gary/.ssh/id_rsa.pub.
The key fingerprint is:
18:fa:6b:68:c7:9f:49:80:bb:0a:1a:2e:15:86:99:e6 gary@apple-mac.local
```

Here, on my Apple Mac, two files are created id_rsa and id_rsa.pub. The .pub file is the public key and can be freely distributed. The id_rsa file is the private key and needs to be protected. In this example I have not used a password. This means that to start the decryption process, no password is needed. The benefit of this is that the client SSH program can connect to the FreeNAS server and it will be authenticated without any input from the user. The disadvantage is that if someone else takes your private key (id_rsa) they can also do the same thing, completely unhindered. It is therefore recommended that if you need extra security, you should include a password for your private key.

The next step is to tell the FreeNAS server your public key. The best way to do this is to copy it to the server using the *SCP* program. SCP stands for Secure Copy and it is a way to copy files in a secure manner from one machine to another. The id_rsa.pub file needs to be copied to the /root/.ssh/authorized_keys2 file on the FreeNAS server.

The main problem is that the /root/.ssh directory doesn't exist and SCP can't copy a file to a non-existent directory. There are several solutions to this, of which the simplest is to go to the FreeNAS console (and if needed press *ENTER* to remove the logo and see the menu). Now choose **6) Shell**. At the # prompt type:

```
mkdir .ssh
```

Now to copy id_rsa.pub file to /root/.ssh/authorized_keys2 file on the FreeNAS server with SCP you need to enter:

```
scp ~/.ssh/id_rsa.pub root@192.168.1.250:.ssh/authorized_keys2
```

where 192.168.1.250 is the address of your FreeNAS server. You will be asked to enter the root password.

The final step is to connect to the FreeNAS server using SSH:

```
ssh -l root 192.168.1.250
```

The `-l` option specifies who to log in as (in this case root) and 192.168.1.250 is the IP address of the FreeNAS server.

When you are connected, you will see something like this:

```
Last login: Wed Mar 19 14:20:52 2008 from 192.168.1.249
Copyright (c) 1980, 1983, 1986, 1988, 1990, 1991, 1993, 1994
    The Regents of the University of California.  All rights reserved.
freenas:~#
```

Summary

In this chapter, we have looked at advanced system configuration including disk encryption, S.M.A.R.T and SSH access.

The next chapter is about troubleshooting and helping you solve the most common FreeNAS problems.

9
General Troubleshooting

It is a common experience amongst all of us that from time to time our computers don't always work as we expect and we need to hunt down and resolve problems with them. Troubleshooting can be time consuming especially if you have limited experience with the software or system you are using. This chapter is a guide on how to solve problems with your FreeNAS server. It covers where to look for information about the problem as well as how to hunt down problems by being methodical. It also looks at the common problems people have with their FreeNAS servers including networking problems and problems with RAID.

Where to Look for Log Information

The first place to head whenever you have a configuration problem with FreeNAS is to the related configuration section and check that it is configured as expected. If, having double checked the settings, the problem persists, the next port of call is the log and information files in the Diagnostics: section of the web interface.

Keep Diagnostics Section Expanded

By default, the menu tree in the Diagnostics section of the web interface is collapsed, meaning the menu items aren't visible. To see the menu items, you need to click the word Diagnostics and the tree will expand. During initial setup and if you are doing lots of troubleshooting, you can save yourself a click by having the Diagnostics section permanently expanded. To set this option, go to System: Advanced and click on the **Navigation - Keep diagnostics in navigation expanded** tick box.

The Diagnostics sections has five sections, the first two are logs and information pages about the status of the FreeNAS server. The other three are networking diagnostic tools and information.

General Troubleshooting

Diagnostics: Logs

This section collates all the different log files that are generated by the FreeNAS server into one convenient place. There are several tabs, one for each different service to log file type. Some of the information can be very technical, especially in the System tab. However, with some key information they can become more readable. The tabs are as follows:

Tab	Meaning
System	When FreeBSD (the underlying OS of FreeNAS) boots, various log entries are recorded here about the hardware of the server and various messages about the boot process.
FTP	This shows the activity on the FTP server including successful logins and failed logins.
RSYNC	The log information for the RSYNC server (see chapter 7) is divided into three sections: Server, Client, and Local. Depending on which type of RSYNC operation you are interested, click the appropriate tab.
SSHD	Here you will find log entries from the SSH server including some limited startup information and records of logins and failed login attempts.
SMARTD	This tab logs the output of the S.M.A.R.T daemon. See chapter 8 for more details on S.M.A.R.T.
Daemon	Any other minor system service like the built-in HTTP server, the Apple Filing Protocol server and Windows networking server (Samab) will log information to this page.
UPnP	The log information from the FreeNAS UPnP server called "MediaTomb" is displayed here. The logging can be quite verbose so careful attention is needed when reading it. Don't be distracted by entires such as "INFO: Config: option not found:" as this is just the server logging that it will be using a default value for that particular attribute.
Settings	The settings tab allows you to change how the log information is displayed including the sort order and the number of entries shown.

What is a Daemon?

In UNIX speak, a Daemon is a system service. It is a program that runs in the background performing certain tasks. The Daemons in FreeNAS don't work with the users in an interactive mode (via the monitor, mouse, and keyboard) and as such need a place to log the results (or problems) of their actives. The FreeNAS Daemons are launched automatically by FreeBSD when it boots and some are dependent on being enabled in the web interface.

Understanding Diagnostics—Logs: System

The most complicated of all the log pages is the System log page. Here, FreeBSD logs information about the system, its hardware, and the startup process. At first, this page can seem intimidating but with a little help, this page can be very helpful particularly in tracking down hardware or driver related problems.

> **50 Log Entries Might Not be Enough**
>
> The default number of log entries shown on the Diagnostics: Logs page is 50. For most situations, this will be sufficient but there can be times when it is not enough. For example in the Diagnostics: Logs: System tab, the total number of log entries made during the boot up process is more than 50. If you want to see how much system memory has been recognized by FreeBSD, you won't find it within the standard 50 entries. The solution is to increase the *Number of log entries to show* parameter on the Diagnostics: Logs: Setting tab.

The best way to learn to read the Diagnostics: Logs: System page is by example, below are several different log entry examples including logs about the CPU, memory, disks, and disk controllers:

`kernel: FreeBSD 6.2-RELEASE-p11 #0: Wed Mar 12 18:17:49 CET 2008`

This first entry shows the heritage of the FreeNAS server. It is based on FreeBSD and in this particular case, we see that this version of FreeNAS is using FreeBSD 6.2. There are plans (which may have already become reality) to use FreeBSD version 7.0 as the base for FreeNAS.

`kernel: CPU: Intel(R) Xeon(TM) CPU 1.70GHz (1680.52-MHz 686-class CPU)`

Here, the type of CPU that was detected by the FreeBSD is displayed. In this case, it is an Intel Xeon CPU running at 1.7GHz.

`kernel: FreeBSD/SMP: Multiprocessor System Detected: 2 CPUs`

If your system has more than one CPU or is a dual core machine then you will see an entry in the log file (like the one above) recognizing the second CPU. If your machine has Hyper-threading technology, then the second logical processor will be reported like this: *Logical CPUs per core: 2*

```
Apr 1 11:06:00      kernel: real memory  = 268435456 (256 MB)
Apr 1 11:06:00      kernel: avail memory = 252907520 (241 MB)
```

General Troubleshooting

These log entries show how much memory the system has detected. The difference in size between real memory and available memory is the difference between the amount of RAM physically installed in the computer and the amount of memory left over after the FreeBSD kernel is loaded.

```
kernel: atapci0: <Intel PIIX4 UDMA33 controller> port 0x1f0-
0x1f7,0x3f6,0x170-0x177,0x376,0x1050-0x105f at device 7.1 on pci0
kernel: ata0: <ATA channel 0> on atapci0
kernel: ata1: <ATA channel 1> on atapci0
```

For disks to work on your FreeNAS server, a disk controller is needed and it will be either a standard ATA/IDE controller, a SATA controller or a SCSI controller. Above are the log entries for a standard ATA controller built into the motherboard. You can see that it is an Intel controller and that two channels have been seen (the primary and the secondary).

```
kernel: atapci1: <SiS 181 SATA150 controller>  irq 17 at device 5.0 on
pci0
kernel: ata2: <ATA channel 0> on atapci1
kernel: ata3: <ATA channel 1> on atapci1
```

Like the ATA controller listed a moment ago, SATA controllers are all recognized at boot up. Here is a SiS 181 SATA 150 controller with two channels. They are listed as devices `ata2` and `ata3`—as `ata0` and `ata1` are used by the standard ATA/IDE controller.

```
kernel: mpt0: <LSILogic 1030 Ultra4 Adapter> irq 17 at device 16.0 on
pci0
```

Like IDE and SATA controllers, all recognized SCSI drivers are listed in the boot up system log. Here, the controller is an LSILogic 1030 Ultra4.

```
kernel: ad0: 476940MB <WDC WD5000AAJB-00YRA0 12.01C02> at ata0-master
UDMA100
kernel: ad4: 476940MB <Seagate ST3500320AS SD04> at ata2-master SATA150
```

Once the disk controllers are recognized by the system, FreeBSD can search to see which disks are attached. Above is an example of a Western Digital 500GB hard drive using the standard ATA100 interface at 100MB/s. There is also a 500GB Seagate drive connected using the SATA interface.

```
acd0: CDROM <TOSHIBA CD-ROM XM-7002B/1005>  at ata1 as master UDMA33
```

When the CDROM (which is normally attached to an ATA/IDE controller) is recognized, it will look like the above.

```
kernel: da0 at ahd0 bus 0 target 0 lun 0
kernel: da0: <MAXTOR ATLAS10K4_73WLS DFL0> Fixed Direct Access SCSI-3
device
```

```
kernel: da0: 320.000MB/s transfers (160.000MHz, offset 127, 16bit),
Tagged Queueing Enabled
kernel: da0: 70149MB (143666192 512 byte sectors: 255H 63S/T 8942C)
```

SCSI addressing is a little more complicated than that of ATA/IDE. In SCSI land, you have a controller, a channel (bus), a disk (target), and the Logical Unit Number (LUN). The example above shows that a disk (which has been assigned the device name da0) is found on the controller ahd0 on bus 0, as target 0 with the LUN 0. SCSI controllers can have multiple buses and multiple targets. Further down, you can see that the disk is a MAXTOR 73GB SCSI-3 disk.

```
kernel: da0 at umass-sim0 bus 0 target 0 lun 0
kernel: da0: <Verbatim Store 'n' Go 1.30> Removable Direct Access SCSI-2
device
kernel: da0: 40.000MB/s transfers
kernel: da0: 963MB (1974271 512 byte sectors: 64H 32S/T 963C)
```

If you are using a USB flash disk for storing the configuration information, it will most likely appear in the log file as a type of SCSI disk. The above example shows a 1GB Verbatim Store 'n' Go disk.

```
kernel: lnc0: <PCNet/PCI Ethernet adapter> irq 18 at device 17.0 on pci0
kernel: lnc0: Ethernet address: 00:0c:29:a5:9a:28
```

Another important device that needs to work correctly on your system is the network interface card. Like disk controllers and disks, it will be logged in the log file when FreeBSD recognizes it. Above is an example of an AMD Lance/PCNet-based Ethernet adapter. Each Ethernet card has a unique address know as the Ethernet address or the MAC address. It is made up of 6 numbers specified using a colon notation. Once found, FreeBSD queries the card to find its MAC address and logs the result. In the above example, it is "00:0c:29:a5:9a:28".

Converting between Device Names and the Real World

In the SCSI example above, the SCSI controller listed is *ahd0*. The trick to understanding these log entries better is to know how to interpret the device name *ahd0*. First of all *ahd0* means it is a device using the *ahd* driver and it is the first one in the system (with numbering starting from 0).

So what is a ahd? The first place to look is further up in the log file. There should be an entry like:

```
kernel: ahd0: <Adaptec 39320 Ultra320 SCSI adapter> irq 11 at device 1.0
on pci2
```

General Troubleshooting

This shows that the particular device is an `Adaptec 39320 SCSI 3` controller. You can also find out more about the the *ahd* driver (and all FreeBSD drivers) at:

`http://www.freebsd.org/releases/6.2R/hardware-i386.html`

Search for *ahd* and you will find which controllers this driver supports (in this case, they are all controllers from Adaptec. If you click on the link provided, you will be taken to a specific help page about this driver.

When FreeNAS moves to FreeBSD 7, then the relevant web page will be:

`http://www.freebsd.org/releases/7.0R/hardware.html`

Networking Problems

Having reliable networking with Network Attached Storage is, of course, essential. This section is aimed at those who are having networking problems.

In general, networking problems can be categorized into two: Physical problems and software problems. In the physical category are such problems as broken cables and faulty hardware and in the software category problems range from device driver problems to network configuration errors.

On the surface, most network problems appear the same, the network doesn't work, you can't connect. To hunt down the problem there are different things you can try.

General Connection Problems

Having booted your FreeNAS server, the first step is to configure the networking. This is covered in detail in chapter 2. Assuming you have configured the networking, the next step is to connect to the FreeNAS server using a web browser. If the web browser connection fails, the web browser (Firefox in this case) will show something like this:

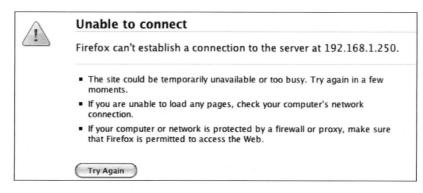

Chapter 9

There are two machines involved in this operation, one is the FreeNAS server and the other is the computer with the web browser. First, test that the machine with the web browser is working normally. Make sure it can access the Internet as well as other machines or devices on your network. If it can't, you need to start there!

If the web browser machine is working then the problem could be with the FreeNAS server, it is time to find the problem. Use this checklist to make sure everything is as it should be:

- Check that the cable is plugged into the network card of the FreeNAS server. It might sound simple, but I have had cases where the cable didn't click in quite correct and so the networking didn't work. Assuming that the other end of the cable is also plugged in correctly, check that the link LED lights on the FreeNAS server and also lights on the switch or hub where it is connected. If you get green lights all round then things are good.
- Check that the network was recognized during the boot up of FreeNAS server. As you can't access the web interface you will need to check this on the console. You are looking for something like this:

```
LAN IPv4 address: 192.168.1.250
LAN IPv6 address: fe80:1::20c:29ff:

Port configuration:

LAN    -> lnc0
```

> **What If My Network Card Isn't Found?**
> This probably means that the network card in your machine isn't supported by FreeNAS or more specifically by FreeBSD. Check the FreeBSD hardware compatibility page for more information: http://www.freebsd.org/releases/6.2R/hardware-i386.html

- If the cabling is right and the network is found, it is time to double check the network settings. The most common mistake is in setting the subnet mask. The subnet mask determines which network a machine is on. When you set the subnet mask using the console menu system, if the subnet mask isn't the same as the machine with the web browser, then connectivity can be lost. Also, incorrect subnet masks can cause odd behavior, for example the machine with web browser might be able to connect to the FreeNAS server but the server may not be able to reply. A typo of 25 (instead of the desired 24) can cause connection problems.
- Is the IP address unique? If you have set a static IP address, have you set the right one? If two machines are assigned the same IP address, strange things can happen. With packets of data destined for one machine arriving at the other and so on. Ensure the IP address is correct and that it is unique.

- If you are using DHCP, ensure that the DHCP server is up and running and it has free addresses to issue. If you see that the FreeNAS server has the address 0.0.0.0, it means that it was unable to get an IP address from the DHCP server.

```
LAN IPv4 address: 0.0.0.0
LAN IPv6 address: fe80:1::20c:29ff:

Port configuration:

LAN   -> lnc0
```

Using Ping

Most operating systems (including Windows, Linux, and OS X) have a tool called *ping* that allows you to test the low level connectivity between two machines. To test the connection to the FreeNAS machine, you can *ping* it and also you can get the FreeNAS server to *ping* other machines.

On Windows XP to run *ping*, click **Run...** and then type **cmd** in the dialog box. Press *Enter* and a black command prompt will appear. The command to *ping* is simply ping followed by the IP address. So to *ping* the FreeNAS server on its standard address of 192.168.1.250 you would type:

```
ping 192.168.1.250
```

If all is well, then the FreeNAS server will *reply*. The output should look something like this:

```
C:\WINDOWS\system32\cmd.exe
Microsoft Windows XP [Version 5.1.2600]
(C) Copyright 1985-2001 Microsoft Corp.

C:\Documents and Settings\Gary>ping 192.168.1.250

Pinging 192.168.1.250 with 32 bytes of data:

Reply from 192.168.1.250: bytes=32 time=18ms TTL=64
Reply from 192.168.1.250: bytes=32 time=23ms TTL=64
Reply from 192.168.1.250: bytes=32 time=1ms TTL=64
Reply from 192.168.1.250: bytes=32 time=23ms TTL=64

Ping statistics for 192.168.1.250:
    Packets: Sent = 4, Received = 4, Lost = 0 (0% loss),
Approximate round trip times in milli-seconds:
    Minimum = 1ms, Maximum = 23ms, Average = 16ms

C:\Documents and Settings\Gary>
```

If the PC can't contact the FreeNAS server then it will report "Request timed out" errors.

You can also use the FreeNAS server to ping other machines on the network. From the console choose option 5. You will then be asked to enter an IP address. The IP address this time won't be that of the FreeNAS server, as this command is running from the FreeNAS server, but rather of another machine on the network. Enter the address and press enter. The output should be something like this:

```
IPv4 address detected...
PING 192.168.1.110 (192.168.1.110): 56 data bytes
64 bytes from 192.168.1.110: icmp_seq=0 ttl=64 time=22.297 ms
64 bytes from 192.168.1.110: icmp_seq=1 ttl=64 time=1.478 ms
64 bytes from 192.168.1.110: icmp_seq=2 ttl=64 time=1.195 ms

--- 192.168.1.110 ping statistics ---
3 packets transmitted, 3 packets received, 0% packet loss
round-trip min/avg/max/stddev = 1.195/8.323/22.297/9.882 ms

Press ENTER to continue.
```

Discovering the IP Address of an XP Machine
To find out the IP address of an XP machine: Click **Start** then **Run**... In the dialog box type **cmd** and press *ENTER*. In the command prompt window, type **ipconfig /all**. The resulting output will reveal the IP address along with the subnet mask and so on.

Using Ping from within the Web Interfaces

If you have access to the FreeNAS server's web interface and you want to *ping* another machine to ensure that the FreeNAS server can contact it, then go to Diagnostics: Ping. Enter the IP address of the machine you wish to ping in *Host* and click *Ping*.

The output for a successful ping will look like this:

```
PING 192.168.1.110 (192.168.1.110): 56 data bytes
64 bytes from 192.168.1.110: icmp_seq=0 ttl=64 time=1.148 ms
64 bytes from 192.168.1.110: icmp_seq=1 ttl=64 time=0.697 ms
64 bytes from 192.168.1.110: icmp_seq=2 ttl=64 time=0.638 ms

--- 192.168.1.110 ping statistics ---
3 packets transmitted, 3 packets received, 0% packet loss
round-trip min/avg/max/stddev = 0.638/0.828/1.148/0.228 ms
```

A failed ping will look like this:

```
PING 192.168.1.100 (192.168.1.100): 56 data bytes

--- 192.168.1.100 ping statistics ---
3 packets transmitted, 0 packets received, 100% packet loss
```

Notice the `100% packet loss`, which means that none of the pings got to their destination.

If you have multiple network cards in your machine, you can select which card to use in the *Interface* drop down box. This can be very useful when you want to check the connectivity on a second Ethernet interface card.

If you want to see which route the network packets are taking (through which switches and gateways), you can use the traceroute tool which is on the Traceroute.

Using ARP Tables to Solve Network Problems

Deep down in the murky depths of internals of Ethernet is a thing known as ARP. The Address Resolution Protocol (ARP) is the standard method for finding a host's hardware address (or MAC address) when only its IP address is known. To send a packet of information to an IP address, the networking software needs to know the physical address of the network card which is serving that IP address. To do this, it sends out and ARP request and gets an ARP response with the MAC address in it.

On the Diagnostics: ARP tables page, there is a table of all the MAC addresses known to the FreeNAS server along with the corresponding IP address. This table is useful as it allows you to see if the networking layers of the FreeNAS server where we are able to at least discover the MAC address of the remote server/PC in question. If the MAC address is known but ping fails, then the problem could be a firewall.

This table is also useful to make sure that two machines don't have the same IP address by mistake. You can tally the IP address with the MAC address to be certain that the right server has been contacted.

What is a MAC Address?

A Media Access Control address (MAC address) or Ethernet address is a globally unique identifier attached to most network adapters by the manufacturer. It can be likened to the postal address of your house, which is unique, so that all things sent to that address are received there by you. The address is made up of 6 numbers specified using a colon notation. An example MAC address is "00:0c:29:a5:9a:28".

`http://www.coffer.com/mac_find/` is a useful website to find out which manufacturer (or vendor as they are known) created any given MAC address.

Gigabit Transfers are Slow

Gigabit networking isn't the silver bullet that some people think it is. Unfortunately, you are never going to get 125MB/s (1000 divided by 8) transfer rates between FreeNAS and your PC. There are several reasons for this, some are theoretical and some practical. To get the best transfers rates over Gigabit Ethernet, to and from your FreeNAS server, you need to consider the following:

- First of all, make sure that you have enabled the tuning of some kernel variables. You will find this option on the System: Advanced: Advanced Setup page. Tick the *Tuning* box and save the settings.
- Make sure your Gigabit Ethernet switch and your Gigabit Ethernet card can handle Jumbo frames. Without Jumbo frame support, the increases over 100Mb/s networking will be marginal.
- Use a PCI Express Gigabit network card when possible.
- Ensure that your CPU is able to handle the load placed on it by the networking and the disk activity.
- Configure your disks in the optimum configuration for speed throughput. This almost certainly means you need to be using some kind of RAID, either hardware or software.

Problems Connecting to Shares (via CIFS)

One of the most popular ways to connect to the FreeNAS server is via the Windows protocol CIFS. In the majority of environments, people will connect to FreeNAS from a Windows machine and probably mount the 'share' as a network drive on the machine.

There are many versions of Microsoft Windows in use today with some people still using Windows 98 or Millennium while others are using Windows 2000, Windows XP or Windows Vista. Each version of Windows has slightly different ideas about networking and a setup—which works with Windows 2000 or Windows 98 *might* not work with Windows Vista.

Here are some problems might be encountered when using Microsoft Windows with FreeNAS.

Windows Vista Asks for My Username and Password for Anonymous Shares

This can happen when the *Null passwords* field is enabled on the Services: CIFS/SMB page (in the advanced settings section). To resolve the problem, disable the *Null password* field.

There are Two FreeNAS Servers on the Network, but Windows Can only See One

During the configuration of these two FreeNAS servers, you probably made sure that each machine had its own IP address and hostname. You also need to make sure that the default name for the CIFS server in FreeNAS isn't the same for both of your servers. Although you can connect to their web interfaces without any problems when you try to use Windows networking, only one machine will be seen.

To solve this, go to Services: CIFS/SMB and set the *NetBiosName* name to something unique for each server.

Turning On Logging to Help Solve Windows Networking Problems

If you find that you have a Windows networking (CIFS) problem that you can't solve then try enabling more logging for the Windows networking server (called Samba) and see if the log files reveal any hints to the problem could be.

To enable logging, go to Services: CIFS/SMB and set the *Log Level* to Normal rather than Minimal. The logging created by Samba will be visible on the Diagnostics: Logs page under the Daemon tab. Entries starting with *smbd* are about the Windows networking server and those starting with *nmdb* are about the Windows networking name service.

If the Normal logging level doesn't help then you can try the Full level and even the Debug level but these will provide lots of output that you might find difficult to comprehend.

If the logging is producing lots of log entries, see the "50 Log entries might not be enough" tip in the Understanding Diagnostics: Logs: System section earlier in this chapter. Also remember that you can clear the logs at any time by pressing the "Clear log" button on any of the Diagnostics: Logs pages.

Don't forget to turn the logging back to Minimal when you are done.

Diagnostics: Information

As well as the Diagnostics: Logs page, there is also an information page in the Diagnostics: section. The Logs concentrates on the output from the various system services in the FreeNAS server where as the information page aims to provide status and configuration information about a variety of sections of the FreeNAS server.

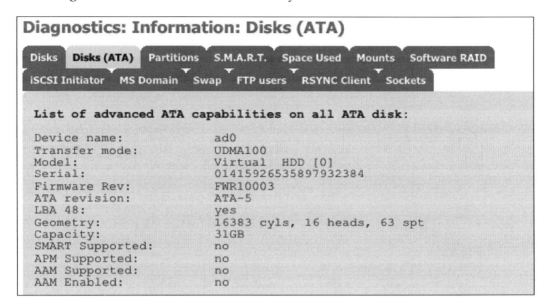

To access this page, go to Diagnostics: Information. At the top, there are lots of tabs. Here is what they mean:

Tab	Information
Disks	A list of the detected hard disks including all ATA/IDE disks, SATA disks, and SCSI disks.
Disks (ATA)	A list of the advanced capabilities on all ATA/IDE disks including the ATA revision, the disk geometry, the disk's capacity, and its S.M.A.R.T capabilities.
Partitions	Information about the partitions on each of the disks.
S.M.A.R.T.	List of SMART capabilities on all detected disks.
Space Used	Information about the disk space usage on the server. Each filesystem is listed with its total size, space used, space available, and what percentage of the disk is used.
Mounts	List of mount points with the filesystem type.

General Troubleshooting

Tab	Information
Software RAID	Information about the software RAID configuration of the FreeNAS server. Each RAID level is listed separately along with data about which disks are used.
iSCSI Initiator	Information about the iSCSI initiator.
MS Domain	Microsoft Active Directory information.
Swap	List of currently configured swap spaces.
FTP users	List of currently connected FTP users.
RSYNC Client	Each configured RSYNC client is listed along with its configuration parameters. The most useful information is the 'Detected shares on this server section'. It shows that the RSYNC client can contact the server and lists the available RSYNC modules.
Sockets	This is a list of the active Internet connections (including servers) as well as the active UNIX domain sockets. From this list, you can see which network servers are running and if there are any connected users to that server.

Replacing a Failed Hard Drive in a RAID Set

The key feature of RAID is the capability of the RAID set to continue working when one of the drives fails. When a drive fails, the RAID set enters a DEGRADED state, meaning the system is working but one of the drives has failed. This drive needs to be replaced as soon as possible.

To check the status of your RAID disks, go to Disks: Software RAID. Click on all the RAID types you have on your FreeNAS server and check that they are in the COMPLETE state. If a RAID set is in the DEGRADED state, you need to replace a disk.

Here is an example of a RAID 1 set in the degraded state:

Volume Name	Type	Size	Status
raid1	1	2048MB	DEGRADED

Note:
Optional configuration step: Configuring a virtual RAID disk using your previously configured disk.
Wait for the 'COMPLETE' status before format and mount it!

Info:
FreeNAS uses GEOM Mirror to create RAID1 arrays.

The first thing you need to know is which disk to replace. Go to Disk: Management page and check the status of each disk. If the disk is healthy, it should have the status of ONLINE. Once you have found the broken disk, you need to replace it. Some disk controllers have the ability to hot swapping, which means that the disk can be unplugged and a new disk added while the system is running. This is often a feature (but not exclusively) of SATA controllers. If you are unsure, then shutdown the FreeNAS server and replace the disk with server switched off.

Rebuilding a RAID 1 Array After Disk Failure

Now that you have replaced the disk, it is time to bring the system up to normal operations levels. This involves 2 steps that are all performed in the tools section of the **RAID 1** tab on the **Disks: Software RAID** page.

The first step is to tell the FreeNAS server to forget any devices that were in this RAID set but are now no longer connected.

1. Go to **Disks: Software RAID** and click on the **RAID 1** tab.
2. Click on the **Tools** tab.
3. Select the name of the degraded array in the **Volume Name** field and select the **Command forget**. The **Disk** field isn't used with the forget command.
4. Click **Send Command!** and the array will be told to forget about non-connected devices.
5. The output from the command should read **Done**.

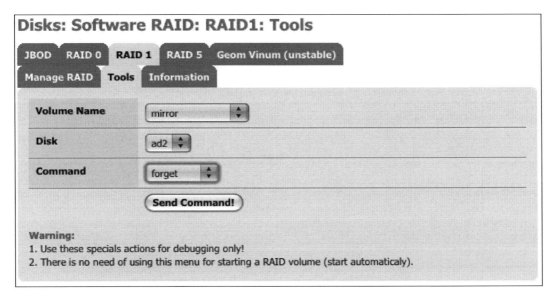

General Troubleshooting

The second step is to insert the new disk back into the array. Remaining in the **Tools** tab of the RAID 1 array:

1. Select the degraded array in the **Volume Name** field.
2. Select the new disk from the **Disk** drop down box.
3. Select the **insert** command and click **Send Command!**
4. The output from the command should read **Done**.

The array will now start rebuilding. You can check that it is rebuilding on the **Diagnostics: Information: Software RAID** page (watch the **Synchronized:** field for percentage completed) and the Manage RAID tab on the **Disks: Software RAID: RAID1**: page will show COMPLETE when the RAID is rebuilt.

Rebuilding a RAID 5 Array After Disk Failure

Having replaced the disk, you are ready to synchronize it with the other disks in the RAID set. This involves a single step that is performed in the tools section of the RAID 5 tab on the **Disks: Software RAID** page.

You need to insert the new disk back into the array. In the **Tools** tab of the RAID 1 array:

1. Select the degraded array in the **Volume Name** field.
2. Select the new disk from the **Disk** drop down box.
3. Select the **insert** command and click **Send Command!**
4. The output from the command should read Done.

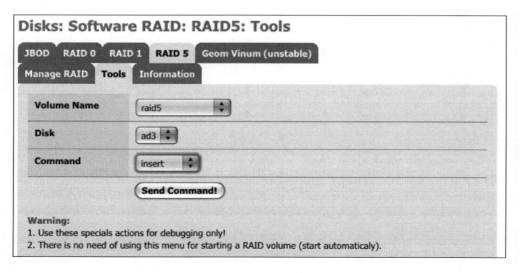

[196]

The array will now start rebuilding. You can check that it is rebuilding on the **Diagnostics: Information: Software RAID** page (watch the **Synchronized**: field for percentage completed) and the Manage RAID tab on the **Disks: Software RAID: RAID 5**: page will show COMPLETE when the RAID is rebuilt.

Where to Go for More Help

If you find yourself really stuck and are not able to track down your problem then the best place for support is the online FreeNAS Help Forums.

These are found at the SourceForge.net site and you need to sign up for a free SourceForge.net account to be able to post to the forums.

To find the support forum, go to the FreeNAS website at `http://freenas.org` and click on the Support link. From there, go to the Help forum.

Summary

In this chapter, we have looked at some of the tools that are available to help track down problems with the configuration of the FreeNAS server. We have looked at networking problems and possible solutions along with how to handle RAID failures.

The next and final chapter is about FreeBSD, the underlying operating system of FreeNAS.

10
FreeBSD and Command Line Tools

FreeBSD is the bedrock of the FreeNAS server. In this chapter, we will look at some simple FreeBSD commands and also some fundamental FreeBSD administration tasks, including stop and starting different services as well as controlling RAID from the command line.

Introduction to FreeBSD

Every computer has what is known as an operating system that is a specialized software to control and manage the different resources in the computer including memory, video, networking, and hard disks. Some popular operating systems today include Microsoft Windows, Apple OS X, Linux, and FreeBSD.

As an operating system, FreeBSD has a very respectable heritage and can trace its parentage to the original UNIX operating system of the late 1970's. Version 1 of FreeBSD saw the light of day in the 1993 and as such has had over 15 years of development. The result is a stable, robust, well-designed, and scalable operating system that can compete with the best.

At its core, FreeBSD is a terminal or console-based operating system. This means that you don't need a fancy graphics card, a high-resolution monitor, and an optical mouse to run FreeBSD. All commands are executed by typing them at the keyboard and hitting *ENTER*. This is essential when FreeBSD is being used as a server. Servers traditionally don't have powerful graphic capabilities and often don't even have a monitor attached to them. So, the ability to be able to connect and administer the server using simple command line tools is very important.

As well as being a solid server operating system, FreeBSD also serves as a desktop OS and comes with a full windowing desktop environment.

FreeBSD and Command Line Tools

Your First FreeBSD Commands

The easiest way to get to the FreeBSD command line is via the FreeNAS console menu. With FreeNAS up and running, go to the FreeNAS machine and press *ENTER* to make the splash screen disappear and the console menu will appear. Option 6 is for Shell, so type 6 and press *ENTER*.

You will now see a prompt like this:

```
freenas:~#
```

Print the Working Directory with pwd

This is FreeBSD! To run your first FreeBSD command type `pwd` and press *ENTER*.

```
freenas:~# pwd
/root
```

`pwd` means Print Working Directory. This tells you your current folder. In this case, it is the folder called `root`. In FreeBSD, the administrator user is known as root. When you connect to FreeBSD via the FreeNAS console, you are automatically logged in as root and you have full administration rights. The `/root` folder is the home directory for the user root.

Consider Disabling the Console Menu

As you can see, by default, the console gives you unfettered access to the FreeBSD command line and gives you full administrator rights from the go. If your FreeNAS server is in an environment where others can access the console menu then you should consider disabling the console (on the **System: Advanced** page in the web interface). This will stop unauthorized and potentially dangerous access to your FreeNAS server.

With the console menu disabled, you will still be able to access the FreeBSD command line via the SSH protocol.

Directory Listings (ls)

To see the contents of the current folder, you use the `ls` (list) command:

```
freenas:~# ls
.cshrc          .dialogrc       .history        .profile
```

By default, there isn't very much in the `/root` folder. Here, we can see that there are 4 files. Notice that they all start with a dot. This means they are hidden files but because you are the administrator, hidden files are shown by default. If a normal user uses the `ls` command then the files starting with dot are not shown.

[200]

To get more information about the files like their size and their read/write permissions, use the -l (long format) option:

```
freenas:~# ls -l
total 8
-rw-r--r--  1 root  wheel  843 Apr 14 10:52 .cshrc
-rw-r--r--  1 root  wheel   57 Feb 22 21:16 .dialogrc
-rw-------  1 root  wheel  123 Apr  2 13:13 .history
-rw-r--r--  1 root  wheel  236 Feb 22 21:16 .profile
```

This long format shows more information about each of the files starting with the file permissions, number of links, owner name, group name, size of the file in bytes, the date and time the file was lost or modified, and of course, the file name.

The file permissions field can look a little complicated but it is easy to understand with a little guidance. The field, if made up of 10 flags, which are either a letter, like r or w, or the hyphen sign (-).

File type (1 flag)	User permissions (3 flags)	Group permissions (3 flags)	Other permissions (3 flags)
d for directory, - for a regular file.	r, w, and x meaning user readable, user writable, and user executable.	r, w, and x meaning group readable, group writable and group executable.	r, w, and x meaning world readable, world writable, and world executable.

For example, the above directory list contains an entry for the .cshrc file.

```
-rw-r--r--  1 root  wheel  843 Apr 14 10:52 .cshrc
```

This means that it is a regular file (as the first flag is -) and that it is readable and writable by the user, but not executable (rw-). It is normal that the file isn't executable as it isn't a program file. The group permissions (r--) mean that users in the same group (wheel) can read the file but can't write to it and the same is true of other users (r--).

Change Directory with cd

To complete the simple file system commands, there is the cd (change directory) command. This will change the current working directory to another directory as specified. To change directory to the very top of the file system you would type:

```
freenas:~# cd /
```

From here, you can see all the folders that exist below the top, in a tree like structure.

```
freenas:/# ls
conf            etc             mnt             usr
bin             ftmp            root            var
boot            dev             lib             sbin
cf              entropy         libexec         tmp
```

To move to another directory, you just enter cd followed by its name:

```
freenas:/# cd /usr
freenas:/usr# ls
X11R6    bin     lib     libexec local   sbin    share
```

And then, deeper still:

```
freenas:/usr# cd bin
freenas:/usr/bin# pwd
/usr/bin
```

To go back up a directory level, use the special name :

```
freenas:/usr/bin# cd ..
freenas:/usr# pwd
/usr
```

You can also go directly to a deep folder by specifying its full path in the cd command. Before that, we changed directory into the /usr directory and then deeper down into the bin directory. To do that in one go type:

```
freenas:/# cd /usr/bin
freenas:/usr/bin# pwd
/usr/bin
```

Copy a File and Change Its Permissions (cp and chmod)

To copy a file, you need to use the cp (copy) command. To copy the .cshrc file to test, you would type:

```
freenas:~# cp .cshrc test
freenas:~# ls
.cshrc          .dialogrc       .history        .profile        test
```

Using the `ls` command afterwards, shows that the file has been copied. To see the file permissions of the file `test` type:

```
freenas:~# ls -l test
-rw-r--r--  1 root   wheel   843 Apr 14 12:06 test
```

To change the file so that only the user has read and write permissions and the no others (including those in the same group) can read it, use the `chmod` (change file mode) command.

```
freenas:~# chmod 600 test
freenas:~# ls -l test
-rw-------  1 root   wheel   843 Apr 14 12:06 test
```

`chmod` takes two parameters: the first is a 3 digit number representing the file permissions you wish to set, and the second is the name of the file or directory you wish to change. Each digit represents the file permissions for either the user, group or world (in that order).

The numbers for the file permissions are as follows:

File permission	Flags	Meaning
0	---	Nothing, no Read, Write or Execute
1	--x	Execute
2	-w-	Write
3	-wx	Execute & Write
4	r--	Read
5	r-x	Execute & Read
6	rw-	Read & Write
7	rwx	Execute & Read & Write

Therefore, setting the file permission to 600 means read and write for the user and nothing for the group or world (rw-------). Similarly 640 means read and write for the user, read for the group, and nothing for others (rw-r-----). The most open you can make a file is 777, which grants read, write, and executable permission to user, group, and world (rwxrwxrwx).

Optionally, chmod all takes a -R flag that can be used on a directory and will cause chmod to set the file permission of all the file and subfolders of the directory.

Connecting to FreeBSD Using Putty

To get access to the FreeBSD command line, without using the console, you can connect to the FreeNAS server via SSH.

SSH (Secure Shell) is a network protocol that allows data to be exchanged over an encrypted (secure) channel between two computers. It is most commonly used as a secure command line interface to a remote computer. This means that you can access the command line interface of the FreeNAS server from a remote computer without having to have access to the keyboard and monitor of the FreeNAS server.

By default, SSH access is disabled, to enable it, go to **Services: SSHD** and enable the **SSH Daemon** (server) by ticking **Enable** in the title of the configuration data table. Click **Save and Restart** to start the SSH server.

There are two types of SSH users on the FreeNAS server. The first is the normal user without administrator access. For each user created on the **Access: Users** page, you can enable Full Shell access that will allow the users to connect and use the FreeBSD command line on the server via SSH.

The second type of user is root. By default, root is not allowed to log in to the FreeNAS server via SSH. To allow root to log in, go to **Services: SSHD** and tick **Permit root login**. Then click **Save and Restart** to finish start the SSH server.

> **Root Password**
> The root password is the same as the web interface password, which by default is *freenas*. If the web interface password is changed, so does the root password.

To connect via SSH on Linux or Apple OS X, you can use the SSH command line program. So, to connect to the FreeNAS server, you would use:

```
ssh -l root 192.168.1.250
```

The `-l` parameter allows you to specify the user name which in this case was root.

Windows doesn't come with a SSH utility by default so you need to use a free utility called PuTTY. PuTTY is a great tool written by Simon Tatham.

You can download PuTTY from http://www.chiark.greenend.org.uk/~sgtatham/putty/

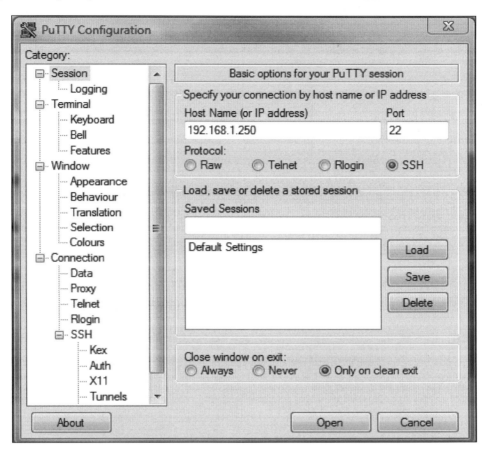

Once downloaded, double click on the executable (there is no installer for PuTTY, you just use the downloaded file). The main PuTTY window has lots of options but all you need to do to use it is enter the IP address of the FreeNAS server in the Host Name field in the top half of the window. Leave everything else as it is and click Open. A window with a black background will appear. If this is the first time you have connected to this FreeNAS server using PuTTY, you will also be asked if you trust the machine to which you have connected. Click Yes.

At the *login as:* prompt type root and press ENTER and then enter the password which will be the same as the web interface password. You will then see the, hopefully now, familiar *freenas:~#* prompt.

From herein, you have access to FreeBSD as you did from the console menu shell.

Monitoring your FreeNAS Server from the Command Line

FreeBSD contains several tools for system monitoring including monitoring the disk space and the system processes.

See Which Disks are Mounted with mount

To see which disks are mounted on the FreeNAS server, use the mount command:

```
freenas:~# mount
/dev/ad0s1a on / (ufs, local, soft-updates)
devfs on /dev (devfs, local)
/dev/raid5/raid5p1 on /mnt/raid5 (ufs, local, soft-updates, acls)
```

This yields the same output as the **Diagnostics: Information: Mounts** page on the web interface. Each device is listed along with its mount point and what type of filing system it is and any options. From the above, we can see the top most directory/(also refereed to as root but not to be confused with the user root) that contains the FreeBSD and FreeNAS software is on the first IDE drive (ad0). We can also see that this FreeNAS server has a raid5 configuration mounted on /mnt/raid.

Check Disk Space Usage with df

Another useful command (which is also available on the web interface at **Diagnostics: Information: Space Used**) is the *df* command. *df* shows the disk space usage. It has an optional parameter -h (the human readable flag), which makes the output more friendly.

```
freenas:~# df -h
Filesystem              Size    Used   Avail Capacity  Mounted on
/dev/ad0s1a             121M     56M     56M    50%    /
devfs                   1.0K    1.0K     0B    100%    /dev
/dev/raid5/raid5p1      3.9G    239M    3.3G    7%    /mnt/raid5
```

Each filesystem is listed with its total size, space used, space available, and what percentage of the disk is used.

Discover the Size of Directories Using du

Another very useful command which **isn't** included in the web interface is the *du* command. The *du* command displays the disk space usage for each file and for each folder given including the subfolders or for the current folder if none is given.

From the example above, we see that the RAID 5 array has 239MB used. If we change directory into the `/mnt/raid5` directory and then run the du command (with the -h flag for human readability and -s for summary) we see that the 239MB listed in the df command is also listed from the du command:

```
freenas:~# cd /mnt/raid5/
freenas:/mnt/raid5# du -hs
239M    .
```

Inside the `/mnt/raid5`, there is a folder called `pictures`, to discover how much disk space is used by the pictures folder use the du command, either by changing directory to that folder or specifying it directly:

```
freenas:~# du -h /mnt/raid5/pictures
2.5M    /mnt/raid5/pictures
```

Process Monitoring Using ps and top

FreeBSD is able to run many programs at the same time. The FreeNAS server includes a web server, an FTP server, and a SSH server etc which all run at the same time. Each of these programs runs as a separate process. Each process uses time on a system's CPU, as well as other system resources such as memory and disk space. If a program goes wrong, it can start to use too much CPU time or memory and so deny other programs the resources they need to run. There are some FreeBSD commands to monitor the status of the process running on your server.

`ps` shows the current processes running on the machine. `ps` has many different options, but one of the most useful invocations is `ps aux`, which shows every process on the system.

A normal FreeNAS server will have some 60 to 70 processes running after boot up, so the output from the ps command can be quite long. Here are the first few lines from a FreeNAS server:

```
freenas:~# ps aux
USER     PID %CPU %MEM   VSZ  RSS  TT  STAT STARTED        TIME COMMAND
root      10 84.6  0.0     0    8  ??  RL   10:28AM    69:12.51 [idle: cpu0]
root       0  0.0  0.0     0    0  ??  WLs  10:28AM     0:00.00 [swapper]
root       1  0.0  0.2   772  388  ??  SLs  10:28AM     0:00.09 /sbin/init --
root       2  0.0  0.0     0    8  ??  DL   10:28AM     0:01.22 [g_event]
root       3  0.0  0.0     0    8  ??  DL   10:28AM     0:01.14 [g_up]
root       4  0.0  0.0     0    8  ??  DL   10:28AM     0:01.60 [g_down]
root       5  0.0  0.0     0    8  ??  DL   10:28AM     0:00.00 [crypto]
root       6  0.0  0.0     0    8  ??  DL   10:28AM     0:00.00 [crypto returns]
```

Here is a brief explanation of each of the columns:

Column	Meaning
USER	This is the name of the user that owns the processes.
PID	Each process has a unique process ID (or PID for short).
%CPU	Shows the CPU utilization of the process. It is a decaying average over up to a minute of previous (real) time.
%MEM	This is the amount of the physical memory the process is using.
VSZ	Shows the virtual memory size of the process in kilobytes.
RSS	This is similar to VSZ, but rather than virtual memory size, RSS shows how much non-swapped, physical memory the process is using in kilobytes.
TT	The controlling terminal. Means there isn't one.
STAT	The status of the process, where S means the process is sleeping and can be woken at any time, L means the process is waiting to acquire a lock. R marks a runnable process.
STARTED	Shows when the process was started.
TIME	Is the accumulated CPU time. This includes time spent running the processes and time spent in the kernel on behalf of that process.
COMMAND	Shows the command which was given to launch the program.

Finding a specific process in such a long list can be a problem. To help, you can use the grep command to look for matches in the text. For example, to look for the ftp server process, use the command:

```
freenas:~# ps aux | grep ftp
root      981   0.0  0.8  3636  1904  ??  Ss    0:00.07 pure-ftpd
root     1407   0.0  0.4  1528   984  p0  R+    0:00.02 grep ftp
```

When you run it, the `grep` command itself will be shown (in this case PID 1407) as it matches the string we are looking for, namely ftp. But of course, it isn't part of the ftp service.

While `ps` shows only a snapshot of the system process, the `top` program provides a dynamic real-time view of a system. It displays a system summary (with CPU usage, memory usage, and other statistics) as well as a list of running processes that changes dynamically as the system is in use. It lists the processes using the most CPU first.

```
The first few lines of top look something like this:
last pid:  1410;  load av:  0.00,  0.00,  0.00    up 0+01:39:09  12:07
23 processes:   2 running, 21 sleeping
CPU:  0.0% user,   0.0% nice,   3.8% sys,   0.0% interrupt, 96.2% idle
```

```
Mem: 10M Active, 12M Inact, 13M Wired, 68K Cache, 9648K Buf, 207M Free
Swap:

  PID USERNAME    THR PRI NICE   SIZE    RES STATE    TIME   WCPU COMMAND
 1087 root         1   4    0  3168K  2212K kqread   0:02  0.00% lighttpd
 1023 root         3  20    0  7160K  4104K kserel   0:01  0.00% mediatom
 1250 root         1  76    0  5640K  2720K RUN      0:01  0.00% sshd
  927 root         1  76    0  5496K  3208K select   0:01  0.00% nmbd
 1253 root         1  20    0  4000K  2780K pause    0:01  0.00% csh
```

The bottom part of the output is similar to the output from the `ps` command.

Advanced FreeBSD Commands for FreeNAS

Up until now, we have really been in read-only mode as far as using the underlying FreeBSD system. We have looked and monitored but we haven't actually changed anything. That is about to change.

Starting and Stopping Services

You will have probably noticed that many of the configuration pages on the web interface say **Save and Restart**. This is because many of the FreeNAS server components need to restart to accept new configurations. As such, it is also possible to restart a service manually using the command line. This might be necessary if a particular service, for example the FTP server or the AFP server stopped responding (this isn't a slur on the FTP server or the AFP server, just merely an example).

Using the command line, it is possible to start, stop, and restart each individual service. All of the scripts to control the various services are kept in /etc/rc.d and to manage a service, you call the respective script directly from that directory. To restart the AFP service, you would type:

```
freenas:~# /etc/rc.d/afpd restart
Stopping afpd.
Starting afpd.
```

Restart is not the only command that is accepted by the scripts:

Command	Meaning
start	Starts the service. If the service is already running, no action will be taken.
stop	Stop the service. If the service isn't running, nothing will happen.
restart	Performs a stop and then a start. If the service isn't running, the stop will fail but the script will continue to start the service.
status	Shows if the service is running.

Here is a table of the possible services you can start and stop:

Name	Service description
afpd	The Apple Filing Protocol Daemon. This provides the connectivity to Apple Mac computers.
lighttpd	The built-in web server for the web interface.
mediatomb.sh	The UPnP server.
nfsd	The NFS server for sharing files with UNIX type clients.
nfslocking	Part of the NFS server and needs to be controlled separately.
pureftpd	The FTP server.
rsync_client	The RSYNC client.
rsync_local	The local RSYNC client for synchronization between two local disks.
rsyncd	The RSYNC server.
samba	The CIFS/SMB server for Windows connectivity.
smartd	The hard disk monitoring service.
sshd	The secure shell service.
unison	The unison synchronization service.

Getting Drastic with kill and killall

The `kill` command attempts to shut down a running process. In FreeBSD, a process is stopped when the operating system sends it a signal telling it to shut down. The default signal for `kill` is TERM (signal 15), meaning software terminate. When the process receives the signal, it should shut down in an orderly way. If the process has become rogue, chances are that it won't respond to being told politely to shut down. In that case, you have to send the KILL signal (signal 9 for short). So to kill off a running process (e.g. process 1234) we would use `kill -9 1234`.

The `killall` command kills running processes by name rather than by PID. This has the advantage that to kill a process you don't need to look for the PID using the `ps` command. As with `kill`, `killall` takes a signal parameter, and `-9` is used to terminate the processes. So to kill off all the ftp processes you would use:

freenas:~# killall -9 pure-ftpd

One thing to note about `killall` is that you need to specify the exact name of the process, using `killall -9 pure` or `killall -9 ftp` will not stop the FTP server.

A couple of useful parameters to `killall` are `-s` and `-v`.

`-s` will show only what would be done, but does not send any signal.

`-v` will show a similar output to that of `-s` but will actually send the signal while reporting what has been done.

freenas:~# killall -9 -s pure-ftpd
kill -KILL 2045

RAID Command Line Tools

Reading the FreeNAS support forums on sourceforge.net seem to show that a fair percentage of users have troubles with RAID configurations. The RAID software in FreeNAS is of the highest quality but things can go wrong. All the RAID functions (and more) that are available in the web interface are available on the command line.

Each different type of RAID level (RAID 0, RAID 1, and so on) uses a different command as it is a specialized program to deal with that RAID level. A utility to manage RAID 1 sets knows nothing RAID 5 and vice-versa. The RAID utilities are: gconcat, gstripe, gmirror, and graid5.

Warning

A word of warning before starting. With the command line, you have complete freedom to manage and control your RAID sets. But this also means you have complete freedom to wreck your RAID sets. Be careful that you don't destroy your RAID sets by mistake. If you are uncomfortable with managing the RAID sets via the command line, you should return to using the web interface as that offers some level of protection.

FreeBSD and Command Line Tools

Another possible problem is that the web interface can become out-of-sync with the current server configuration when you are using the command line. In one sense it is like doing things behind the back of the web interface and it doesn't know what has changed. For example if disk *da0* fails in a RAID set, and another disk *da1* is added to the system and that disk is used to repair the RAID array, then although the RAID will function correctly, the web interface will know nothing about the disk *da1*. At its worst, this is just an annoyance, especially if the new disk *da1* saved your valuable data.

List and Status Commands

Although each of the utilities for managing RAID levels is different, they do have some common commands. Every utility accepts the `list` and `status` commands.

The `status` command provides a short summary of the disks that make up the RAID set and the current status of the RAID set. Here is the example output of status for a RAID 5 array:

```
freenas:~# graid5 status
        Name            Status    Components
raid5/myraid5   COMPLETE CALM   da0
                                ad3
                                ad1
```

From this, we can see that the RAID5 is COMPLETE (no disks missing), which also means it isn't rebuilding, and that disks *da0*, *ad3*, and *ad1* make up the RAID set.

The output from the list command is more comprehensive and in many ways is debug information. When your RAID array is working well, this information isn't very interesting, but when you are having troubles with your RAID set, this information can be very valuable.

To get the list information for a RAID 5, you would type:

```
freenas:~# graid5 list
```

I have split the output into different sections to aid easier reading:

```
Geom name: myraid5
State: COMPLETE CALM
Status: Total=3, Online=3
```

This first section shows us that this RAID set is called `myraid5` and that it is COMPLETE and CALM. It is made up of 3 disks of which all 3 are online.

```
Type: AUTOMATIC
Pending: (wqp 0 // 0)
Stripesize: 131072
MemUse: 0 (msl 0)
Newest: -1
ID: 1419279684
```

The next section shows different internal information about how the RAID set is implemented. Each RAID level will have different information in this section.

```
Providers:
1. Name: raid5/myraid5
   Mediasize: 4294705152 (4.0G)
   Sectorsize: 512
   Mode: r1w1e2
```

This section shows us what this RAID set provides for the system. It provides a RAID 5 array that is 4 Gigabytes in size.

```
Consumers:
1. Name: da0
   Mediasize: 2147483648 (2.0G)
   Sectorsize: 512
   Mode: r2w2e3
   DiskNo: 2
   Error: No
2. Name: ad3
   Mediasize: 2147483648 (2.0G)
   Sectorsize: 512
   Mode: r2w2e3
   DiskNo: 1
   Error: No
3. Name: ad1
   Mediasize: 2147483648 (2.0G)
   Sectorsize: 512
   Mode: r2w2e3
   DiskNo: 0
   Error: No
```

The consumers are the disks that are used to make this RAID set. The disk name is listed along with its size, disk number (the order the disks are used in), and its error state.

JBOD and gconcat

Because JBOD (Just a Bunch of Disks) doesn't offer any kind of protection against disk failure, there isn't much that can be done on the command line. The status of the JBOD array can be checked using `gconcat status` as follows:

```
freenas:~# gconcat status
         Name   Status  Components
concat/myjbod     UP    ad3
                        ad1
```

It is possible to create, format, and mount JBOD arrays completely from the command line but it is of little value as the web interface will know nothing about the newly created array and as such it can be used (via the web interface). Also, because the array isn't saved in the FreeNAS configuration it will be forgotten when the machine is rebooted.

RAID 0 and gstripe

Like JBOD, RAID 0 doesn't provide any protection against disk failure and so there is little that can be done on the command line. The status of the RAID 0 array can be checked using the `gstripe status` command:

```
freenas:~# gstripe status
         Name    Status  Components
stripe/myraid0     UP    da0
                         da1
```

It is possible to create, format, and mount RAID1 arrays completely from the command line but it is of little value as the web interface will know nothing about the newly created array and as such, it can be used (via the web interface). Also, because the array isn't saved in the FreeNAS configuration, it will be forgotten when the machine is rebooted.

RAID 1 and gmirror

RAID 1 (mirroring) is the first of the 4 basic RAID levels provided by FreeBSD/FreeNAS that offers some kind of protection against disk failure.

Here is the output from gmirror status when one of the disks (da0) from the mirror set is missing:

```
freenas:~# gmirror status
           Name      Status    Components
mirror/mymirror    DEGRADED    ad1
```

The steps to rebuild a mirror array are the same as those set down is chapter 9. The command line can be used to rebuild the array rather than the web interface. Once the new disk has been put back into the system, you need to use the `forget` command. This command sounds a bit harsh but don't worry it isn't going to forget the whole mirror set, only the drives that are not currently available. Having issued the forget command, you can insert the new disk and the array will rebuild.

```
freenas:~# gmirror forget mymirror
freenas:~# gmirror insert mymirror da0
freenas:~# gmirror status
         Name        Status    Components
mirror/mymirror   DEGRADED   ad0
                             da0 (17%)
```

Once the mirror set is rebuilt, the status will be like this:

```
freenas:~# gmirror status
         Name        Status    Components
mirror/mymirror   COMPLETE   ad1
                             da1
```

RAID 5 and graid5

The procedure to repair a RAID 5 array after disk failure is exactly the same as described in chapter 9 but this time we will use the command line rather than the web interface.

Using the status command, we can see that there is a problem with this array:

```
freenas:~# graid5 status
       Name              Status    Components
raid5/myraid5    DEGRADED CALM    ad3
                                  ad1
```

The disk `da0` is missing and the RAID is running in a degraded state. Having replaced the disk, we are ready to synchronize it with the other disks in the RAID set.

The new disk needs to be placed back into the array. This is done using the `graid5 insert` command.

```
freenas:~# graid5 insert myraid5 da0
```

FreeBSD and Command Line Tools

The array will now start rebuilding. You can check that it is rebuilding by using the `graid5 status` command again:

```
freenas:~# graid5 status
       Name              Status    Components
raid5/myraid5       REBUILDING CALM   ad3
                                      ad1
                                      da0 (543162368 / 25% (p:0))
```

Once the array is rebuilt, it will return to its COMPLETE status.

```
freenas:~# graid5 status
       Name              Status    Components
raid5/myraid5       COMPLETE CALM     ad3
                                      ad1
                                      da0
```

Where the FreeNAS Stores Things

There are several places like /etc/rc.d where the FreeNAS server stores important files. Here is a summary of some key directories from FreeBSD that the FreeNAS server uses.

Directory	Importance
/root	The home directory of the root user
/mnt	All disks and RAID sets are mounted under this directory
/bin & /usr/bin	Store all the user runnable utilities like *chmod* and *kill*
/sbin & /usr/sbin	Store all the root runnable utiliteis like the RAID utilities
/etc	This directory contains the various configuration files needed by FreeNAS. Many of them are created at bootup.
/usr/local/www	Here are the web pages for the FreeNAS web interface.
/var/log	Here and in directories below it are all the log files stored by the FreeNAS server.

Note that the embedded version of FreeNAS only runs from RAM (and is initially loaded from the hard disk or USB flash disk) and any changes made to the operating system files will only be temporary, and when the system is rebooted it will return to its original state.

Miscellaneous & Sundries

There are a variety of commands that can be useful when using the command line but they aren't quite big enough to warrant a section of their own, so I have grouped them all together here.

Using ping and arp from the Command Line

In chapter 9, we looked at the ping and arp commands. These are available from the web interface but they are also available from the command line. To ping another machine from the command line type:

```
freenas:~# ping 192.168.1.42
PING 192.168.1.42 (192.168.1.42): 56 data bytes
64 bytes from 192.168.1.42: icmp_seq=0 ttl=64 time=0.718 ms
64 bytes from 192.168.1.42: icmp_seq=1 ttl=64 time=0.613 ms
64 bytes from 192.168.1.42: icmp_seq=2 ttl=64 time=0.536 ms
64 bytes from 192.168.1.42: icmp_seq=3 ttl=64 time=0.697 ms
^C
--- 192.168.1.42 ping statistics ---
4 packets transmitted, 4 packets received, 0% packet loss
round-trip min/avg/max/stddev = 0.536/0.641/0.718/0.072 ms
```

The ping command is a bit different to that of other platforms (like Windows) in that it will keep on pinging until you press *CTRL+C* and then it will stop. Alternatively, you can use the -c parameter that sends only the specified number of pings:

```
freenas:~# ping -c 1 192.168.1.42
PING 192.168.1.42 (192.168.1.42): 56 data bytes
64 bytes from 192.168.1.42: icmp_seq=0 ttl=64 time=0.685 ms

--- 192.168.1.42 ping statistics ---
1 packets transmitted, 1 packets received, 0% packet loss
round-trip min/avg/max/stddev = 0.685/0.685/0.685/0.000 ms
```

Also, to look at the arp tables type:

```
freenas:~# arp -a
? (192.168.1.42) at 00:08:02:5a:9b:f5 on lnc0 [ethernet]
Mac-Mini.lan (192.168.1.110) at 00:16:cb:a3:72:1c on lnc0
Toshiba-Laptop.lan (192.168.1.242) at 00:1b:9e:36:d9:ad on lnc0
speedtouch.lan (192.168.1.254) at 00:14:7f:2e:32:2d on lnc0
```

Creating Directories and Deleting Things

Earlier on, we looked at some simple file system command like change directory (cd), print working directory (pwd), and copy (cp). Here are a few more commands that you might find useful when working with the file system from the command line:

Command	Description
mv	Move a file from one place to another, which also has the effect of doing a rename. eg. *mv oldfilename newfilename*
mkdir	Create a directory. eg. *mkdir temp*
rmdir	Remove a directory. The directory must be empty. eg. *rmdir temp*
rm	Remove (delete) a file. eg. *rm deleteme*
rm -rf	Remove (delete) a non empty directory and delete all the file and sub directories in it. Use with care! eg. *rm -rf goodbyeworld*

Editing Files Using nano

Included in the FreeNAS software is a small text editor called nano. Provided by GNU, nano is small and friendly. Besides basic text editing, nano offers many extra features like an interactive search and replace, go to line and column number, auto-indentation, feature toggles, internationalization support, and filename tab completion.

To edit a file, say a text file on one of your disks you would type:

```
freenas:~# nano /mnt/store/readme.txt
```

The basic keys are displayed at the bottom of the text editor to help you quickly find the key you need. This is especially handy if you are not familiar with the editor. The ^ symbol means press the *CTRL* key and the letter mentioned at the same time, so ^X means *CTRL+X*.

Basic keys include:

>^O WriteOut (Save)
>
>^R Read File
>
>^Y Prev Page
>
>^X Exit
>
>^J Justify
>
>^V Next Page

You can get more information on nano at: `http://www.nano-editor.org/`

Shutting Down Using the Command Line

We are now at the last section of the last chapter this book and as the book draws to an end, it seems appropriate to show you how to shutdown the FreeNAS server from the command line. To shutdown the server, use the `shutdown` command. Used with the `-p` parameter, the server will be shut down and powered off (if the hardware supports it) and with `-r` the server will be rebooted. The command also needs a time on when to shutdown, and for immediate shutdowns use the word `now`.

`freenas:~# shutdown -p now`

or

`freenas:~# shutdown -r now`

If you don't want to shutdown now but want to schedule the shutdown for some time in the future then you can change the word `now` to be a number of minutes until shutdown with a plus sign in front. So to shutdown in 5 minutes from now use:

`freenas:~# shutdown -p +5`

Finally, if you want to schedule a shutdown for a certain day at a certain time then the time of shutdown can be specified as *yymmddhhmm* if you leave out the *yymmdd* then the time will be take to be today.

Shutdown at 23:15 tonight is:

`freenas:~# shutdown -p 2315`

And to shutdown on the 1st May 2009 at 22:30 (which happens to be a Friday) is:

`freenas:~# shutdown -p 0905012230`

Summary

In this chapter, we have looked at FreeBSD. We have covered the basic commands for file manipulation as well as some more complex commands for managing processing including starting and stopping the various FreeNAS services. We also looked at commands for managing RAID sets.

Index

A

Address Resolution Protocol. *See* **ARP**
administration tasks
  Bonjour/Zeroconf, disabling 119
  console menu, disabling 117
  date and time configuration 115, 116
  DNS server, setting 113
  hostname of server, setting 112
  languages for web interface, setting 115
  predefined network hosts, adding 117
  rebooting/shutting down server 111
  server, resetting to factory defaults 118
  shutdown beeps, stopping 117
  simple network administration 118
  start up beeps, stopping 117
  status categories 120
  status information, getting 119
  status report, sending by email 121
  web GUI user name/password, changing 110
  web interface, configuring to use HTTPS 112
  web interface port, changing 113
advanced FreeBSD commands, FreeNAS server
  killall command 211
  kill command 210
  RAID command line tools 211
  restart command 210
  services, starting 210
  services, stopping 210
  start command 210
  status command 210
  stop command 210
advanced system configuration
  disk encryption 161
  FreeBSD, tweaking 170
  SSH, enabling 176
  swap file, adding 175
AFP
  about 89
  parameters 90
AMI BIOS 47
ARP
  about 190
  MAC address used 190

B

backups
  copy backup 149
  daily backup 149
  differential backup 149
  incremental backup 149
  normal backup 149
  types 149
basic configuration, FreeNAS
  about 51
  CIFS access, testing 60
  disks, accessing via CIFS 58, 59
  disks, accessing via FTP 61
  disks, adding 54
  disks, working with 54-58
  FTP access, testing 62
  web interface 52

C

CIFS 6
  about 70, 99
  CIFS connection, from OS X 80
  configuring, on FreeNAS server 71, 72, 99

connecting with, via Windows
    Millennium 76, 77
network drive, mapping 75
options, when adding shares 75
using, with Windows XP 77
Common Internet File System. *See* **CIFS**

D

DHCP
about 49
advantages 50
Diagnostics
information page 181, 193
logs page 181
directory size, discovering
du command used 206, 207
disk, FreeNAS server
acoustic level 126
advanced power management 126
avalability, on network 129
disk, formatting 126, 128
hard disk standby time 126
mounting 128
mounting, fields 128
parameters 126
pre-formatted FS 126
UDMA mode 126
disk encryption
about 161
consumer 166
 data, adding 162
encryption tools 164
password, entering 163, 164
provider 166
disk encryption, FreeNAS
about 162, 163
parameters 162, 163
disk names,FreeBSD 41
disk space usage, discovering
df command used 206
Dynamic Host Configuration Protocol.
    See **DHCP**

E

encryption tools, disk encryption
attach 165

deattach 165
disk, unlocking 165
list command 165
list command, example 165
password, changing 165
setkey command 165
status, checking 165
status command, example 165
eXtensible Markup Language. *See* **XML**

F

files
accessing, built-in web server used 98
accessing, HTTP used 98
File System Consistency checK. *See* **fsck**
FreeBSD
about 199
commands 200
connecting to, using PuTTY 204, 205
directory size, discovering 206, 207
disk space usage, checking 206
FreeNAS server, monitoring from
    command line 206
kernel tuning, enabling 172
key directories 216
mount command used 206
overview 199
process,monitoring with ps command 207
tweaking 170
tweaking parameters 171, 172
FreeBSD, columns
%CPU 208
%MEM 208
COMMAND 208
PID 208
RSS 208
STARTED 208
STAT 208
TIME 208
TT 208
USER 208
VSZ 208
FreeBSD, commands 200
arp command, using from command
    line 217
cd(change directory) command 201, 202

change file mode(chmod) command 203
cp(copy) command 202
df command used 206
du command used 206, 207
file permission, numbers 203
files editing, using nano 218
grep command 208
ls(list) command 200, 201
mkdir command 218
mounted disks, checking 206
mv command 218
ping command, using from command line 217
process, monitoring with top command 207
ps command 207
pwd command 200
rm-rf command 218
rm command 218
rmdir command 218
shut down command used 219
top command 208
FreeNAS
  about 9
  backing up 145
  backup planning 27, 28
  backup server, setting up 154
  capacity planning 18, 19
  consolidation 16
  disk, encryption 162
  downloading 9, 35
  embedded versus full version 66
  features 10-12
  function 12
  hardware, required 35, 36
  hardware requirements 20
  installing to hard disk 63, 64
  local share 156
  local user management 101
  needs, fulfilling 14
  network considerations 31
  planning 17
  prerequisites 14
  RAID 28
  remote module name 156
  remote RSYNC sever 156
  synchronization time 156
  tasks 12, 13

upgrading from previous version 66
FreeNAS server, backing up
  external hard disk drive 148
  hard disk 148
  shared network drive 148
  strategies 145
  Windows XP built-in backup utility, using 145-148
FreeNAS configuration files
  configuration, backing up 152
  configuration, restoring 153
FreeNAS configuration files, backing up
  XML 152
FreeNAS help forums 197
FreeNAS installation. *See* **installation, FreeNAS**
FreeNAS server
  accessing via CIFS, in Windows Vista 78
  accessing via CIFS from Linux 79
  administration tasks 110
  advanced FreeBSD commands 209
  backing up 145
  basic configuration 51
  built-in Windows backup software, using 153
  CIFS, configuring 71, 99
  configuring 129
  configuring files, backing up 152
  connecting via AFP 89
  disk, adding 161
  group, creating 102
  iSCSI 142
  media streaming, UPnP used 90
  mounting via NFS, on Linux 87
  overview 10, 123
  practical uses 15
  problems, tracking 181
  protocols 69, 99
  RAID, configuring 130
  RSYNC server, configuring 154
  RSYNC server, creating 157
  RSYNC server, debugging 157, 158
  RSYNCD, used for backups 88
  servers, interfacing 153
  share connection, problems 191, 192
  storage, adding 123, 124
  swapping 175

Unison, used for backups 89
UNIX device names 124
Unison, used for synchronization 89
user, creating 102
using, as backup server 153
using, with Microsoft Active
    Directory 108, 109
FreeNAS web interface
  about 52
  access 53
  advanced 54
  diagnostics 54
  disks 53
  interfaces 53
  sections 52
  services 53
  status 54
  system 53
FreeNAS web interface example 7, 8
FSB 21
fsck
  about 169
  checking 169
  output 170
  running 170
  using 169
FTP
  about 11, 80
  advanced options 81
  command line FTP client, using 82, 83
  configuring 81
  FTP commands 84
  uses 80
  web browser, using for FTP 84, 85

H

hard drive parameters
  read error rate, S.M.A.R.T attributes 169
  reallocated sectors count, S.M.A.R.T
      attributes 169
  S.M.A.R.T 166
  S.M.A.R.T, enabling 167
  S.M.A.R.T, using 167
  S.M.A.R.T attributes 169
  spin retry count, S.M.A.R.T attributes 169
  uncorrectable sector count, S.M.A.R.T
      attributes 169
hardware requirements, FreeNAS
  buses 22
  CPU 20
  disks 21
  drives 24
  drives, seek time 24
  drives, spindle speed 24
  drives, transfer speed 25
  factors, hard drive permormance 24, 25
  guidelines, for CPU 21
  IDE/ATA 22
  memory 26
  multiple disk drives 25
  network card 26
  PATA 23
  PCI 26
  SATA 22
  SCSI 22
  USB 26

I

information page, Diagnostics
  about 193
  disks(ATA) tab 193
  disks tab 193
  FTP users tab 194
  iSCSI initiator tab 194
  mounts tab 193
  MS Domain tab 194
  partitions tab 193
  RSYNC client tab 194
  S.M.A.R.T tab 193
  sockets tab 194
  software RAID tab 194
  space used tab 193
  swap tab 194
installation, FreeNAS
  AMI BIOS, setup programs 47
  booting, from CD 45
  booting process 36, 39
  boot process 47
  CD burning 45
  FreeNAS, configuring 39, 41
  IP address 49-51
  ISO image, burning into CD 37

LAN IP address 49
network, configuring 47, 48
Phoenix-Award BIOS, setup programs 47
Phoenix BIOS, setup programs 46
share, testing 43
Windows machines, sharing with 42

IPv4 51

IPv6 51

iSCSI
 about 11, 92
 configuration 92
 iSCSI initiator 142
 iSCSI initiator, configuring 143
 iSCSI target 92
 iSCSI target, configuring 92, 93
 iSCSI target, configuring steps 92
 iSCSI target, testing with another FreeNAS server 94, 95
 iSCSI target, testing with Windows Vista 96, 97

J

JBOD 130
 about 130

Just a Bunch of Disks. *See* **JBOD**

K

key directories, FreeBSD
 /bin &/usr/bin 216
 /etc 216
 /mnt 216
 /root 216
 /sbin &/usr/bin 216
 /var/log 216
 usr/local/www 216

L

LAN IP address 49

logs page, Diagnostics
 ahd0 device 185
 Daemon tab 182
 disk controller used 184
 files, collating 182
 FTP tab 182
 log system tab 182
 network interface card used 185
 RSYNC tab 182
 settings tab 182
 SMARTD tab 182
 SSHD tab 182
 System log page 183
 System log page, reading 183
 UPnP tab 182

M

MAC 1901 191

Media Access Control. *See* **MAC;** *See* **MAC**

mirroring vs conventional backups 160

mounted disks, checking
 mount command used 206

mounting fields, FreeNAS server
 description 129
 disk 128
 file system 129
 name 129
 partition 129
 read only 129
 type 128

N

NAS
 about 5, 6
 advantages 9
 NAS servers 8

Network Attached Storage. *See* **NAS**

network considerations, FreeNAS
 hub 31
 switch 32
 wireless 32

Network Filing System. *See* **NFS**

networking problems
 ARP tables, using 190
 checklist, connection problem 187
 connection, problem 187
 gigabit transfers 191
 physical problems 186
 ping tool, using 188, 189
 ping tool, using within web interfaces 189, 190
 software problems 186

network settings
  device polling 173
  duplex 173
  MTU 173
  parameters, changing 172
  speed 173
  static route, adding 173
  tweaking 172
NFS
  about 11, 85
  configuring 85
  list of authorized networks, parameters 86
  MAP all users to root, parameters 86
  parameters 86
  using, from OS X 86

P

Phoenix-Award BIOS 47
Phoenix BIOS 46
protocols
  AFP 89, 99
  CIFS 70, 99
  FTP 80, 99
  iSCSI 92, 99
  NFS 85, 99
  RSYNCD 88, 99
  Unison 89, 99
  UPnP 90, 99

R

RAID
  about 28, 130
  balance algorithm option, RAID 1 133
  combination levels 136
  hardware RAID 30
  JBOB, levels 130
  JBOD, configuring 135
  levels 28, 130
  nesting levels 136
  RADI 0, levels 130
  RADI 1, levels 130
  RADI 5, levels 130
  RAID 0+1, configuring 138, 139
  RAID 0+1, creating 138
  RAID 0, configuring 135
  RAID 0, levels 29
  RAID 1+0, configuring 137
  RAID 1+0, creating 137
  RAID 1, configuring 132, 133, 134, 138
  RAID 1, defining 132, 133, 134, 138
  RAID 1, levels 29
  RAID 10+0 142
  RAID 10, levels 30
  RAID 100 142
  RAID 5+0, configuring 139, 140
  RAID 5+0, creating 139
  RAID 5+1, configuring 140, 142
  RAID 5, configuring 134
  RAID 5, defining 134
  RAID 5, levels 29
  RAID 6, levels 29
  RAID controller 30
RAID, configuring
  disks, adding 130, 131
RAID command line tools, advanced FreeBSD commands
  forget command used 215
  gconcat status command used 214
  graid5 insert command used 215, 216
  gstripe status command used 214
  JBOD status, checking 214
  list command 212
  RAID 0 status, checking 214
  status command 212
  warning 211
RAID set
  failed hard drive, replacing 194, 195
  RAID 1, rebuilding after disk failure 195, 196
  RAID 5, rebuilding after disk failure 196, 197
RSYNCD 88
RSYNC server
  configuring 154
  configuring, fields 154
  creating 156
  data, synchronizing 158
  debugging 157, 158
  destination share, internal setup, 159
  internal setup 158, 159
  internal setup, debugging 159, 160
  source share, internal setup, 159
  synchronization time, internal setup, 159

S

S.M.A.R.T 166
Samba 70, 99
Secure SHell. *See* **SSH**
Self-Monitoring, Analysis, and Reporting Technology. *See* **S.M.A.R.T**
share connection, problems
 FreeNAS server, visibility 192
 logging, turning on 192
 NetBiosName, setting 192
 Null password field, disabling 192
 Null password field, enabling 192
SSH
 about 107, 176
 authentication, types 177
 enabling 176
 root login, allowing 176
SSH authentication
 keyboard-interactive authentication 177
 public key authentication 177-179
 ssh-keygen command 177
static route, network settings
 destination network 174
 gateway 174
 interface 174
swap file
 adding 175

U

Unison 89
UPnP
 about 90
 parameters 91
user management features
 AFP users, authenticating 105, 106
 CIFS, using with local users 103
 SSH 106, 107
 user login with FTP 104, 105

V

virtualization 36
VMWare 36

W

wireless card
 configuring 174

X

XML 152
XP's built-in backup utility, FreeNAS server 151
 restoring 151
 setting 148, 149, 150

Packt Open Source Project Royalties

When we sell a book written on an Open Source project, we pay a royalty directly to that project. Therefore by purchasing Learning FreeNAS, Packt will have given some of the money received to the FreeNAS Project.

In the long term, we see ourselves and you—customers and readers of our books—as part of the Open Source ecosystem, providing sustainable revenue for the projects we publish on. Our aim at Packt is to establish publishing royalties as an essential part of the service and support a business model that sustains Open Source.

If you're working with an Open Source project that you would like us to publish on, and subsequently pay royalties to, please get in touch with us.

Writing for Packt

We welcome all inquiries from people who are interested in authoring. Book proposals should be sent to authors@packtpub.com. If your book idea is still at an early stage and you would like to discuss it first before writing a formal book proposal, contact us; one of our commissioning editors will get in touch with you.

We're not just looking for published authors; if you have strong technical skills but no writing experience, our experienced editors can help you develop a writing career, or simply get some additional reward for your expertise.

About Packt Publishing

Packt, pronounced 'packed', published its first book "Mastering phpMyAdmin for Effective MySQL Management" in April 2004 and subsequently continued to specialize in publishing highly focused books on specific technologies and solutions.

Our books and publications share the experiences of your fellow IT professionals in adapting and customizing today's systems, applications, and frameworks. Our solution-based books give you the knowledge and power to customize the software and technologies you're using to get the job done. Packt books are more specific and less general than the IT books you have seen in the past. Our unique business model allows us to bring you more focused information, giving you more of what you need to know, and less of what you don't.

Packt is a modern, yet unique publishing company, which focuses on producing quality, cutting-edge books for communities of developers, administrators, and newbies alike. For more information, please visit our website: www.PacktPub.com.

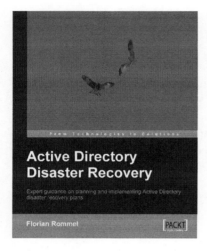

Active Directory Disaster Recovery

ISBN: 978-1-847193-27-8   Paperback: 236 pages

Expert guidance on planning and implementing Active Directory disaster recovery plans

1. Essential disaster recovery planning/response book
2. Configure and strengthen Active Directory to increase resilience
3. Practical diagnosis of failures
4. Design and implement an organizational Disaster Recovery plan
5. Symptom-Cause-Recovery approach

Mastering OpenLDAP

ISBN: 184-7191-02-9   Paperback: 400 pages

Install, Configure, Build, and Integrate Secure Directory Services with OpenLDAP server in a networked environment

1. Up-to-date with the latest OpenLDAP release
2. Installing and configuring the OpenLDAP server
3. Synchronizing multiple OpenLDAP servers over the network
4. Creating custom LDAP schemas to model your own information

Please check **www.PacktPub.com** for information on our titles

Configuring IPCop Firewalls

ISBN: 1-904811-36-1   Paperback: 154 pages

How to setup, configure and manage your Linux firewall, web proxy, DHCP, DNS, time server, and VPN with this powerful Open Source solution

1. Learn how to install, configure, and set up IPCop on your Linux servers
2. Use IPCop as a web proxy, DHCP, DNS, time server, and VPN
3. Advanced add-on management

Network Administration with FreeBSD 7

ISBN: 978-1-847192-64-6   Paperback: 280 pages

Building, securing, and maintaining networks with the FreeBSD operating system

1. Set up and manage networking on FreeBSD
2. Virtualization with FreeBSD Jails, IPFW and PF
3. Configure interfaces, protocols, and routing

Please check **www.PacktPub.com** for information on our titles

Printed in Germany by
Amazon Distribution
GmbH, Leipzig